A WOMAN SCORNED

THE MURDER OF GEORGE SAXTON
—A TRUE CRIME MELODRAMA—

JOHN STARK BELLAMY II

A Woman Scorned

ISBN 13:978-1456541941   ISBN 10:1456541943

By the same author:

They Died Crawling

The Maniac in the Bushes

The Corpse in the Cellar

The Killer in the Attic

Death Ride at Euclid Beach

Women Behaving Badly

Vintage Vermont Villainies

Cleveland's Greatest Disasters

The Last Days of Cleveland

Anyone wishing to contact the author may do so at this email address: jstarkbi@tops-tele.com

To Laura,
with all my love

Table of Contents

Preface

Over the past two decades my compulsion to rediscover and share the most melodramatic and intriguing incidents of northeastern Ohio history has provoked the writing of eight books containing a dozen dozens' true tales of Western Reserve murder, calamity and woe. But I have to admit that not a single one of those seven score-plus stories has come even close to the George Saxton tragedy for fascination, scandal and suspense. The Saxton murder remains the best Ohio murder of the 19th century — and would claim prize as the best All-American homicide if it were not for the antics of Fall River spinster Lizzie Borden in 1892. The Saxton homicide had everything: George Saxton, a Social Register victim with a lurid love life; Anna George, a fetching femme fatale howling from the gutter where he'd kicked her; and all the events of their fatal collision played out on the stage of a staid small town — which nonetheless seethed with the subterraneous doings of shady politicians, dodgy police officials, dope-crazed house-wives and women of dubious chastity — not to mention William McKinley, President of the United States, the corpse's embarrassed brother-in-law.

The ensuing murder trial of murder suspect Anna George seethed deliciously with sex, celebrity and sensation and remains one of the most exciting criminal trials in the annals of both tab-loid-style journalism and American jurisprudence. Lasting three weeks and fought to the bitter finish by quartet of ferocious law-yers, it held courtroom spectators and a curious nation rapt with its many unexpected twists, improbable witnesses and bombshell disclosures. Finding and writing this incredible story has been the sublime literary adventure of my life and my hope is that you will find as much pleasure in reading it as I did in writing it.

John Stark Bellamy II
January 15, 2011

Heaven has no rage like love to hatred turned,

Nor hell a fury like a woman scorned.

William Congreve, *The Mourning Bride* [1697]

He left the name, at which the world grew pale,

To point a moral, or adorn a tale.

Samuel Johnson, *The Vanity of Human Wishes* [1749]

"A highly popular murder had been committed."

Charles Dickens, *Great Expectations* [1862]

"Annie listened and was tempted —

She was tempted and she fell,

As the angel fell from heaven

To the blackest depths of hell.

George Robert Sims, "Ostler Joe" [1890]

MRS. ANNA E. GEORGE.

Mrs. Anna E. George
(Cleveland Leader: April 29, 1899)

Prologue

Washington, D. C.
October 7, 1898
8 P.M.

It was a lousy way to end a party. It had been, most of the guests would later agree, all that a White House entertainment should be. The East Room that early October night was flooded with electric light as over a thousand guests surged toward the President at the end of the room. There, as was his custom, William McKinley shook hands firmly with each one of them as the hours passed by. Nearby was his wife, gowned in stunning white satin, her high white collar secured by a necklace of glittering diamonds. Although notoriously a semi-invalid of precarious health and uncertain temper, Ida McKinley was in good form this evening, graciously greeting her guests, her sister Mary ("Pina") often at her side to monitor her unpredictable moods and stamina.

The occasion was a formal-dress reception for the delegates to the Triennial Protestant Episcopal Convention, although attendance was hardly limited to men of that denominational cloth. The year was 1898, and the crowd at the White House that evening reflected the almost perfect congruence between American religious and political elites. J. Pierpont Morgan, the foremost human icon of American capitalism was only the most prominent Protestant layman present in the 1000-plus throng and there were many U. S. Army generals and Navy admirals present. Although there was some disappointment that space considerations had dictated that it be an all-male affair, all present agreed it was a brilliant one.

It was shortly after 8 p.m. when the President's private secretary, J. Addison Porter, discreetly entered the room. Although often dismissed by the Washington press corps as a pompous incompetent, Porter knew how to handle his present task in the unruffled McKinley style. Sidling silently to the President's side, he leaned toward McKinley's ear, just as McKinley was unclasping the hand of one guest to take the hand of the next. Porter whispered a few words, inaudible to all but the President. Even as he reached for the next outstretched hand, McKinley almost imperceptibly stiffened—and continued to grasp one hand after the other from the seemingly endless receiving line. Turning his head quickly for a moment, he muttered to Porter, "Mrs. McKinley *must* not be told!" and continued to greet his guests with reliably genial small talk and his famously firm handshake.

Two hours later, the last guest finally departed from the East Room. Hurrying to the White House living quarters, McKinley sought out his sister-in-law Pina. Mrs. Barber was paying an extended visit to the White House, while her son John recovered in a Washington, D. C. hospital from typhoid fever he had contracted in Puerto Rico on active service in the just-concluded Spanish-American War. It was always a comfort to the President to have Pina around, incomparably experienced as she was in managing her fragile, temperamental sister. Mrs. McKinley, long a protected recluse and subject to chronic aliments, was also vulnerable to epileptic-like seizures. Such episodes were often triggered or aggravated by stress, and William McKinley had long since learned to be cautious when giving his wife ill tidings.

But this time it couldn't be avoided or procrastinated. Already the news was spreading throughout the United States via a thousand telegraph wires and it would be the headline in all of tomorrow's newspapers. "It's bad news from home, Pina," said the President of the United States. We just received a telegram from Canton. Your brother George has been shot to death, apparently by *that* woman!"

Chapter 1   A Rogue's Genesis

When it was all over, after George D. Saxton was dead and buried, everyone seemed to agree how inevitable, even predictable his murder had been. His immediate family, his sisters Ida and Pina, had wrung their hands for years over his scandalous behavior, wondering just where and how his wicked carryings-on would end. His respectable brothers-in-law, Marshall C. Barber and President William McKinley, continually shuddered at the potential social and political fallout George's notoriously raffish conduct might provoke. Saxton's best friend James J. Grant, the confidant of his most lurid secrets and also the very discreet attorney who dealt with the legal consequences of his shenanigans, worried much over the nemesis his wayward friend seemed intent on ceaselessly courting. Even Saxton himself, a man not given much to introspection, often spoke to his friends of his unpleasant premonition that something "unusual" and probably malign was fated to happen to him. And yet, notwithstanding such baleful auguries, the scorn of "decent" society and the vengeful feelings of abandoned mistresses too numerous to recall, George D. Saxton had somehow managed to survive to within 24 days of his 48th birthday. How had this heartless libertine managed to live so long without serious consequences, and what — or more precisely *who* — had finally brought him to his largely unmourned grave?

The answer to the last question may never be answered with certainty. But the why of George Saxton's death and some clues to puzzle of his fate can be reconstructed from various historical sources. We must begin by going back to northeast Ohio in the early 19th century.

Actually, the George D. Saxton story began in Huntington, Pennsylvania in 1815. It was there on August 15 of that year that John Saxton, the son of immigrant George Saxton (the original English surname was Sexton), married Margaret Laird, following

GEORGE D. SAXTON.

George D. Saxton
(Cleveland Daily World, April 28, 1899)

his honorable service in the War of 1812. Immediately after their wedding John and Margaret journeyed on horseback to Stark County, Ohio. There, John Saxton soon made his fortune in Canton, acquiring large real estate holdings and establishing the *Ohio*

Chapter 1   A Rogue's Genesis

Repository newspaper (later the *Canton Repository*, still Canton's chief newspaper.)

John and Margaret Saxton had nine children, the most important to this narrative being James Ashbury Saxton, born in 1816. James likewise flourished materially, becoming the principal stockholder and President of the Stark County Bank and a leader in Canton's civic affairs. James took for his bride Catherine, the daughter of Walter DeWalt, another well-to-do and prominent Canton citizen and they were blessed with three children during their marriage of 26 years. The first was Ida, born in 1847, and destined to become the wife of President William McKinley. Her sister Mary was born a year later and the final child and only son, George DeWalt Saxton, arrived on October 31, 1850. He was destined to bring upon his family a disgrace nearly equal in magnitude to the matrimonial celebrity of his elder sister Ida.

But there was no inkling of George's ultimate fate as he grew up, if not matured, in the Canton of the 1850s and '60s. Educated in the excellent common schools of Canton, George was slated and groomed from infancy to inherit his father's civic and business interests. There is little known of the family dynamics of the Saxtons. Such a modern psychological inquiry, to say the least, would have baffled and probably appalled upper-middle-class citizens of 19th century Canton such as the Saxtons. And the surviving biographical facts and assertions about the early years of George and Ida are conventionally pious and flattering. But it seems probable, judging from the adult characters of Ida and George, that these children of the Canton elite were indulged and petted from the beginning. Although both of them were capable of exhibiting quite winning ways on occasion, their adult personalities were imbued with a remarkable selfishness and an uncomprehending blindness to the needs, desires and deserts of others. Ida McKinley, under the pressures of early marriage and the deaths of two children (a not uncommon experience for women of her era) evolved into what Margaret Leech (the best of the McKinley biographers) would characterize as a "feeble, self-centered nerv-

11

ous invalid." Indeed, one of the reasons her husband William was so admired by bourgeois Americans of the Victorian Age was because of his saintly patience with the sort of wife who might have driven a successful man of lesser character to seek personal consolations elsewhere.

Whatever Ida's failings, however, George's more public misbehaviors chronically eclipsed her personality defects. After completing public school and serving a stint as a Sunday school teacher, he spent several years in his father's bank, to master the arts of finance and the administration of the substantial family properties. George seems to have been a competent businessman, and he handled the family investments well, mostly concentrated in real estate and insurance, both in his apprentice years and after his father died in 1887. But the same competence could not be detected in his personal life at any time.

Some people never mature. George Saxton was a classic case. Spoiled from an early age, he evolved gradually but inexorably, in Margaret Leech's shrewd phrase, into "the kind of man who slides into middle age without having quite grown up." Never really leaving home, he lived with his parents until their deaths and after that with his sister Pina and her husband in the old Saxton home at 333 South Market Street. He also, however, maintained a second residence for more personal concerns, after 1880, in the new Saxton Block, a substantial commercial-residential block erected by his father on South Market Street between West 8th and West 9th Streets. Given the dominant social and financial position of his family in Canton and Stark County, it was naturally expected that George Saxton would seek and find a wife of similar background. And the limited evidence available suggests that he made efforts to do so in the early years of his manhood. "His first engagement was with a beautiful young lady of Canton, his equal socially and financially." So wrote "Coe," the discreet and anonymous chronicler of Saxton's sexual misdeeds and sensational death (*Canton's Great Tragedy: The Murder of George D. Saxton*; Coe's real name was Thurlow K. Albaugh, a journalist familiar with the details of the George Saxton saga.) The beautiful young lady was Alice ("Allie") Schaeffer, the nineteen-year-old daughter of Louis Schaeffer. Schaeffer was a well-to-do Canton businessman and the alliance was enthusiastically promoted by both sets of parents. Alice and George had known each other since childhood, and their formal engagement in the early 1870s fulfilled all family hopes and expectations.

It was not to be. George, now in his early twenties, was already displaying the sensuality and promiscuity that would soon brand him the archetypal Lothario of Stark County. His taste in women already ran to more worldly and obvious types than the sweetly virginal Alice and his visits to his doting fiancée became increasingly infrequent. Worse yet, the callow George did not try to conceal his relations with women of lesser caste or virtue. Newspaperman "Coe," writing for the proper middle-class audience of his day, narrated the denouement of the engagement in the sort of melodramatic cadences that must have been deeply pleasing to his moralistic audience:

> His conduct toward her and his seeming indifference were a cruel blow to her future happiness. She could not believe that he would disregard so readily the sacred vows which he had so earnestly made. The knowledge of his associations with others and his abandonment of her, threw her into an illness from which she never recovered. She died of a broken heart.

Perhaps so. It is a fact that Alice Schaefer died in the mid-1870s. It is likewise true that she is buried in West Lawn Cemetery, not far from where her jilting swain George Saxton lies. But it is left to the reader to decide whether she died of a broken heart. It would later be gossiped that the heartsick Alice was persuaded to break off the engagement by her brother-in-law, William Rufus Day. It was said that Day, a future U. S. Secretary of State, U. S.

Supreme Court Justice, close McKinley friend and the husband of Alice's elder sister Mary Elizabeth, persuaded Alice to cast her unworthy lover aside. This dramatic scenario seems unlikely: a quarter of a century later Judge Day, now a prominent jurist, would represent George D. Saxton as the defendant in a squalid alienation-of-affection suit filed by irate and injured husband Sample C. George, hardly the behavior expected toward a vulgar fornicator who had driven one's sister-in-law to an early grave.

An even juicier, if equally implausible tale whispered around Canton was that an angry Louis Schaeffer barred a sincerely sorrowing George Saxton from Allie's funeral, held at the Schaeffer home. Saxton, frantic with grief, followed the cortege to the West Lawn Cemetery. There, he was confronted by the furious Louis, who pronounced this menacing malediction on him: "Leave this place. If you do not, you will be killed. You cannot remain here. And I say to you now, George Saxton, that you will die with your boots on!" Several nights later, it was said, Saxton returned to the cemetery, where he bribed the sexton to open sweet Allie's coffin for a final farewell. As any reader of Edgar Allan Poe might expect, Saxton then smothered the corpse's face and hair with repentant kisses until the horrified sexton dragged him away.

Canton gossips would always maintain that the courtship of Alice Schaeffer was the closest George Saxton really ever came to wedlock. Be that as it may, he soon became engaged to another well-connected debutante, a Miss Louisa Miller of Massillon. Alas, his second betrothal fared no better than the first. Often seen in the company of "low" or "fast" women, Saxton repeated his callous treatment of Allie with the ease born of habit. Louisa eventually tired of his inattentions and broke off the engagement. It was rumored, however, that she was so shattered by George's spurning that she immediately eloped with her father's coachman, Joe Grogrem, on the rebound, perhaps a fate worse than death to proper upper-crust Cantonians. It was later rumored that yet a third engagement with a woman named Elizabeth Frantz flared up briefly before it flickered to ashes on the cold altar of George Saxton's heart.

GEORGE SAXTON AND HIS FIRST LOVE AFFAIR.

Four Views of George D. Saxton and a Sketch of Miss Allie Schaeffer (Cleveland Daily World, April 17, 1899)

All, some or none of such stories about George Saxton's love life may be true. It is fair to say, however, that by the mid-1880s, Saxton was well-established in public regard as a charming, convivial but shallow-hearted and callow playboy. By that time he had set up his bijou bachelor lair in the Saxton block and settled into a comfortable pattern of serial and casual sexual relationships. The home of his sister Pina on South Market Street remained a convenient base for his more respectable activities and associations but his heart was in the Saxton block. There, on most weekends, it was said, one might find him with his latest conquest, whiling away the sweet hours with copious draughts of beer, champagne and sex.

Although he would one day be excoriated as a serial homewrecker, a despoiler of innocent daughters and virtuous housewives, such a judgment seems too harsh on Saxton's lubricious lifestyle. With the exception of the woman accused of killing him, George Saxton's sexual proclivities don't seem to have ever run much to either housewives or virgins. True, he was a confirmed lecher and libertine. Such moral lapses were bad enough in themselves, but more particularly reprehensible in the brother-in-law of William McKinley, a rising political superstar. McKinley had married Ida Saxton in 1871 and his political ascent since his 1876 election to the U. S. House of Representatives had followed a steady course. Even before McKinley became Governor of Ohio in 1892, George's licentious lifestyle provoked concern among McKinley's political handlers and George's relatives. But, for all the anxious moralizing and fear of scandal, George's sexual affairs seem to have focused on women of like mind and appetites. The names of many women connected with his nocturnal diversions would be coarsely bandied on the lips of scandalized Cantonians as the years rolled by. But not one of them was an "unsoiled dove" — as Saxton's contemporaries might have put it — before encountering the randy, ready George. And so things might have gone on for decades more, an endless parade of available, tarnished women coming and going through room No. 7, the site of Saxon's assignations in the Saxton block. But in 1887 Saxton met Annie George.

Chapter 2   A Small Town Girl Goes Bad

George Saxton usually went looking for the kind of woman he wanted. Annie George, however, dropped into his life and lap without warning one day in 1887. His ignorance of her up to that moment was all the more remarkable, as she had actually been living under his own roof for some months.

Thirteen years later, in a deposition read at Annie George's murder trial, dry goods merchant Jacob Goldberg would recall that day in precise detail. Jacob and his brother Abraham were tenants of George Saxton's, having run their dry goods store out of several rooms in the Saxton block since 1881. It was just another business day in the retail shop and Jacob stood chatting with the ever affable George about inconsequential matters. Suddenly, a striking, well-dressed woman entered the shop and began looking at merchandise. Brown-haired and brown-eyed, she possessed a voluptuous figure that many would find stunning even after she passed the age of forty.

George D. Saxton considered himself an experienced connoisseur of female beauty. But as Jacob Goldberg recalled, his usually voluble landlord remained mute with admiration as his eyes tracked the enchanting female apparition around the Goldberg store. Several minutes later, the woman exited the store and Saxton turned to Jacob and said, "Jacob, that is a deuced pretty woman. I wonder who she is. I should like to get acquainted with her!" Jacob replied, "She is Mrs. George, the wife of a carpenter. She and her husband recently moved here and she lives here in this building."

Annie George had come far in her twenty-nine years before falling under the lustful gaze of George Saxton. Born on September 18, 1858 to farming folk in Hanoverton, Columbiana County, Ohio, she was christened Anna Eliza and grew up with hopes of a destiny no more grandiose than the modest estate of her parents, William and Lucinda Ehrhart. When she was a little girl, her father moved to town to start a hotel, reportedly so that his son and two daughters could take advantage of better schools there. Annie grew up, it was said, somewhat the "pet" of her family. Beautiful and winning even as a child, she matured into the acknowledged "belle" of Columbiana County by the late 1870s. And it was there that she captivated local carpenter Sample C. George and married him on April 8, 1878.

Little is known of Annie George's early married life. Her defenders, when she was on trial for her life, would acclaim her as the unsullied model of a contented, virtuous spouse during that first decade after she married Sample C. George. One child, Warren G., died in infancy but their son Newton Robert was born in 1881. A second son, Charles Howard, arrived in 1884. Sample was in Salem, Ohio at the time of Charles' birth, and later critics of the George marriage would make much of this absence as implying a conjugal estrangement. But there was never any evidence produced to significantly alter Sample's characterization of his early married life as "pleasant and happy."

Maybe it was the arrival of son Charles Howard. Perhaps it was the not unusual ambition of small-town folk to leave bucolic scenes behind them and make a new and more prosperous life in the city. Millions of Americans fled from farms and small towns for just such reasons during the 19th century. Whatever their motives, Sample, Annie and their two sons moved to Canton in 1886. The plan was for Sample was to find work there as a carpenter, while Annie prosecuted her considerable skill as a seamstress. She had been gifted at needlework even as a child and had enjoyed some modest success in selling her handiwork, in addition to handsomely clothing herself and her family.

The Georges apparently lived in several locations in Canton before moving into rooms on the third floor of the Saxton block on April 18, 1886. Their life there initially developed according to plan. Sample found carpentry work and Annie began enlisting patrons for her needlework. The children went to the Canton public schools and all seemed, indeed, "pleasant and happy."

Chapter 2 A Small Town Girl Goes Bad

Did George Saxton have to work hard to seduce Annie George? Her defense attorneys would later insist it was so. "When she came here," John Cullen Welty would rhapsodize on an April afternoon in 1899, "she was as pure, upright and virtuous as any woman who ever lived and was until she met this man Saxton." Perhaps so. But Atlee Pomerene, who struggled mightily to send Annie George to the electric chair, made a telling riposte to Welty's portrait of wifely innocence when he remarked that a truly pure and virtuous woman would never have allowed a man like George D. Saxton to "mash" her. And there is certainly no question that Saxton did and quite thoroughly mash Annie George. Smitten from the second he laid eyes on her, he set about her seduction in methodical, persistent fashion. Very shortly after seeing her at the Goldberg Brothers store, Saxton dropped in to pay a friendly call on his third-floor Saxton block tenants. He was pleasant, he was charming, he was generous--and above all, disarming. Sample George apparently suffered no suspicions as his landlord followed up his initial contact with visits of increasing frequency and duration. Whether the sometimes absent Sample was aware of just how frequent Saxton's visits became is an unanswered question. But it is clear that they were the stage for a two-year amorous siege that culminated in Annie's sexual capitulation.

In Annie's defense, it must be said that it might have been difficult for even a reasonably chaste domestic angel to have resisted Saxton's personal and material blandishments. Annie was a relatively unsophisticated girl from the "sticks" and anyone from her provincial background might have been dazzled by the attentions of such a man. However soiled his name became in life or after his death, George Saxton was — when he chose to be--an attractive man. Socially prominent, well-to-do, an easy conversationalist with a democratic manner, he generally charmed men and women alike with his manners, his calculated generosity and his extroverted, sunny temperament. Added to that were his more personal attractions. Although he may not have been, like Richard Cory, "imperially slim," George's somewhat portly figure and mustache were well within the parameters of masculine attractiveness in his era. It is likely, too, if only on the basis of his greater experience, that many women found his sexuality more intriguing and promising than that of more prosaic males like Sample C. George.

Even with all these attractions, however, it took George Saxton two years to accomplish Annie's downfall. Saxton's approach to her was a powerful appeal to both her material desires and her human vanity. His shrewd campaign began innocently enough. During one of his early visits, he asked her if she would mend a pair of gloves for him. This Annie did, and George showed his pleasure with her work by giving her several additional commissions of like nature. The breakthrough came one subsequent evening when Saxton dropped by with an expensive sealskin sacque (a short, loose fitting coat for females). He had purchased it, he told the guileless Annie, for a female acquaintance, a woman, he continued, of just about her size and shape. It required, however, some alteration — and would she be so kind as to do it for him? Sometime later, he dropped by the Georges' flat to retrieve it. To assure himself that it would fit properly, he insisted that Annie try it on herself. "Ah," he purred, admiring the sacque draping her shapely shoulders, "the fit is so perfect on yourself, it would be too bad to take it from you and give it to someone else." Despite her alleged misgivings, Annie eventually agreed and accepted the costly present.

"Coe," the sometimes willfully naïve chronicler of the Saxton saga, would later comment with a distinct, if prim humor on the transaction:

> Mr. and Mrs. George were very much surprised and pleased at Mr. Saxton's generosity. They could hardly understand what prompted him to become so much interested in their welfare. They modestly accepted the valuable gift in a spirit of gratitude; never

dreaming of the true object that inspired him to make it.

Whatever their true feelings, Saxton's generous gift created no apparent rift in his relations with the Georges. Indeed, the frequency of his visits, especially during Sample George's absences, increased apace. During those visits, he solicited the favor of young Newton and Charles with gifts of fruit, candy and occasional tickets to the circus. In more private moments with Annie, he began a full-blown campaign to lure her away from her husband. Continuing to lavish presents on her, he appealed directly to her vanity by insisting that a woman of her beauty and accomplishments deserved to occupy a higher sphere than that of the wife of a humble, poor and unappreciative carpenter. Saxton's appeals at this time were no doubt aided by Sample's prolonged absence on business during the winter of 1886-7.

No one ever accused Sample C. George of being acutely perceptive. It seems to have been some time before he became suspicious about his landlord's frequent visits and numerous presents to his wife. But sometime after his return to Canton in 1887, Sample put his foot down. People in Canton were starting to gossip about Annie and Saxton and Sample was becoming concerned about his wife's reputation. After some angry scenes with Annie he extracted a promise to renounce her friendship with Saxton and the George family immediately moved out of the Saxton block to a flat on West Ninth Street.

It was too late. The worm had entered the apple of Mrs. George's marriage and it would rapidly decay for all of Canton to see. She soon broke her promise to Sample and resumed her discourse with Saxton. There were more scenes with Sample, more vows to reform and more relapses into the company of Saxton. In 1889, at the Meyer's Lake Casino Hotel, a resort near Canton, Annie George entered into a sexual relationship with George Saxton. Soon afterwards, in the spring of 1890, she separated from her husband, Sample took the children back to Hanoverton and

Annie moved into Room No. 7 on the second floor of the Saxton block.

Annie would always claim that her seduction by Saxton was based on his explicit promise to marry her, made at the outset of their affair. If this were true, the canny Saxton was never imprudent enough to put any such commitment in writing or to avow it in the presence of other witnesses. But his actions following the public rupture of Annie's marriage to Sample are persuasive evidence that Saxton initially did intend to marry her in the "first, fine, careless rapture" of their adulterous affair.

After a year of more or less openly consorting in his Saxton block rooms, Annie and George began implementing their marital timeline. In his initial rage at his wife's adultery Sample George had filed a suit for divorce but quickly withdrawn it when he realized how gratified Annie and George were at his taking the initiative. So Saxton contrived his own scheme: Annie was to go to South Dakota, then notorious for having the most liberal divorce laws in the United States. Living there at Saxton's expense, she would complete the necessary six months' residence and divorce Sample. She would then marry Saxton, confound her critics and take her rightful place in the front ranks of Canton society.

It didn't work out that way. Annie didn't leave Canton for South Dakota until October, 1891. Acting under the direction of Saxton's personal attorney, James J. Grant, she took the long train ride out there and registered at the Harland House hotel in Canton, the center of South Dakota's "divorce colony." Annie was there for the better part of a year, considerably longer than the minimum residency requirement. Saxton visited her several times there, chastely occupying Room No. 14 while Annie remained in Room No. 10. But at least once, Saxton took her to a hotel in Sioux City, South Dakota, where they spent a night together as "George D. Saxton and wife, Canton." During her Dakota sojourn Annie lived on remittances from Saxton, regularly sent in the form of checks and money orders, which were as regularly cashed by Annie as she waited out her ordeal.

And an ordeal it must have been, even for the once shy woman who had by now learned to brazen out her role as the scarlet paramour of Canton's premier playboy. Divorce may have been comparatively easy to obtain in South Dakota but the process was still by no means respectable or pleasant, even for a woman who was the injured party in a divorce, which Annie decidedly was not. An anonymous journalist for the *New York Herald* described South Dakota's divorce colony in bitter words:

> To one who has never breathed the same air, nor lived side by side with the men and women who compose the "divorce colonies" in South Dakota, it is almost impossible to describe the mortification felt by the sensitive, refined, shrinking, well-bred woman who exiles herself to this far-way prairie town, and finds herself the cynosure of all eyes; the daily pinpricks in the innuendoes; the slurs, the slights, the ostracisms to which she is subjected by; the inhabitants and the press; the constant annoyance at finding herself an object of public property, her comings and goings criticized, her dress and manners questioned, her motives pronounced without trial to be the worst possible to be imputed to woman.

Annie George's mortifications were no doubt intensified by her unenviable position in the social order of South Dakota divorcees. As the *New York Herald* correspondent noted, such soiled doves as Annie were scorned as untouchables even by their seeming sisters:

> The second class [of divorcees] is composed of women who have violated their marriage vows, who have formed a mad infatuation for some man, and whose only object in coming here is to take advantage of the loose divorce laws, and in nine cases

out of ten to live in open shame with their paramours; while putting themselves under the protection of these laws, their daily life being an open
defiance to any law, human or divine. To these
women, the opinion, good, bad, or indifferent, of
man or woman, is a matter of perfect indifference,
their notoriety and the criticism they call forth being
only so much incense burned before the shrine of
their sensual vanity. And to these women may be
given the credit for the ignominious scourge which
flays their honest, suffering sisters.

Annie's unhappiness at being a social pariah in a strange
place could not have been much soothed by her letters from
Saxton. A more perceptive woman might have noted that her
supposed lover seemed far more concerned with the financial and
legal facets of their relationship than their emotional bond. On
May 30, 1892, he wrote:

Dear Annie: -- I enclose you a draft payable to
Brown [cashier Oscar K. Brown of the Lincoln County National Bank, Canton, South Dakota] for
$100.00. Do you know that since the 1st of January,
1891, you have spent almost $1,200.00? I got a letter
from B. yesterday, in which he rakes us for my mistake in Sioux City [imprudently registering with
Annie at the hotel there as man and wife]. I am sorry
you had to leave Canton, as I think that was a better
place for you than Sioux Falls, but go and visit your
cousin. Jennie is here; she came yesterday and is going to Alliance today. I have not been well for the
past three or four weeks, and I think I will go up to
Mt. Clemens, Michigan, for a couple of weeks, and
take a course of baths, but do not know just when I
can leave.   With love and kisses, George.

The very same day Saxton unburdened himself about his legal woes in another letter to Annie:

Dear Annie—I wrote you a letter Wednesday and suppose you think I am scolding you all the time, but I don't want to scold you, for I consider you have enough trouble without any scolding from me. I will send my attorney [James J. Grant] down to Hanoverton the 9th of next month to see the witnesses and have a talk with them and take their depositions [concerning Sample C. George's alienation of affection suit]. I don't think you are going to have any trouble with your [divorce] case out there, but of course I don't know of Sample's arrangements, but I don't think he cares whether or not you get a divorce if he can get some money on the other case, and I will want to take your deposition in relation to the letter and offer that Sample made you. You told me that he offered you $1000 if you would go before his attorney and say I was the cause of your leaving him. Was that what the letter said? If we only had that letter it would be valuable evidence.   With love and kisses. George.

It is worth noting that no such letter containing a bribe offer from Sample C. George was ever produced by any of the concerned principals; it probably never existed.

Whatever her Dakota mortifications, Annie endured them stoically, her goal of marriage to Saxton seemingly in prospect, and the months passed slowly by. She could not have been amused by the news that her husband Sample had filed a $30,000 alienation-of-affection suit against Saxton in February, 1892. [Although now generally barred, alienation-of-affection lawsuits were once common in American courts. Such suits allowed the injured spouses of adulterous husbands or wives to sue their lovers for financial damages]. Specifically, Sample's lawsuit accused Saxton of alienating Annie's affections in April, 1891. Even more concretely, it accused Saxton of committing adultery with Annie in November of the same year and at various other times.

It was the first genuinely public ventilation of the adultery, allowing the previously cautious Canton press to inform its readers, by virtue of its now legal character, of the progress of the city's favorite scandal. Worse yet for Annie, it gave Saxton a fresh pretext for delaying the promised wedding. So even after her divorce from Sample was granted on September 28, 1892, it was clear that her purgatory as Saxton's doxy — not his wife — would continue for an indefinite period. Annie had no idea just how long it would last, but she was agreeable to relocating to Cleveland, Ohio until the legal situation cooled off. Residing there first at the Hollenden Hotel, then at the Doan, she finally moved into a residential hotel at Payne Avenue and North Perry Street (East 21st Street) with a maternal aunt and awaited events.

The months went by. 1892 faded into 1893, then 1893 waned into 1894. Working fitfully as a seamstress, Annie was barely supported by Saxton as she endured the lengthy repercussions of Sample's lawsuit against Saxton. As her material circumstances deteriorated, she drifted first to a less commodious flat on Euclid Avenue and later to still less imposing quarters on Huron Road. Sometimes she was forced to make ends meet by working at various menial jobs. Saxton wrote to her how sorry he was that she "had to stand on her feet in the store all day long" but he did not adequately relieve her financial want. After various legal machinations on both sides, Sample's suit was dismissed in March, 1894 — but without prejudice. Sample soon refiled his suit, this time for $20,000 damages, and it began its laborious progress through the courts. Even as it slowly moved forward, William McKinley's friends began to take an interest in the case. It was obvious by now that McKinley would be a serious candidate for the Republican Presidential nomination in 1896. The last thing his patrons and friends wanted was a scandalous lawsuit associated with his extended family. Quiet negotiations with Sample's lawyers commenced, but the months continued to pass without any resolution.

Shortly after the dismissal of Sample's first lawsuit, Annie moved back to Canton and into the Saxton block. Although she conducted a nominal sewing business there with an assistant, Tishie Hull, she was still being modestly supported by Saxton. However much his original passion for her had cooled, he had been cautious with Annie since her Dakota divorce, painfully conscious that he needed her good will — indeed, would probably have to rely on her willingness to perjure herself — in defending himself against Sample's lawsuit. With the dismissal of Sample George's first suit, however, Saxton felt less restraint with Annie and it was soon demonstrated. Not long after her return to the Saxton block, Saxton orchestrated, or the very least, took advantage of a quarrel with her, and ejected her from her lodging in his building. It was probably on this occasion, or so she would later claim, that he literally kicked her down the stairs from her second-floor room.

The breach may have been some calculated pretext, the kind of feigned but angry spat that has terminated many a failing liaison since time immemorial. More likely, the culminating dispute evolved out of Annie's inescapable realization that there were other women in Saxton's life. The exact details are unknown, except that the inevitable rupture came one night in late 1894. Canton City policeman H. A. Smallfield would one day be asked to recall in court how he encountered a tearful Mrs. George that night and how he arranged for her to stay at a hotel after Saxton threw her out on the street.

Saxton may have thought that his troubles were over. He was wrong. Annie George was not a woman easily scorned, and he and she had only completed the opening act of the tragedy that would climax with his death on a dark, wet street four years later.

Chapter 3   A Woman Scorned

George D. Saxton had run through a lot of women in his life. With the exception of Annie George, though, virtually all of them had no reputation to lose. Annie C. George was probably the first "decent" woman he had actively pursued — and she paid a bitter price for her fallen status. The sexual code for middle-class Americans of the 1890s was inflexible, at least for women. Back then, a woman's chastity, like a maiden's virginity, admitted of no degrees. Once a wife's reputation for sexual fidelity was compromised, her social ruin was total and permanent; she fell, in Shakespeare's bleak phrase, "like Lucifer, never to hope again."

By the time Saxton ejected Annie from bed and board in Room No. 7, she was already the most notorious woman in Canton, if not Stark County and all of northeastern Ohio. She and Saxton had practiced little discretion, either before or after her husband's discovery of their adultery, and she had dispensed with all caution from the moment she became Saxton's kept mistress in the Saxton block. Even before she left to get her Dakota divorce, she was acutely aware of the judgment of those around her. She knew she was talked about, made the butt of rude jests and the theme of moral lessons by persons at all levels of Canton society. In just a few years she had evolved from a provincial ingénue to "that woman" — and her pain at Saxton's emphatic rejection was intensified by the social obloquy she now endured.

Annie's veritable social death was not even her most pressing problem. Without a husband and newly abandoned by her erstwhile lover, she had little visible means of support. Owing to the shabby circumstances of her "quickie" divorce, she had no alimony. True, Sample now had custody of their sons, but Annie still had to cope with the day-to-day problem of getting the necessities of life: food, clothing and shelter.

George Saxton, too, soon found that his problems had only just begun with Annie's ejection from Room 7. From the moment he turned her out of his life, she refused to accept his rejection. Never in the three years of life remaining to him would Annie ever accept or even admit, publicly or privately, that he had spurned her once and for all. Nor would she ever stop insisting, to anyone who would listen, that she still loved George Saxton and wished only that he would keep his promise to make her his lawfully wedded wife. That was her story and she stuck to it with implacable ferocity. As one observer later put it, she worshiped Saxton, "as a whipped spaniel will love an ugly master, cringing and piteously following him."

Annie's efforts to reclaim Saxton commenced from the moment he ejected her from the Saxton block. She had apparently decided that all was fair in her love war and she pursued both a formal legal strategy and an informal campaign of harassment. In late 1894 she filed a $50,000 breach-of-promise suit against Saxton. [Up until the 1940's, such lawsuits were common in English and American courts. If a defendant in such a case were proven to have made an unfulfilled promise of marriage, he was liable for financial damages. Fans of vintage motion pictures like *Goldiggers of 1933* or *Footlight Parade* will recall that such lawsuits were once a central plot device of film comedy]. More annoying to Saxton was her simultaneous and prolonged assault on his privacy. Although no longer a resident of the Saxton block, she now became a fixture there, both day and night. Persistently haunting the hall by Saxton's private rooms on the 2nd floor, she accosted him whenever he showed himself and loudly beseeched him to return to her loving arms.

The breach-of-promise suit was bad enough. True, Saxton had never promised to marry Annie in writing or in front of witnesses. But Saxton had plenty more reasons to worry. The first was that he had registered with Annie as man and wife at several hotels in South Dakota, Ohio and Pennsylvania during their affair. Worse yet, he knew she possessed letters from him in which he had addressed her as his "dear wife." Working through his attorney, James J. Grant, Saxton succeeded in getting the breach-of promise suit quashed on technical grounds in 1895. But it was soon refiled on December 21, 1895, and Saxton's legal apprehensions were amplified by the revival of Sample C. George's alienation-of-affection suit about the same time.

At least Saxton had James J. Grant to serve as his personal firewall in facing his legal difficulties. He was far more vulnerable on a day-to-day basis to Annie's soon chronic disruption of his personal life. Appearing early in the morning at the Saxton block, she would sometimes remain all day, even invading his private rooms and refusing to leave. On at least one occasion, Saxton had to call a policeman to remove her from the building. There were scenes, ugly, screaming, shouting episodes, especially when Saxton tried to escort other women to his private quarters.

William F. Cook, who roomed in the Saxton block during the mid-1890s, would later recall more ominous behavior on Annie's part. Once, he came in late at night to find that all the lights on the second floor were out. Turning a light on, he discovered Annie George standing motionless and silent in front of Saxton's door. On yet another occasion, Cook returned from the theater late one night to find Annie standing by Saxton's door with a pistol in her hand. She tried to hide the weapon but Cook saw it clearly and later told Saxton about it. There were more angry public scenes in the Saxton block, especially after Saxton began squiring around his latest inamorata, Mrs. Eva B. Althouse.

By late 1895, Saxton had had enough. On December 5 his lawyer filed a request with Judge Thomas T. McCarty of the Stark County Common Pleas Court for a restraining order barring Mrs. Annie E. George from the Saxton block. Stating that he was the owner of a commercial-residential building, he accused Mrs. George of repeatedly entering the building merely to annoy and molest him.

Annie's answer to Saxton's petition made it clear she would give no quarter in her battle to reclaim him for her own. Denying that she annoyed or molested him, she stated that her former swain's rooms in the Saxton block, far from being the innocent residential quarters described by him, were in fact a venue for prostitution, gambling and the resort of immoral characters. She further insisted that her own visits to the Saxton block were for the sole purpose of looking after her valuable personal property there, which she accused Saxton of sequestering from her access.

Eventually, early in 1896, Saxton was granted the restraining order he sought. His troubles with Annie, however, did not cease. Although barred from his bachelor pad, she still considered Saxton fair prey if she met him outside it, which she took continuous and considerable pains to do. Moreover, she now found a fresh focus for her boundless hostility: Eva B. Althouse.

Mrs. Eva B. Althouse
(Cleveland Daily World, April 6, 1899)

Just when Saxton became enamored of Mrs. Althouse is unclear. A newspaper account would later assert that he made her acquaintance in July of 1890. That seems unlikely, as Mrs. Althouse was then otherwise engaged. Indeed, she was at that very time acquiring the just the sort of personal resume that might have made her attractive to a broad-minded roué like George Saxton.

As journalist "Coe" would later coyly put it, Eva, "like a good many others connected with this strange case, has a peculiar history." Roughly the same age as Annie George and of no less respectable antecedents, Eva Best had wed a young man of Canton named Nighman in the 1880s. Sometime after their marriage Mr. Nighman was alerted by friends to the fact that Eva was receiving visits from a young Canton bachelor. Hiring a private detective to investigate, Nighman quickly discovered that his worst suspicions were true. With the assistance of the Canton police force, Nighman had a watch placed upon his home. The surveillance bore fruit on July 4, 1890, when a watchful Canton constable saw George W. Althouse enter the home. Employing a key furnished by Mr. Nighman, the police entered the house and discovered Eva in a state of anxious dishabille. Searching the house, the police found nothing suspicious, save a locked bathroom door. When Eva refused to unlock it, one of the policemen threatened to detach it with a screwdriver. Eva then relented and the door was opened to reveal George W. Althouse in a state of embarrassed undress. The upshot was that Nighman divorced Eva. She survived her disgrace handsomely, however, subsequently marrying George W. Althouse and settling into presumed domestic bliss at 319 Lincoln Avenue.

Eva's connubial pleasures ended abruptly in the early 1890s, when her husband George, like her, an avid bicyclist, was hit and fatally injured by a Canton streetcar on Tuscarawas Street while pedaling his "wheel." Sometime after that, as Eva would later recall under oath, she consulted George D. Saxton, whom she had known casually since childhood, about a financial matter. They hit it off immediately. While not quite as good-looking as

Chapter 3   A Woman Scorned

Annie George, Eva Althouse, by all accounts was an attractive female. An independent woman with her own residence, moreover, she also shared with Saxton a taste for night life, bicycling and an apparent indifference to public censure and the strictures of the Seventh Commandment. They were soon seen together everywhere.

There were other women in Saxton's life during the period around his break-up with Annie George. The names of Elizabeth Parks, Corrine Smith and Emma Saltzmann would later be bruited in connection with his nocturnal adventures in the Saxton block during the mid-1890s. But Eva Althouse eventually pushed potential rivals from the scene and from 1896 on, Saxton seems to have focused exclusively on her.

It was quickly apparent to Annie after Eva and Saxton began their affair that Eva represented the chief threat to her supposed claims on Saxton. Eva was a far more practiced and shrewd hand at sexual intrigue than Annie, and Annie passionately hated and feared her new rival. Abandoning her erstwhile stakeout of the Saxton building, Annie thenceforth concentrated on shadowing and stalking George and Eva wherever and whenever she could find them. Her noisy confrontations with the couple became a frequent and presumably entertaining sight to curious Cantonians. William Cook would recall watching Annie stalk them as they sauntered one summer evening amid the twilight diversions at the Meyer's Lake resort. Hiding behind a tree, Annie kept them carefully in sight until they eluded her by pedaling away on their bicycles.

As George and Eva became a more serious item between 1895 and 1897, Annie stepped up the pressure. Walking almost every evening to the vicinity of Eva's Lincoln Avenue home, Annie would wait for George to arrive there on his bicycle. Accosting him, she would entreat him not to enter Eva's house and to return to her and keep his pledge to marry her. Sometimes, George would evade Annie's surveillance and manage to get into Eva's house before she arrived. On such occasions, Annie would stand outside for hours, varying her anguished cries for George's return with angry and often obscene abuse of Eva.

Meanwhile, the increasingly embittered and tangled relations between Annie and Saxton were also quickening on the legal front. In response to the injunction barring her from the Saxton block, Annie filed two replevin suits against Saxton, accusing him of unlawfully sequestering her personal belongings in her former quarters there. The suits were filed in Canton Justice of the Peace Frank H. Darr's court on November 16 and November 23, 1895. Saxton's reply to her suits was a legal rejoinder that he was holding some of her belongings as security for a $300 loan he had made to her. He said she was free to visit the block with a disinterested party and to repossess some of her belongings but he insisted on holding the remainder until the alleged debt was satisfied. Annie eventually showed up with Canton Police officer Adam Jackman with an appropriate writ to reclaim her goods. After taking some of them away she requested some of the remaining items and inquired why her sewing machine was broken. Saxton replied in surly fashion that a step-ladder had fallen on it. Saxton's attorney, James J. Grant, also present on the occasion, had had enough of Annie, whom he considered a completely impossible, grasping woman. "She got everything but the paper on the wall," he jeered to Jackman, "and now she wants that." Annie left the Saxton block without getting all of her goods.

Matters waxed still uglier in 1896. Annie's personal siege of Saxton was beginning to complicate his life in a manner he deemed unacceptable. Her breach of promise case, vexing enough in itself, now seriously undermined his efforts to contest Sample C. George's alienation-of-affection suit. Annie had originally agreed to give supporting testimony to Saxton's side of the case; it was now rumored she was shopping contrary evidence to Sample's lawyers. Her replevin suits remained legally unresolved. And although George had an injunction barring Annie from the Saxton block, she remained free, willing and able to harass him anywhere else, especially at the Althouse residence. Early that year, shortly after securing his restraining order against Annie, George undertook more aggressive counter-measures.

Saxton's first ploy was an attempt to destroy Annie's breach-of-promise suit by contriving evidence of her promiscuity. Operatives working out of Jake Mintz's celebrated private detective agency in Cleveland labored hard to establish that Annie had enjoyed sexual relationships with other men during the years she was involved with Saxton. Mintz initially promised Saxton quick returns on his retainer, assuring him that he had secured hard evidence linking Annie to a man who "would put her out of your way forever." But Mintz's investigation fizzled out in early March, 1896; although some suggestive correspondence with other men was discovered, Mintz's men were unable to find the kind of evidence needed to destroy Annie's public portrait of herself as Saxton's exclusive worshipper.

Saxton's second stratagem was more subtle. Disguised as a complete surrender, it actually bought more time for him to maneuver against both Sample and Annie. In March, 1896, alarmed by fresh rumors that Annie might be willing to offer testimony supporting her ex-husband's alienation-of-affection suit, he sent a message through unknown intermediaries that he wished to make up with her. The upshot was that on the night of March 23, Annie boarded an eastbound train in Canton. Six hours later, she got off at Allegheny, Pennsylvania. There, at the Federal Hotel, she met Saxton and they registered there for a room as "George B. Smith and wife" of Toledo, Ohio. Their registration was witnessed by clerk J. S. Hubbel. The next morning, Saxton and Annie were also seen together breakfasting in the hotel dining room by Freeman A. Leeser of Canal Fulton, Ohio.

If ever Annie George clearly proved herself a sincere patsy for George Saxton's love, it was on the occasion of their Hotel Federal meeting. During their colloquy there they reached an agreement that, in her eyes, seemed to resolve their differences once and for all. Annie's later version of events was that in return for Saxton's renewed promise to marry her and to support her financially until the resolution of Sample C. George's suit, she agreed to all of his demands. But none of Saxton's concessions was put in writing—and in return Annie surrendered virtually her entire interests in their dispute. Turning over to Saxton all such correspondence as might compromise him in both the breach of promise suit and Sample George's suit against him, (the letters, for example, containing the salutation "My Dear Wife"), Annie also signed two documents which constituted a complete abandonment of her legal claims against Saxton. The two documents were almost identical. The second one read:

> April 2, 1896
> Received of George D. Saxton the sum of one dollar and other valuable considerations, the receipt of which is hereby acknowledged in full satisfaction of all claims and suits against him whatsoever. By this is meant particularly the two replevin suits against him and the breach of promise case now pending in Common Pleas Court of Stark county, Ohio. The settlement is in full of everything against him.

The only difference between the two documents was that the dollar amount was not specified in the first one. Annie would also later claim that Saxton agreed to settle $3,000 worth of Canton real estate on Mrs. George's two sons. Like the alleged promises to marry and support her, this clause was not put in writing or any other legally binding form. Saxton destroyed the incriminating letters he retrieved from Annie but copies of them would survive to be disputed as evidence at Annie's murder trial.

Soon after withdrawing her lawsuits against Saxton, Annie discovered anew what his promises were worth. Although he briefly paid for her to board with a Mrs. Mary Finley on South Street in Canton, all financial support soon ceased. Neither the property promised to her sons nor preparations to espouse Annie were forthcoming and she eventually renewed her campaign of public harassment against Saxton with increased virulence and new tactics.

One of Annie's new measures was an attempt to enlist the Canton media on her side. Long accustomed to broadcasting her Saxton woes to any available ear, Annie now approached Canton's newspapermen. Two of them were Charles Lloyd of the *Canton Repository* and Perry Van Horne of the *Canton News-Democrat*. During Annie's murder trial in 1899, Lloyd and Van Horne would recall Annie repeatedly contacting them to retail her latest bickering with Saxton and pleading with them to write something about it sympathetic to her in their newspapers, especially something that would "roast" George D. Saxton. Nothing much came of that; neither Canton newspaper was likely to assail a prominent and well-to-do citizen like George D. Saxton, and most Canton newspaper reporters, like their fellow citizens, thought Annie's woes comic distraction at best, rather than a public concern demanding extensive media coverage or investigation.

Annie's other new tactic consisted of numerous and continual threats against George Saxton's life. They began soon after the collapse of her Allegheny agreement with Saxton and continued virtually up until the day of his death, three years later. Anna made threats to shoot Saxton in the presence of both Van Horne and Lloyd; in June, 1898, during a conversation with Lloyd on Market Street, she exclaimed, "If George Saxton does not keep his promise of marriage to me, I'll kill him, damn him, I'll kill him!" Such threats would usually come after Annie had worked herself up into a state of semi-hysteria, priming her anger with emotional recitations of Saxton's alleged wrongs against her.

Annie did not confine her threats strictly to an audience of newspaper reporters. Shortly after coming to live at Mary Finley's house, Annie met Nettie McAllister of South Cherry Street, who came over to Finley's to meet this notorious woman, the subject of so much delightful Canton gossip. During their ensuing conversation Annie waxed emotional on the subject of Saxton's wrongs and vowed she would kill Saxton if he didn't marry her when Sample C. George's alienation-of-affection suit was settled.

As the months continued to pass and Saxton failed to honor his Allegheny promises, Annie increased the frequency of such threats. She was present at a quilting bee in February, 1897 at Mary Nauman's house on South Walnut Street when her woes with Saxton surfaced in the conversation. Someone asked Annie what she would do when her ex-husband's alienation-of-affection suit was settled. Two years later, Nauman would recall the ferocity of Annie's response:

> After the case is settled there will be a wedding or a funeral. If he does not marry me he'll not walk the streets of Canton another day. I'll shoot him dead, and [Harry] Clark [a friend of Mrs. George] will get [me] the revolver.

When Nauman remonstrated that Annie would get in trouble if she shot Saxton, Annie retorted that she had always gotten out of trouble before and that she would get out of that, too. She told Nauman that even if she were sent to the penitentiary, she would "knock everyone's eyes out" there.

During the two and half years that elapsed between the Allegheny agreement and the murder of Saxton, Annie often repeated her threats to shoot him dead. Virtually all of her threats, however, were made conditionally; an always overwrought and often weeping Annie would tell her audience that she would kill Saxton *if* he did not honor his promise to marry her and *after* Sample C. George's suit was settled.

By the summer of 1897, it was obvious that Annie's new strategies to woo Saxton back were not working any better than the old ones. A fresh approach was needed, especially with the settlement of Sample's suit a real possibility. So Annie now decided to focus on what she considered the most serious short-term threat to her dreams of conjugal bliss with George D. Saxton: Eva B. Althouse.

Stepping up her verbal abuse of Eva, Annie now seized every opportunity of publicly confronting and upbraiding her rival, often in obscene and profane language. Lurking in Eva's coal shed or nearby outbuildings, Annie would emerge on George's visiting nights. Stomping right up to the door of Eva's Lincoln Avenue home, Annie would loudly demand that he come out of that "whore's" house and honor his promise to marry her.

One night in August of 1897, Annie went a bit further. Accosting George and Eva as they returned to Eva's home from a moonlight bicycle excursion, Annie grabbed George's arm as Eva fled into her house and locked the door. "Look here; you're not going to go in there tonight!" cried Annie to Saxton. He stared at her for a moment, and then said, "Hello, here's Mayor Rice's whore! (probably a spontaneous slur triggered by the fact that James Rice, who combined a private law practice with his mayoral duties, sometimes represented Anna in her lawsuits against Saxton.) "There's another in there!" riposted Annie. "George, go home with me tonight!" she pleaded, and clutched at his arm. Saxton was carrying an umbrella and as he shook off her hand he began beating Anna with it. After several blows, she pulled out a revolver and forced him to walk down the street with her. As they approached the Tuscarawas Street bridge, she asked Saxton if he wanted to die right then and there. Saxton's response was a bewildered, "Who are you? I don't know you!" When they arrived at the bridge, Annie's revolver, which had been wrapped in her shawl, fell out. As it clattered to the street, Saxton picked it up, put it in his pocket and kept on walking. Annie followed him to the Saxton block, where, however, she observed the restraining injunction by making no attempt to enter the building. The next morning, Annie gleefully recounted the episode to her landlady, Mary Finley, once again threatening to kill Saxon and repeating her conviction that she could get away with it:

I will not stand by and see George Saxton going with this woman. He has promised to marry me just as soon as my former husband's case against him is settled and if he fails to keep that promise I will kill him. I'll do it if I hang the next day, but I do not think any jury on earth would convict me after hearing my story.

Shortly after that, Annie summoned newspaper reporter Perry Van Horne and recounted the details of the incident to him in the vain hope that he would write up a sympathetic account of it in the *News-Democrat*. She also repeated her threat to kill Saxton if he didn't marry her after Sample's lawsuit was settled.

The revolver episode may have been the final straw for both Saxton and Eva. Annie's increasingly belligerent tactics were scary enough—but the revolver episode, possibly leaked by Annie herself, eventually provoked a front page headline in the August 15, 1897 edition of the *Cleveland Plain Dealer*. An angry George Saxton now contacted United States Post Office officials to complain of unsigned and threatening letters that Annie had sent to him and Eva; these messages included obscene abuse of both of them and a more specific intention to cut out Eva's heart and "hang it on a telephone pole." On August 23, 1897 Annie was arrested in Canton by Deputy United States Marshal John J. Keeley and taken to Massillon for an arraignment before Commissioner Folger. Bailed out by her friend Mayor James Rice of Canton, Annie was indicted that fall by a Cleveland federal grand jury on a charge of sending obscene material through the mail. She posted bond and her trial was set for the spring term of 1898. But Annie was never tried on that charge. The reason she was never prosecuted remains unknown, although her indictment remained active at the time of Saxton's murder, a year later.

Perhaps the reason Annie's misuse of the mails was not aggressively pursued was that Canton officials already thought that they finally had the Annie George situation under control. The problem for the Canton authorities, as for Saxton's relatives, had always been that any efforts to suppress Annie's hostile behavior had to be measured against any possible negative publicity for the Saxton and McKinley families such measures might generate. William McKinley became President of the United States on March 4, 1897 and any publicity about the tawdry affairs of his wife's playboy brother George was potential political poison for McKinley and the Republican Party. Always, throughout the George Saxton-Annie George conflict, it was thought necessary to temper prosecutorial zeal with political caution and Annie seems to have been the greater beneficiary of such discretion.

The seeming solution to the Annie George problem was a local one. In April, 1898 Eva B. Althouse filed peace proceedings against Annie George in the Stark County Probate Court. After listening to witnesses and perusing some of the threatening letters allegedly written by Annie, Justice of the Peace James Robertson ordered her to post a bond committing her to keeping the peace with Eva. Interestingly, both Mary Finley and a woman named Christina Eckroate testified at the peace bond hearing. Finley, still friendly with Mrs. George, testified that Annie acted like a lady, was a peaceable woman and would not harm anyone. Finley would not always entertain this opinion and Annie would later encounter both her and Christine Eckroate in even more dramatic circumstances.

In Annie's defense, it must be said that Saxton was willing to play as rough a game as she. His experience with Jake Mintz's detectives had shown him that it was no simple task to besmirch Annie's reputation for fidelity by entangling her with other men. So, sometime in early 1898, he tried a more drastic tactic. Saxton had word sent to Annie that he was to meet her in Massillon. When she arrived there, a man purporting to be Saxton's agent told her that a friend of hers was getting married in Mansfield and that he was to escort her to the nuptials. The man brought her to Mansfield, where he took her to a house. Five minutes after he left her there, the place was raided by Mansfield lawmen, who arrested Annie and charged her with being resident in a house of ill repute. Contrary to Saxton's hopes, however, Annie was not jailed or sent to the workhouse, but allowed to leave Mansfield after pledging her watch as security for a $15 fine.

Progressively stymied in her efforts to directly harass Saxton and Eva Althouse, Annie stepped up her litany of public threats. In the fall of 1897, she elaborated on her previous conversation with Mary Finley during another emotional outburst at the latter's home. She told Mary:

> Just wait till the case of Sample C. George and Saxton is settled; I will see Saxton. I am going to ask Mayor [James] Rice to go with me to Saxton's office. I am going to ask Saxton what he will do for me, and if he does nothing I will shoot him so full of lead that he will stand stiff.

Once again remonstrating with Mrs. George, Finley replied, "Mrs. George, you must not do that, you will go to the penitentiary." "Only a few years if I do," riposted Annie, "and what is that?"

Early in 1898, Annie again repeated to Finley her vow to kill Saxton if he didn't marry her. This time she mentioned Harry Clark again, noted that he often went to Chicago, could obtain a revolver there for her, and "nobody will know anything about it." Annie added that she wanted a self-acting revolver and that if Clark could not obtain one she might try and get one from her friend Mayor Rice. As he was also the acting police chief of Canton, she thought he might easily supply her with one confiscated from a criminal. About a month later Finley teased Annie, opining that Saxton would ultimately marry Mrs. Althouse instead of her. A riled Annie repeated her threat to shoot Saxton, vowing, "I'll not do it like a coward; I'll go up in front of him and let him know who did it."

Chapter 3   A Woman Scorned

Sometime during early 1898 Annie was living in a shabby downtown room in a Canton bath house. There, she struck up an acquaintance with Mary E. Grable, the manager's wife. One day, the two women were sitting together at a window looking out on the street when they saw George Saxton pass by. "There goes George Saxton," said Mrs. George bitterly. "He ruined my life. If he doesn't do what is right and marry me, I will fill him full of lead!"

Whatever culpability Saxton may have had for Annie's plight, there seems little doubt that Annie was being sincere when she described her life as "ruined." Stigmatized by much of "decent" Canton society as a fallen woman, she had nothing but bitter memories to show for her decade-long relationship with that society's most glittering bachelor. Separated from her children, she barely eked out an existence as a low-paid seamstress, always in debt, living in a succession of rented rooms and eating inexpensive meals at cheap restaurants. Then, in October, 1898, the final blow fell upon Annie without warning.

Chapter 4   Prelude to a Murder

Sample C. George's alienation-of-affection lawsuit was probably a distant memory to most Cantonians by the fall of 1898. Originally filed in 1892, dismissed without prejudice in 1894 and refiled for an adjusted amount of $20,000 in 1895, the suit had meandered its way though the court system with no hint of resolution for three years. Saxton's initial legal strategy against George's renewed suit was to ignore its merits, insisting simply that the adulterous acts alleged in the suit had occurred too long ago to fall within the statute of limitations. The Stark County Common Pleas court initially sustained Saxton's claim, but was subsequently reversed by the circuit court and the suit resumed its slow progress through the legal system.

Shepherded skillfully on Sample's behalf by Stark County attorney James A. Sterling and opposed with equal vigor by Saxton's lawyer James J. Grant (with assistance during the early phases by William R. Day) Sample's case finally appeared on the docket of the Ohio Supreme Court in early 1898. There it was argued in June—only to be remanded back to the Stark County Court of Common Pleas for a hearing on its merits. There seemed no end in sight for the wearisome litigation. All sides began preparing for the next round, including Annie, who again summoned reporter Charles Lloyd to repeat her warning that she would kill Saxton if he didn't marry her when the case was decided. Then, without warning, it was abruptly settled in October.

Unexpectedly, the offer to settle came from Sample's attorney, James Sterling, and Saxton must have been astonished by its modesty. After ten years of public scandal and six years of legal combat, Sample C. George now stated that he was willing to settle his $20,000 lawsuit for $1,825.00—considerably less than even ten cents on each dollar of the original demand, but paid in cash. Attorney Grant immediately opened negotiations and the deal was sealed on October 4. The final agreement read as follows:

Canton, O. Oct. 4, 1898
Sample C. George vs. George D. Saxton

Received of George D. Saxton, defendant in the above entitled action, the sum of eighteen hundred and twenty-five ($1,825.00) dollars in full satisfaction of any and all claims and demands of any nature whatsoever against the said George D. Saxton, and more especially in full settlement of the claim and demand set out against the defendant in the action aforesaid, except docket costs amounting to $13.59, to be paid by defendant; it being further agreed by me, Sample C. George, for the consideration aforesaid, that the above action shall be marked "settled;" without record.

[Signed] Sample C. George, James Sterling, Welty & Albaugh, Nat. C. McLean

It all seemed too good to be true — and it was, at least in one sense. True, Saxton's lawyers had been willing to settle for considerably more than the final sum agreed upon. The pressure from Saxton's family and Republican politicos concerned about the scandal potential of Sample's suit had been growing in tandem with both William McKinley's rapid political ascent and lurid developments in the Saxton-George imbroglio. It seemed, indeed, like a bargain settlement until all parties had signed on the dotted line. It was at that point, however, that a smiling Sample C. George turned to Grant and announced that he had been remarried for more than a year to Lucy T. Graham of Alliance. The only reason Sample had settled for such a diminished sum, he now confessed, was because he feared he could not keep his new marriage a secret for much longer. Grant, Saxton's chagrined attorney could only agree, stating that he would never have advised any financial settlement had he known of Sample's remarriage in September, 1897. All the attorneys in the case agreed that no jury would have ever awarded significant damages to a plaintiff who had found such emphatic consolation for his injured conjugal feelings.

Whatever his private feelings about the money and Sample George's deception, George Saxton's public stance on the terms of the settlement was a model of understated propriety. While he continued to deny any obligation whatsoever to pay Sample a penny, he expressed relief to his friends that his legal ordeal was over and that his family would be spared further "unnecessary annoyance." But the most interesting remark made at the lawsuit settlement ceremony in James J. Grant's office was Sample C. George's comment, "I believe Annie will kill Saxton if he does not marry her, now that our suit has been settled."

The news that Sample C. George's lawsuit had been settled took most Cantonians by surprise. Probably no one was more stunned than Annie, whose whole life had been focused on that event for more than six years. Indeed, so unanticipated was a resolution of the lawsuit that Annie had only recently made plans to return to her mother's home in Hanoverton. With no means of support but her meager earnings as a seamstress, Annie was practically destitute in Canton. She had to get out of there, and she had already arranged for her furniture to be shipped to her mother's house that very week. Annie was now boarding at the home of Cora Oberlin at 1516 West Tuscarawas Street. It was a double house, and she had moved there in early 1898 to the home of a Mrs. Taylor after a personal breach with Mary Finley left her without a residence. After her furniture was shipped out on Monday, October 3, she made arrangements to rent a bedroom from Mrs. Oberlin on a day-to-day basis. It was rumored that the notorious Annie had been forced to pay double the regular amount of rent, as Mrs. Oberlin was reluctant to rent the room to a woman of her fragrant reputation.

The day after Sample's settlement was announced, Annie went to see attorney James Sterling in his Dannemiller block office. The details of her discussion with Sterling are unknown, but Annie later discussed her ex-husband's settlement with her landlady Cora Oberlin that night. Although she did not repeat her threats against Saxton, Annie did express wistful surprise that the suit was settled and that Sample had remarried without her knowledge. Annie did not disclose more of her feelings to Mrs. Oberlin but it seems likely that she must have felt more isolated than ever. With the withdrawal of the most serious legal threats against him, George Saxton was now free to do as he wished with the opposite sex.

What Annie did not tell Cora Oberlin was that she had already tried to see Saxton after she had heard of the settlement. At 5:30 that same Thursday evening, she had accosted Canton Police Patrolman Charles Dickerhoff on a downtown street as he made his rounds. Dickerhoff, a veteran of some three years on the force, had known Mrs. George for four or five years and was friendly with her. She told Dickerhoff that she had been to see Mayor Rice that afternoon and that he had detailed the policeman to accompany her on a proposed visit to the Saxton block. All of which was true, including Annie's flattering remark that she had specifically asked for Dickerhoff. Her stated motive for a police escort was her fear of Saxton's using violence against her and Mayor Rice apparently agreed to her request, notwithstanding the injunction against her entering the Saxton block, which was still in force.

Dickerhoff returned to headquarters, notified the desk sergeant that he was on detached duty, and then met Mrs. George by prearrangement at Market and Ninth Street at 6:30 p.m. The ninety minutes that followed were a futile and lugubrious comedy, as Dickerhoff and Annie, sometimes together and sometimes separately, walked around and around the Saxton block, searching for signs of its elusive owner. Eventually, after another prowl down the alley adjacent to Saxton's quarters, Annie reported that there was now a light on in one of his rooms. But she did not ask Dickerhoff to enter the building to find Saxton, nor did she violate the injunction by going in after him herself. Dickerhoff was somewhat puzzled by her behavior but retained his amiable manner towards Annie. After more fruitless prowling around, she finally decided to call it quits for the night, thanked him and arranged to have him meet her again the following night at Ninth and Market Streets for a repeat performance. As all Canton would eventually learn, Dickerhoff kept that appointment; Annie George did not.

Autumn is usually the most beautiful and clement of seasons in northeast Ohio. The winters are frequently quite brutal and the summers are all too often marathons of broiling temperatures and excruciating humidity. But Friday, October 7 was not the kind of perfect fall day for which the region is justly famous. Although the temperature never dipped below the 50s, there were two intervals of rainfall during the day. There was a light sprinkling shortly after daylight and then a more prolonged and heavier downpour after 2 p.m., the latter amounting to .15 inch. Most observers would later agree that the rain caused some muddiness, but not an excessive amount, especially in Canton's vacant lots. Skies remained cloudy after the afternoon rainfall and the wind was negligible, leaving most of the leaves still on Canton trees as the early fall evening set in. Darkness would arrive just about 6 p.m.

As befitting a future murder defendant, more is known about Mrs. George's movements that October day than those of any other Cantonian. Annie left Cora Oberlin's house at about 9 a.m. that morning, telling Mrs. Oberlin she would be back that evening. Going downtown, she dropped into the Davis block to see John J. Jackson, the janitor of the building. She was on friendly terms with Jackson, as she was with many Cantonians, whatever their private views or hurtful gossip about her notoriety. He had known Mrs. George for about ten years and she would drop in to chat with him, usually once or twice a week. Now, as was her custom, she poured out her Saxton woes to a willing ear. After asking for some writing paper so she could write a request to have her umbrella fetched, she mentioned her ex-husband's settlement with Saxton and said that he had vowed to marry her after it was concluded. She said she was going to try and see him as soon as possible. Jackson, knowing both Annie's temper and the still-

48

standing injunction against her, advised against it. "Why don't you write to him, instead?" he said. Annie replied that Saxton probably wouldn't answer any note she wrote him. She paused pensively for a moment, and then she said, "Jack, I am beginning to realize what you always told me, that he is not going to marry me." She then complained that she was tired of being "baffled" by Saxton and would take her revenge if he didn't marry her. When Jackson cautioned her that killing him wouldn't help her, she replied resolutely, "Well, he'll get his deserts in hell or in eternity."

Sometime early that Friday afternoon, Annie dropped in on her friend Lena Lindeman. Just when she arrived at Lena's South Market Street home and when she left it would later be matters of intense legal debate. Both women were seen at Lindeman's house that afternoon. J. C. Moore observed the two women sitting together sometime between 4:30 and 5 p.m. Lena and Annie had been friends for some time and they chatted in a friendly manner as Lena, who did George Saxton's ironing, worked on a pile of tidies from his Saxton block lodgings. [A tidy is a protective covering, often fancily embroidered, for the arms or headrest of a chair]. As Lena was ironing one of them, Annie stared at it intently, and then exclaimed happily that it was one of several she had stitched for Saxton during her long Dakota sojourn at the Harland Hotel. She noticed that the tidy was becoming a little ragged at the edge and she took it from Lena and trimmed it neatly. She asked Lena to observe carefully when she returned the tidies to Saxton and report back to her whether George had noticed that the tidy had been repaired.

It was an entirely different Annie George who conversed with a sympathetic Lena Lindeman that long afternoon. No longer the unrelenting, familiar Medea of her recent chat with John Jackson, Annie now chattered happily of the halcyon times she now saw in prospect. Annie, Lena later recalled, chattered like a lovestruck teenager about George Saxton and said she expected to be married to him soon. Annie hoped to meet with Saxton about their future the next day and she promised to meet Lena on Market Street afterwards and tell her all about it.

Sometime during that long afternoon, or so Lena would later testify, Annie loitered for a few minutes in Lena's backyard. Like many a yard and vacant lot in Canton, it was overgrown, particularly at its borders, with a profusion of weedy vegetation, predominantly Spanish needles and burrs. The question of whether the fabric of Annie's black dress accumulated a quantity of those sticky weeds in the Lindeman yard would later bring her very close to the electric chair.

Did Annie George go to the downtown Canton post office sometime that Friday afternoon? Were she and Lena Lindeman truthful in their assertion that Annie spent the whole afternoon at Lena's house? Canton Post Office money order clerk Michael Barr later told a different story. Barr had been involved as a government witness in the obscene mail charge against Annie in 1897 and he knew Annie well by sight. According to Barr, he saw Annie twice at the downtown post office that afternoon, the first time at 2:45 and the second at 3:15. Neither sighting, if valid, would have had anything to do with the subsequent murder of George Saxton. But if Barr was telling the truth, why was Annie at the post office at a time she claimed to have been at Lena Lindeman's house? And why would the two women have lied about it?

What we do know for certain is that Annie took leave of Lena sometime before 5 p.m., probably closer to 4:30. She walked back downtown to the Star Restaurant, where she was in the habit of inexpensively dining each evening, using a punched meal ticket. Waitress Lena Mauger greeted Mrs. George when she arrived that day, about 4:40 p.m. Knowing that the Star Restaurant did not begin serving suppers until 5 p.m, Lena asked Annie if she were in a hurry. Annie replied that she was not, but in any case she was served her meal shortly before the hour. Annie was also seen at the Star Restaurant by waitress Ida Hug, who took Annie's order and brought her meal. Ida didn't recall when Annie finished her meal and left the restaurant. Nor did restaurant cook Lucile

Monter and waitress Clara Weiser, who took note of their regular customer. But Star Restaurant owner Samuel A. Kirk did, later remembering that Annie walked out of his restaurant at 5:15 p.m.

Five minutes later pedestrian Effie Darr passed Mrs. George as she walked westward on Tuscarawas Street. Ten minutes later, she was seen, still walking there, by Frank M. Wyant, the treasurer of the Wrought Iron Bridge Company. Five minutes after that, Mrs. George dropped in on Stark County Common Pleas Judge Thomas T. McCarty at his Tuscarawas Street home. Thanks to her copious litigation, Annie was no stranger to McCarty; he had granted Saxton the injunction barring Annie from the Saxton block. But McCarty and Annie remained on friendly terms and he welcomed her, despite the interruption of his supper. Getting immediately to the point, Annie mentioned that her ex-husband's lawsuit against Sample had been settled. Would it be all right, in view of that fact, if she could now enter the Saxton block and talk to George?

"You must not do that, Mrs. George," McCarty sternly cautioned. "The injunction has not been resolved."

"He promised to have it dissolved!" said Mrs. George.

"Well, he has not done so."

"But I want to see Saxton and I do not know how I can arrange it."

"I suggest you write him a note and make an appointment for a meeting."

"I don't think he'll meet with me. May I not meet him?"

"Mrs. George," McCarty wearily returned, "you had better leave Saxton alone."

Recognizing the note of finality in McCarty's voice, Annie conceded quietly. Insisting that she did not wish to violate the terms of Saxton's injunction, she took leave of McCarty and left his house, walking west on Tuscarawas Street. The last words he said to her were, "Be careful," referring to the precarious front steps of his house. The entire exchange had taken no more than five minutes. Just about the time Annie left McCarty's home, Frank

Wyant, the Treasurer of the Wrought Iron Bridge Company, encountered George Saxton at Copthorne's tailoring store on Tuscarawas Street. A minute later, Grand Opera House treasurer William Choffin looked out a window from his seat in a barber shop near Market and Eighth Streets and saw Saxton enter the south door of the Saxton block. He soon exited, carrying a satchel in his hand, mounted his bicycle and began pedaling north up Market Street. It was now about 5:40 p.m.

Five minutes later, Canton streetcar No. 21 left the Canton Public Square on its regular 5:45 westbound run down Tuscarawas Street. It carried only a crew of one that October evening, Motorman Charles F. Rittenhouse. At that very moment Adams Express Company clerk Ed Bour was driving his delivery wagon east on Tuscarawas Street. As he drove through the oncoming darkness he passed George D. Saxton, pedaling westward.

It was about 5:50 p.m. when Annie George boarded Streetcar No. 21 at High and Tuscarawas Streets. There were about seven passengers on it and most of these witnesses, as well as the motorman, later agreed she was wearing a black dress, carrying a dark cape and wearing a light sailor hat. Rittenhouse saw her get on his car. He did not know Mrs. George by sight, but that was a deficiency soon remedied in a town as small as Canton. As she settled into her seat, off-duty streetcar conductor James Shetler — who was riding as a passenger — turned to Motorman Rittenhouse and muttered, *sotto voce*, the identity of their notorious passenger. Edward J. Landor, the president of the Wrought Iron Bridge Company, saw Mrs. George get on the streetcar as he got off it, as did Lorin Wise, a Canton attorney. Jesse C. Taylor, the night streetcar barn man for the Canton-Massillon Street Railway Company, also saw Mrs. George get on Car No. 21. Taylor also noticed her attire but he got off before she did, just east of the Valley Railroad crossing at Tuscarawas Street.

The regularly scheduled Valley Railroad freight was a little late that night. Due at 5:44 p.m., it didn't pull into the freight depot siding until at least 5:56, perhaps as late as 5:58 p.m. Its tardiness created a delay for the passengers of streetcar No. 21, for its freight cars blocked the Tuscarawas Street intersection for the four or five minutes it took to unload its cargo. There would later be much dispute as to when the Valley train arrived, when it left the depot, and how long it blocked the streetcar line. Valley Railroad gate keeper John Treeman was in charge of the crossing gate that day and his recollection was probably the most accurate. He recalled that the freight arrived no earlier than 5:56 and cleared the Tuscarawas Street intersection no earlier than 6:02 or 6:03 p.m. That would have been just about the time Patrolman Dickerhoff showed up at Market and Ninth Streets for his abortive second rendezvous with Mrs. George.

Charles Huth was also at the crossing that October evening, and his subsequent recollection supported Treeman's chronology concerning the blockage of the streetcar tracks. Huth, a driver for the United States Express Company, was there with his express wagon to pick up items from the Valley Railroad freight train. His memory of the occasion would be reinforced by his wife, who was there, as promised, to bring him his dinner. Sometime during the interval while the freight was being unloaded, George Saxton bicycled westbound, passing Canton resident Florence Klingler on Tuscarawas Street. Perhaps five minutes later, just before the freight cleared the tracks, carpenter Jacob Adams also saw Saxton, riding on his bicycle at Dueber Avenue and Tuscarawas Street. Hailing Saxton, he asked him if he had attended the Stark County Fair at Minerva. "Yes," hollered Saxton, and pedaled on. Adams was probably the last person to see Saxton alive, save his slayer.

Sometime between 6:05 and 6:10 p.m., Annie George got off the streetcar at Hazlette Avenue and Tuscarawas Street. Why she had boarded the trolley in the first place would never be known. It seems improbable that she was going home, for the streetcar had passed Mrs. Oberlin's Tuscarawas Street home by several blocks before Annie arose to disembark. Motorman Rittenhouse would recall that Annie did not ring the streetcar bell and that she exited at the "wrong" end of the streetcar for disembarking passengers.

Rittenhouse saw Annie get off the car, as did conductor Shetler. Passenger John A. Shanafelt, the secretary-treasurer of the Canton Steel Roofing Company, also saw Annie get off the car. Shanafelt did not notice what she was wearing and no one on the car noticed in which direction she went after the streetcar proceeded on its way. Two blocks and one thousand feet away, George D. Saxton was approaching the home of Eva Althouse on his bicycle . . .

Chapter 5 Death of a Ladies' Man

Each October evening the autumn dusk comes earlier and earlier to Ohio. On this October 7, 1898, daylight was already rapidly fading as 6:00 p.m. arrived in Canton. It was a Friday evening in the northeast Ohio city, and its citizens were bustling in the still-growing city of nearly 35,000 souls. Most of Canton's laboring population was still at work or just getting off, this being the pre-modern era when the work week extended to 50 or even 60 hours for most unskilled workers. But many of the people still on the darkening Canton streets were middle-class housewives returning from downtown shopping expeditions and small businessmen homeward bound from work. One of those new-fangled horseless carriage "automobiles" would have been an unusual sight on the Canton streets but there was still plenty of noisy traffic, horse-drawn vehicles dominating the thoroughfares and pedestrians thronging the stone and wooden sidewalks.

Most Cantonians would later agree that the weather was temperate as twilight waned. Most of the women and many of the men on the streets would have been wearing hats, regardless of the temperature but there was no need but that of display that clement evening for the often elaborate headgear of the day. Some pedestrians wore shawls and there were a few mackintoshes and other forms of raingear to be seen. But the rain had ceased and most of the ground was not very muddy, although the Spanish needles and burrs crowing the sidewalks of many a Canton street were an annoying hazard to clothing, especially the voluminous skirts of Canton women. It was a quiet autumn evening, distinctly unmemorable until murder made it an unforgettable moment in the lives of many Cantonians.

The first shots came at 6:10 p.m. Loud enough to reverberate throughout a circumference of several blocks on Canton's northwest side, they aroused the immediate attention of several persons in the vicinity of Eva B. Althouse's home at 319 Lincoln

Avenue. Most of them were familiar with the sound of firearms being discharged and they stopped whatever they were doing, cocked an attentive ear . . . and waited . . . for something more to happen. They didn't have to wait long: thirty seconds later, two, perhaps three more shots resounded in the fall night air. Although no one actually saw the first shots fired, many of those who heard them seemed to think they came from the area around Eva B. Althouse's home.

HOUSE OF MRS. ALTHOUSE. **X** INDICATES THE SPOT WHERE SAXTON'S BODY WAS FOUND.

The Murder Scene: The Althouse Residence at 319 Lincoln Avenue (Cleveland Daily World, April 7, 1899)

One of those who heard the first shots was Henry J. Bederman. He was probably also the auditor nearest them, as he was standing with his young daughter just inside the door of the Eckroate grocery store, across Lincoln Avenue from the Althouse home and no more than 200 feet away from the shooting site. The first shots came as Bederman was conversing with August Boron, who ran the little grocery out of a rear first-floor room in the home of his father-in-law, Joseph Eckroate. Bederman, who lived just around the corner at 1809 West Third Street, later recalled his first thought upon hearing the sound of gunfire. It was probably a notion shared by many of Eva Althouse's neighbors: "Saxton is getting it!" Like everyone in Eva's neighborhood, Bederman had long been a weary witness of the noisy nightly shenanigans occurring as Annie George stalked George Saxton on his visits to Lincoln Avenue's merry widow. Like many a Cantonian, Bederman had been expecting Annie to shoot Saxton for some time, and he immediately ran outside Eckroate's grocery.

Bederman saw nothing but some flashes from a revolver being fired as he peered across the street towards the Althouse residence. But about thirty seconds after the initial shots, he thought he heard a moaning cry of "Help!" coming from that direction. Then, as he stepped warily towards the street, he saw a shadowy, darkly dressed figure striding rapidly towards the two stone steps that connected the public sidewalk to the slate walk running up to Mrs. Althouse's front porch. The figure seemed to be a woman in dark clothing, who, he would later admit, he immediately assumed was Annie George. Seemingly unaware of Bederman, the figure approached the stone steps and leaned down. Bederman could now see that there was another figure prone on the sidewalk by the steps. The dark, female-looking figure leaned farther and seemed to clutch at the arm of the prone figure. She then straightened up and fired two more shots in the direction of the figure on the ground. Even as Bederman stared in unbelieving shock, the female figure turned around and scurried away. He continue to gape as the figure ran south to the residence of Mrs. R. M. Quinn, the house next door, turned west and disappeared, running through an adjacent vacant lot toward Lawn Avenue. Bederman ran back to the Eckroate grocery, retrieved his daughter and groceries and rushed to his nearby home. Turning his daughter over to her mother, he ran back towards the Althouse steps.

William Glick heard the shots from inside his home at 323 Lincoln Avenue, just north of the Althouse house. He was reading the evening newspaper when he heard two shots, followed thirty seconds later by two more shots. "There must be something wrong here!" he exclaimed, and ran out of the house toward the Althouse steps. Frank Hildenbrad was another person who heard the shots on Lincoln Avenue. Sitting in his home at 217 Meyers Court, a street to the rear of the Eckroate grocery, he almost immediately started running in the direction he thought they were coming from. As he dashed around the corner of Lincoln Avenue, he almost ran into a woman. As he passed her, she screamed, "My God! Someone has been shot! He is lying there dead!" Seconds later, Hildenbrad found the body lying on the sidewalk.

Henry Bederman got to the body just seconds after Hildenbrad. As they stared at it, thirteen-year-old Russell Hogan arrived breathless at the scene. Russell, the son of Canton Councilman Martin Hogan, had been at his 216 Lincoln Avenue home, a few houses south and across the street from Althouse house, when he heard the shots. Rushing out of his house, he thought he saw a figure running down the street and then west through the vacant lot by the Quinn house. William Glick was right behind him as he arrived at the Althouse steps.

It was too dark to see who was lying on the sidewalk. Although there was a street light at the intersection of West Third Street and Lincoln Avenue, a lamp in the window of the Eckroate grocery and some illumination from neighborhood homes, little light reached the area by the Althouse steps. Whoever was lying there, however, was not moving or making a sound. Even when Hildenbrad turned the body over, there wasn't enough light to identify it. Finally, he fumbled in his pockets and pulled out some matches. August Boron, who had by now arrived on the scene, also pulled matches and struck one. As the first one flared, he, Hildenbrad, Bederman and Hogan stared at the body below. "My God!" blurted out Bederman as he recognized the face. "It's George Saxton!"

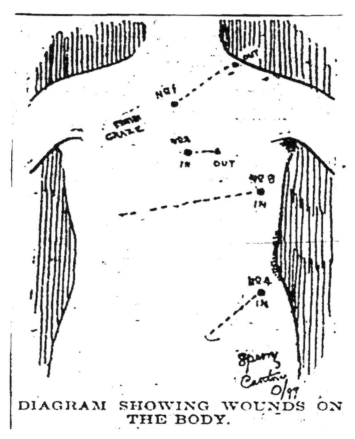

DIAGRAM SHOWING WOUNDS ON THE BODY.

Diagram Showing George D. Saxton's Bullet Wounds
(Cleveland Daily World, April 11, 1899)

Saxton was lying fully extended across the sidewalk, between the stone steps and the curb. He was laying on his right side, his face to the sidewalk and his hands drawn up to it, as if to protect himself from something or someone. His feet were toward the Althouse residence, his right foot on the first step, his left on the lawn. He was wearing a bicycle cap and a light overcoat. There were no obvious signs of violence and his body looked as if it had fallen from the steps. Propped against a tree by the curb was his bicycle, where he had apparently left it before mounting the steps. Near his body was a satchel, containing a nightshirt and a bottle of champagne.

Within three or four minutes of Hildenbrad's arrival, a crowd drawn by the shots had gathered around Saxton's body. Some of the men there was lighting match to afford a better view of the body and everyone was talking about Saxton being shot. Two of those present were sisters Augusta and Louisa Suskey. They had been walking home from downtown and had turned north on to Hazlette Avenue from Tuscarawas Street when they heard what they thought were the sounds of three shots being fired as they neared the intersection with West Third Street. As they passed near Henry Bederman's house by the corner of Third and Lincoln, they heard two more. Drawn by the noise of the crowd, they walked west and then turned onto Lincoln Avenue. Although it was dark, both of them could recognize several persons by sight in the crowd across the street by the Althouse front steps.

It may have been Henry Bederman who finally decided to take charge in what was becoming an unseemly, even ghoulish spectacle, as the crowd swarmed around Saxton's body for a closer look. He, or possibly some other spectator, turned to Russell Hogan and told him to run to Weiss's saloon, about a block away, and tell Weiss to call the Canton police. Accompanied by Joseph Schmidt, 12, Russell did as he was bid. The call came into the downtown Canton Police station at about 6:20 p.m.

The word that George D. Saxton had been shot was big news and the Canton police responded immediately. Canton City humane officer Charles R. Frazer was the chief officer on duty that night. Although his duties usually involved stray pets and instances of cruelty to animals, he had full police powers and he quickly collected a posse of officers, including Canton Marshal William H. Reed and Superintendent of Patrol Service Romey. Jumping into a horse wagon, they rushed first to the Canton home of Dr. Edward Brant at 114 North Cleveland Avenue, the Canton physician on call to the police department that night. The four men arrived on the chaotic scene by 6:25 p.m. They were soon joined by Canton Police Sergeant William J. Hasler.

Dr. Brant was used to such scenes and did not stand on ceremony. Pushing his way through the crowd, he stooped to the body and turned it over. As Brant touched Saxton's vest, a bullet rolled off it and onto the sidewalk. Brant made a rapid check for vital signs and then said, "It is George Saxton, sure enough, and he is dead." A minute later, the police put Saxton's body on a stretcher, hustled it into their wagon and sped it on its way to Shilling's Morgue. After conferring there with fellow physician, Dr. Austin C. Brant, Dr. Edward pronounced Saxton officially dead.

It was obvious to the physicians that Saxton had been shot to death and it was clear that an autopsy would have to be performed as soon as possible. Local politics, however, immediately intruded and delayed the post-mortem for the better part of an hour. Although Stark County Coroner T. T. McQuate was nominally in charge, local custom had long dictated that the first physician on the scene could choose the members of the autopsy team. The prestige of performing the autopsy on one of Canton's most prominent citizens—a post-mortem that would garner national publicity—was at stake. McQuate argued fiercely for the honor but eventually conceded to custom.

The autopsy commenced shortly after 9 p.m., with Dr. Brant in charge and wielding the scalpel. Also assisting were Canton physicians Dr. Alonzo B. Walker, Dr. Austin C. Brant, Dr. W. O. Foulks, Dr. A. H. Gaus of Massillon and Coroner McQuate. Saxton's muscles were already stiffening into the rigors of death and the post-mortem crew worked methodically but hurriedly as they examined Saxton's corpse. Carefully removing his worsted suit, vest, negligee shirt and pants, they set to work. The evidence of what had killed Saxton was only too clear but they labored conscientiously and meticulously, as they knew it were their duty to be likewise certain what had *not* killed him. Their scrutiny of Saxton's corpse clearly indicated that he was a mature man in good health, his organs and brains normal and healthy and showing no signs of disease or injury other than his obvious gunshot wounds. It was the body of a middle-aged man: a bit above average height, a little portly, with a sandy complexion, a round face and bushy mustache.

Four bullets had hit George D. Saxton. It was not clear, then or ever, the exact order in which the shots had been fired, so Dr. Brant and his crew arbitrarily assigned a numerical sequence to the bullet paths they found. As they reconstructed that sequence, they concluded that the "first" bullet had entered sideways, just above the right breast, bounced off a suspender buckle and exited about two inches above the entry wound. Its path was no deeper than a half inch. That was probably the bullet that rolled off Saxton's vest at the murder scene. The second bullet had entered sideways at the left breast, glanced along the ribs and then exited out the left shoulder. Its path, too, was only about a half inch deep. This bullet was found on Saxton's left breast, inside his clothing during the autopsy. Saxton's physicians believed that both these first and second wounds were superficial and could not have caused death or even very serious injury.

The third bullet had entered under the left arm, penetrated the lungs and diaphragm, severed several large arteries and come to rest in Saxton's liver. It had plowed six inches into his body and its path was about a half inch in diameter.

The fourth bullet had entered Saxton's left side five inches above the third rib and penetrated the stomach, the iliac artery and the small intestine several times. The half-inch slug had smashed through almost a foot of viscera. The immediate cause of death was the severing of the iliac artery but either the third or fourth bullets would have been fatal; the fourth immediately and the third within 24 hours. The third was dug out of his corpse but the fourth and most fatal bullet was never found. The bullets found were all .38 caliber but Dr. Brant was unable to discern the caliber of the fourth bullet or even whether it matched that of the others. The bullets had been fired close enough to cause burn marks on Saxton's coat and underwear.

The members of Saxton's autopsy team were, no doubt, feeling increasing pressure as the minutes of the postmortem slipped away. The initial spat with McQuate had set a bad tone and additional political overtones crept into the room as the work proceeded. Stark County Prosecutor Atlee Pomerene came into observe, and Saxton's attorney James J. Grant arrived soon after. Both of them spoke to the doctors and made it clear that they wanted unequivocal forensic evidence from Saxton's postmortem. Dr. Brant and his assistants tried for over a half hour to find the missing fourth bullet, even to the extent of dislocating the left hip joint and removing the left leg, before giving up. The next day's edition of the *Canton Repository* reported that some of Saxton's friends dropped by to witness the autopsy; not surprisingly, most of them soon abandoned such gruesome duty.

There was little other evidence of the extreme violence of Saxton's death. Although there were apparent powder burns on his vest, there was no blood on his clothing and Brant could find only about two teaspoons of blood on the exterior of Saxton's body. Virtually all of Saxton's bleeding had been internal, and almost all of it caused by the third and fourth bullets.

Saxton's clothing and personal effects offered no additional clues to his death. In his pockets were found a gold watch and chain, some inconsequential letters, two memorandum books, a diamond ring, a diamond collar button and two bunches of keys containing about 30 keys altogether.

The doctors carving up Saxton's corpse weren't the only ones feeling political heat that October evening. James J. Grant was breathing fire when he swept into the autopsy room. Grant, as he would ceaselessly reiterate in coming days, had probably been George D. Saxton's best friend. Grant sincerely loved his erring chum, and had been a close and constant witness of his tangled relationship with Mrs. George from its lurid beginning to its apparent violent end. Grant's office was in the Saxton block and he was a personal friend of William McKinley. There was no doubt in his mind who the killer was and his first words to McQuate were an angry demand that he immediately arrest Annie George on a charge of murdering George Saxton.

McQuate was not one to be intimated by an attorney, even a politically well-connected one. Citing the lack of any concrete evidence against Mrs. George, he rebuffed Grant's demand, insisting he would reserve his judgment until the completion of the Saxton murder inquest, already scheduled to begin on the following afternoon at 2 p.m.

Grant exploded. He had watched what he considered Mrs. George's unwarranted and brazen persecution of Saxton for years, outspokenly outraged by the law's impotence in protecting his client from her relentless, malignant harassment. And now that "that woman" had shot down his beloved friend in cold blood on a public street, the law — as embodied by Coroner McQuate — was unwilling to do its duty. Beside himself with wrath, Grant turned to the freshly dissected body of Saxton. Placing his hand on the corpse, he loudly swore that he would do everything in his power to convict Mrs. George of murder and that if, God willing, she were convicted, he would go to Columbus and push the button on the electric chair himself. Pomerene had already left for the Canton police station and Grant soon followed.

Meanwhile, the search for Mrs. George had begun in earnest. Henry Bederman's first thought, upon hearing gunfire, that Mrs. George had shot George Saxton, was a suspicion shared by many Cantonians that tumultuous Friday night. There was never really any other suspects from the moment the first shot resounded, and the first police patrolmen who came to the scene with Charles Frazer were soon joined by other officers in a dragnet for

Mrs. George. Fanning out through Canton, they staked out the Saxton block and Cora Oberlin's rooming house. Eager civilians also joined in the search, especially around the Althouse residence. But there was little for them to find there. A policeman tardily knocking on Eva's door was soon informed by a neighbor, Mrs. Mary Glick, that Eva had been absent from home for days. All the doors of her house were locked and there was no sign of anyone within. All that was left at the scene were the mute items of evidence found near Saxton's body: his bicycle and the valise containing his nightshirt and a bottle of champagne.

One of those who searched the Lincoln Avenue area was Canton Police Sergeant William J. Hasler. Arriving there soon after the first policemen got to the scene, he grabbed a lantern and began combing the area around the Althouse home. Finding no clues, he took Saxton's bicycle to a grocery for future examination and then walked eastward down Tuscarawas Street to Cora Oberlin's house. There he joined a group of patrolman who had already staked out Mrs. George's most likely destination.

Where *was* Annie George? That was the question on the lips of most Cantonians as the sensational news of Saxton's shooting spread throughout the city. Just where she was from the time she disembarked from streetcar No. 21 at Hazlette Avenue and Tuscarawas Street until the moment of her arrest would be the crux of her coming legal battle to stay out of the electric chair. Two violently conflicting narratives would be presented at her trial to chronicle her movements from 6 to 8 p.m. on Saxton's final evening. The core of the dispute, never quite resolved, was her exact whereabouts at the time Saxton was shot. We can be reasonably certain, however, about most of Annie's movements during the two hours after Saxton's murder.

Sometime between 6:20 and 6:30 p.m. Mrs. George arrived at the home of her friend Florence Klingler. Klingler, who made her living as a private nurse to invalid Cantonians, lived at 311 Marion Street, a little over a mile from the murder scene at 319 Lincoln Avenue. Klingler, a woman in her early twenties, was a likely friend for Annie. Of humble antecedents and dubious reputation, she had much in common with the pariah seamstress, including a marriage that had gone bad. Although Klingler does not seem to have been expecting Annie, she invited her in and asked her to share her supper. Annie declined, saying she had just eaten and the two women chatted while Florence ate her dinner. Some minutes after Annie's arrival, Florence's boyfriend, Ira Howenstine arrived at the house. His later recollection would be that he got there at 6:35 p.m. and chatted with the two women for several minutes. Finally, Annie arose and said she must be leaving. She said she was going to see her lawyer, James Sterling in his Dannemiller block office on South Market Street.

Annie was true to her word. Dannemiller block janitor Harry E. Noble was on Fifth Avenue when he saw Annie passing by, about 6:50 p.m. and headed westward. He was sure about the time, as he looked at the courthouse clock a moment later. Ten minutes later, Annie entered the block and went to the elevator. Harry's wife Virginia was operating it in his absence, and Annie asked her to take her to the second floor. Stepping off the elevator there, she knocked on Sterling's door. When no answer came, she realized he was absent and left. Both Virginia and Harry saw Annie leave the building, probably no later than 7:10 p.m.

Sometime around 8: 00 p.m. Mrs. George was seen by carpenter Jacob Adams. She was at the corner of Lynch Street and walking westward on Tuscarawas Street in the direction of the Oberlin house. Adams would recall that she seemed calm and unagitated. Ten minutes later, Annie was seen further west on Tuscarawas Street by Mrs. Maud Randall. Annie said "Good evening" to Randall and she saw nothing unusual in Mrs. George's appearance as she passed by. As it happened, Randall was more concerned about her dress than the appearance of passers-by. As she walked down the sidewalk her dress was picking up Spanish needles and burrs from the dense weeds which grew in the adjacent vacant lots.

Another woman who passed by Mrs. George on Tuscara-was Street about the same time was schoolteacher Miss Mattie Grimes. Grimes noticed that Mrs. George was wearing dark clothing and carrying a cape. She also noticed that Annie's face was flushed, as it well might have been, considering the amount of walking Annie had been doing that evening. Miss Grimes would later admit that she, like most Cantonians, already knew about the murder on Lincoln Avenue. But unlike most Cantonians, she believed Mrs. Eva Althouse to be the prime suspect. So when Annie greeted her as she passed by, Mattie simply responded in kind and both women continued on their way.

Shortly after encountering Miss Grimes, Annie walked past Joseph Lippert's Tuscarawas Street grocery, just beyond the Valley Railroad crossing. There was still a large puddle of water from the afternoon rain on the sidewalk there. Lippert watched as Annie daintily stepped around the puddle, bringing her skirt close to the edge of the sidewalk, which like much of that section of Tuscara-was Street, was covered by a bounteous fall crop of Spanish needles and burrs. Lippert noticed nothing unusual about Annie and she continued on her way to Cora Oberlin's house. Neither did his son Frank, who also saw Annie pass by the grocery. Sever-al minutes later, Annie was seen walking on Tuscarawas Street by Jesse Taylor, who had seen her two hours earlier on streetcar No. 21. Taylor was probably the last person to see Annie before she arrived at the Oberlin house.

Annie found quite a welcoming committee waiting for her when she arrived there about 9 p.m. Canton Police officers Fred McCloud [a future Canton Police Chief], Aaron Rohn, Henry Piero and Lewis Smiley had already been there for several hours, inter-rogating Cora Oberlin and searching the neighborhood. They had also taken the liberty of searching Annie's room and personal possessions. They were still chatting with Cora, when they spied Mrs. George gliding through the darkness towards a side door of the house. Piero moved fast and was right behind her as she came through the door and he immediately accosted her in the hallway.

Piero knew Mrs. George by sight, but he initially played his part by the book. "Are you Mrs. George?" he asked her. Without waiting for an answer, he added, "Yes, you are Mrs. George, and you are under arrest." Annie said nothing. Piero added, "Yes, for suspicion." Officer McCloud then placed his hand on Annie's left arm and Piero grasped her right arm. Annie looked at them calmly and said, "I will go with you, gentlemen."

It must have been an odd looking procession down Tuscarawas Street that night. Surrounded by four hulking police officers, Mrs. George walked eastward the better part of two miles through downtown Canton to the police station. Gawked at by a huge crowd of curious Cantonians lining the street, she remained regally silent during the half hour the journey consumed. She offered no resistance to her arrest, no objection to her forced march to the police station and asked no questions whatsoever about why she was being arrested. Nor did she allude in any way to Saxton's shooting, a topic which was on the minds and lips of virtually all Cantonians at that hour. Perhaps odder still, her arresting officers did not even tell her what she was being arrested on suspicion of.

The legal environment at the time of Annie's arrest was not quite the same as that of the 21st century, especially with regard to civil liberties and what we now term the "rights of the accused." True, it was generally understood that accused persons had the right to counsel and a constitutional protection against self-incrimination. But those were technical safeguards, rarely invoked or even recognized by many law officers of the era, especially in newly urbanized areas like Canton, Ohio. Most lawmen of that era, whether in big cities like New York or in the innumerable tiny townships of the country, had virtually no training in proper interrogation procedure or the cautioning of suspects against self-incrimination.

The policemen who arrested Annie were no exceptions to the contemporary level of police practice, and they went at Mrs. George directly. They had not even reached the sidewalk at Mrs.

Oberlin's house when officer McCloud asked Annie why she had entered the house by the side door. No answer. He tried again. "Why did you go in between the houses, instead of the front door?" No answer. More questions followed as the strange procession continued its way down Tuscarawas Street. Where had she been that evening? Had she been downtown? Had she been out on Lincoln Avenue? Annie continued her silence for a while and then simply said, "Excuse me, sir; I will talk when the proper time comes."

Annie's arresting officers were also observing her as they marched through downtown Canton that October night. To them, she seemed agitated, tense and visibly perspiring. Somewhere between the Oberlin house and the police station, moreover, Piero and McCloud took the occasion to examine Annie's hands. They both noted that the right hand was discolored, smudged with what looked to them like gunpowder. Both officers also took the liberty of smelling that hand, agreeing that it smelled like gunpowder. And they both noticed that the right side of her skirt was covered with Spanish needles and burrs.

Annie George was brought into the police station at 9:30 that night. As soon as she saw Marshal Reed, she requested that her attorney, Canton Mayor James Rice, be sent for and that he is present to protect her rights. Reed ignored her request, and ushered her into a small room, where a seething Atlee Pomerene awaited her. Pomerene was the only elected Democratic county official in Stark County but he remained on good personal terms with the overwhelmingly Republican officials of the county, not to mention the McKinley family. He intended to remain so, and he was acutely aware that he needed to crack the Saxton murder quickly. Accordingly, he went at Mrs. George directly. "Mrs. George, you know why you are here?"

Annie did not answer him. Instead, she turned to Police Jail Turnkey Samuel Becherer and whispered something in his ear. Becherer repeated her words to Pomerene, a request that her attorney be present. Pomerene ignored her request, telling Becherer that there was already too much of a crowd at the police station. He then barked out the next question. "Did you go out on a street car this evening about five o'clock?"

Annie replied calmly, "Pardon me, sir, I will talk at the proper time. I do not care to answer any questions in the absence of my attorney."

Pomerene again ignored her request and asked, "Did you go out on a street car this evening about five o'clock?"

No answer.

"I will say to you, Mrs. George, that if you had nothing to do with this case I do not want to detain you a minute; all I want is the truth about this matter. Do you know that George Saxton is dead?"

No answer. By this time J. J. Grant had arrived in the room and he had a whispered colloquy with Pomerene. Then Pomerene tried again "It has been said, Mrs. George, that you threatened to kill Mr. Saxton; is there any truth in that report?" Still no answer.

"Why did you get off the car this evening at John Weiss' corner and go across the lots?" No answer.

"Did you have any business out there at that time?"

No answer. Pomerene's next question was based on misinformation he had received from the arresting officers.

"Why did you come up through the swamp to Tuscarawas Street just before you were arrested?" No answer.

"Where did you come from?" No answer.

Pomerene was getting nowhere and he knew it. Furthermore, he realized that his window of opportunity to interrogate Mrs. George was closing fast. It was only a question of time, perhaps only minutes, before her lawyer arrived and put an end to his preemptory interrogation. Pomerene decided to try a more conciliatory tack.

"Now Mrs. George, if you know nothing about this, I want the officers to let you go. If you explain satisfactorily your whereabouts at six o'clock tonight, I will have the officers go out and verify it, and let you go within an hour." No answer.

"I notice there are a good many burrs on your dress; where did they come from?" Still no answer, and the stolid Anna did not even move her head to look at the alleged burrs. Pomerene gave up at this point and turned her over to jail physician, Dr. Maria Pontius.

DR. MARIA G. PONTIUS.
She scraped the black substance, which may be burned powder, from Mrs. George's hand, after the latter's arrest.

Canton Jail Physician Dr. Maria G. Pontius
(Cleveland Press, April 12, 1899)

Pontius was a most professional physician and there is no evidence that her treatment of Mrs. George was discriminatory or prejudiced. Still, it might have been better for the subsequent judicial process if she had demonstrated more sensitivity in handling Mrs. George. Several of her arresting officers remained in the room while Dr. Pontius stripped Mrs. George down to her undergarments and felt under her corset and underclothing for suspicious items. In her physical examination Pontius paid special attention to Mrs. George's hands. The left land was clean but the thumb and first two fingers of the right hand seemed to be discolored with some dark substance. Dr. Pontius carefully scraped the discolored area with a scalpel and put the scrapings into an envelope. Pontius wasn't sure there was enough matter to make a successful chemical analysis but she wrote an identifying label on the envelope and put it aside for prosecutor Pomerene. Pontius also noticed the many burrs and Spanish needles adhering to Annie's skirt. Approximately forty or fifty of them were scraped off and likewise put in an envelope for Pomerene's perusal. Interestingly, Mrs. George made no protest whatsoever during the search of her person and calmly conversed with Dr. Pontius and her audience of gawking policemen. She carefully refused, however, to respond to any queries about Saxton's shooting.

Meanwhile, James J. Grant and Pomerene, still angry over Coroner McQuate's refusal to arrest Annie George, confronted City Marshal William H. Reed. Both lawyers wanted Annie taken to the county jail, as if she were a formally accused criminal. The less emotional Reed knew that she was not: despite popular prejudices as to her assumed guilt, he was well aware that she was being held on the only sure charge against her: suspicion. Pomerene then demanded not only that she be incarcerated in the county jail but that no one — including her lawyers — be allowed access to her. Reed promptly declined but Pomerene kept pushing. "I ask this because no one seems to have any authority here," spluttered Pomerene. In fact Pomerene knew very well who had the authority: it was Mayor Rice, who, in addition to being the Chief of Police and a Police Court judge, was also said to be Annie George's legal representative. But Pomerene's strategy now was to bully Rice — and Rice's policemen — into either cooperating with his treatment of Mrs. George or to provoke an outright refusal for the purpose of generating negative publicity.

Reed was no fool. He knew the law and he knew who his boss was. It wasn't Pomerene, and he replied, "Why, you know well enough that I have no authority over the policemen."

Pomerene quickly countered, "And no one else seems to have, and when I make a request of this kind I think you ought to honor it." "She is safe here, just as safe as she would be in [county] jail," replied Reed.

The livid Grant had heard enough. As far as he was concerned, he'd already had a bellyful of Canton justice that evening. He thundered, "Well, we want her treated as any other common murderess!" "How do you know she is a murderess?" riposted Reed. Grant shot right back, "I know she is. For two years she has been flourishing her gun out on that street, saying that no policeman in this town would arrest her, and that the mayor would not order her arrest."

Reed couldn't let this slur on the police and Mayor Rice pass. "You don't know anything of the kind," he said. It now degenerated into a shouting match between Grant and Reed.

"She has been using this police court for a fence for two years!"

"You don't know anything of the kind, you only think so!"

"Well, I know what I know, and I want her taken to the jail!

"She will not be taken to the jail. She is only in here on suspicion, and we will hold her here until the mayor orders what shall be done with her. She is not charged with murder!"

Grant wasn't ready to concede the fight. He launched into a detailed indictment of how he believed the Canton police, under Mayor Rice's direction, had consistently mishandled Mrs. George. He spoke of her constant threats to kill Saxton, her harassment of him and her nightly escapades, with or without a gun, out on Lincoln Avenue. He ranted of his many warnings about Mrs. George over the years, warnings that had fallen on the ears of a deaf Canton officialdom.

It was all in vain. Having put Mayor Rice's back up and ventilated their views to the press, Pomerene and Grant prudently decided to compromise. Having little law on their side in the controversy they agreed that it would be all right if Mrs. George remained in the city jail overnight, as long as she was watched by a guard and visitors were kept away. Shortly before midnight, she was led to a cell, where she fell asleep on a rude jail cot several hours later. During the night she was guarded by officer Henry Piero, one of her arresting officers; his presence was mainly to insure that she did not try to commit suicide. He was relieved at 6:30 a.m. on Saturday by Police officer Elmer E. Willis. When Mrs. George woke up a little later, she asked Willis to read the newspapers aloud to her. She listened silently to an account of Saxton's murder but when Willis got to the part describing the wounds in detail, she murmured, "Never mind, I don't want to hear that part of it."

The wily Pomerene had not been quite on the level with Marshal Reed. He may have wanted to keep Mayor Rice and any other counsel away from Mrs. George, but he didn't mind infiltrating someone less sympathetic into Mrs. George's company. Shortly after she entered her cell, she looked up to see Perry Van Horne, the reporter to whom she had confided some of her threats and harassments of George Saxton in bygone days. Van Horne had witnessed Pomerene's interrogation of Mrs. George and the prosecutor believed that she still trusted the reporter in whom she had previously confided. Now, at Pomerene's request, Van Horne approached her cell and began talking to her. He said he was sorry to see her there and talked for some time about their previous meetings. Then, he looked at Annie and said, "Mrs. George, do you remember that at our last meeting, about six months ago, how you said you would shoot George Saxton if he didn't marry you after Sample George's case was settled?" Annie did not audibly reply, Van Horne later told Pomerene, but she did nod her head and compress her lips tightly in response to his question.

Chapter 6   Rush to Judgment

Thirty-five thousand Cantonians awoke to new, exciting and distracting realities as Saturday, October 8 dawned. Within just twelve hours their somewhat sleepy northeastern Ohio city had suddenly turned into the cynosure of national, indeed world attention. Even as Canton's two newspapers struggled to chronicle the previous night's shocking events, a dozen correspondents from the nation's larger metropolitan newspapers — New York, Pittsburgh, Chicago and Cleveland--began arriving in Canton to furnish breathless copy for millions of American readers. For the better part of the next seven months, these reporters would observe the raw material of the Saxton murder and transform it into briskly written melodrama suitable to the moralistic Victorianism of their readers.

What the shape of that melodrama would be was still an open question as the day opened. The chief practical difficulty for those reporting the Saxton murder was initially simply one of focus — which facet of this lurid story to cover. There was the fact of the murder itself: the celebrity of its victim and the irony of his kinship to McKinley, the complete and contrasting icon of sexual probity. And the likelihood that the hard fact of the homicide would produce the delectable drama of a good-looking woman on trial for her life. But for now, better yet was the sordid back story: one part vile seducer, one part fallen woman, ready to serve steamy and delicious to a public already habituated to weeping over period songs and poetry chronicling the same. It was almost as if Annie George and George Saxton had leapt as living beings out of the verses of a popular ballad like "Village-Born Beauty," a staple of Gay Nineties parlor poetry:

> See the star-breasted villain,
> To yonder cot bound,
> Where the sweet honeysuckle

Entwines it round, Yet sweeter, far sweeter,
Than flower e'er seen,
Is the poor hedger's daughter,
The pride of the green.
But more, never more,
Will she there please all eyes;
Her peace of mind withers,
Her happiness flies!
She pauses, sighs, trembles,
And yet dares to roam,
The village-born beauty's
Seduced from her home.

Then, inevitably, as Annie George had found:

But soon from indifference,
Caprice, or what not—
By her keeper forgot.

And what was the betrayed Sample George's lot but a real-
life replication of "We Never Speak As We Pass By," a staple of
Gilded Age music hall song:

The spell is past, the dream is o'er.
And tho' we meet we love no more!
One heart is crushed to droop and die,
And for relief, must heav'nward fly!
The once bright smile has faded — gone!
And given way to looks forlorn!
Despite her grandeur's wicked flame,
She stoops to blush beneath her shame.

We never speak as we pass by,
Altho' a tear bedims her eye;
I know she thinks of her past life,

When we were loving man and wife.
In guileless youth I sought her side,
And she became my virtuous bride;
Our lot was peace so fair, so bright!
One sunny day, no gloomy night!
No life on earth more pure than ours,
In that dear home, midst field and flow'r,
Until the tempter came to Nell;
It dazzled her — alas! she fell!
In gilded hall, midst wealth she dwells;
How her heart aches, her sad face tells.
She fain would smile, seem bright and gay,
But conscience steals her peace away.
And when the flatt'rer casts aside
My fallen and dishonored bride,
I'll close her eyes in death, forgive,
And in my heart her name shall live.

The newspaper reporters who covered the Saxton murder would eventually sort out their priorities, settling for a nice balance between the salacious backstory of the case — generally masquerading as instructive moral lesson — and the suspenseful, astonishing developments of its ensuing murder trial. Their first task, however, as the murder after-morning arrived, was to chronicle its most immediate consequence: the return of President McKinley's family to Canton for George Saxton's funeral.

The first word to the White House concerning George Saxton's murder had come in the form of telegrams sent there by Marshall C. Barber. Barber, a successful businessman and husband of Ida's sister Pina, had been left alone at the North Market Street house for some weeks while his wife tended to the welfare of their son John in a Washington, D. C. hospital. John Barber, an aide to U. S. Army General Guy V. Henry, had contracted typhoid fever during the recent campaign in Puerto Rico, and Pina had descended on the Garfield Hospital there to nurse him in person. Marshall's telegrams about the murder were necessarily cryptically discreet and the President's attempt to secure more information via a primitive long-distance telephone hookup was unsuccessful. But McKinley knew his first task was to tell Ida.

The President was always careful with his emotionally and physically fragile wife. During their twenty-eight years of marriage and her early decline into semi-invalidism, he had assiduously woven a protective social cocoon around her. Based on what is known about his previous handling of her at vulnerable moments, it is likely that he gave the bad news to Ida in installments, first warning her that something unfortunate had happened, then that George had been wounded, and finally, that he had been shot to death, presumably by Annie George. Such was Ida McKinley's reputation as psychologically frail, however, that it would soon be gossiped around Canton that Ida did not realize that George had been shot, refusing, as was believed to be her wont, to accept sordid reality. Even longtime McKinley intimates were fooled by Ida's stolidly withdrawn mask; McKinley aide Charles Bawsel would write to his wife only two weeks later, "Do you mean to say that Mrs. McK does not know George was shot? What care and grief she is spared by the ignorance. . . . Mrs. McK's is truly a bed of roses." But Ida McKinley, as historian Margaret Leech once observed, was not as obtuse as she liked to appear. Whatever her husband told her, she knew all she needed to know about her brother's death. Like many of George Saxton's kith and kin, she had long and wearily fretted over her black-sheep brother's scandalous escapades, and it is significant that after his funeral the deeply conventional Ida avoided all the usual public rituals of mourning with regard to dress and social engagements.

Arrangements were quickly made for the President's family to come to Canton for the obsequies. Before George Saxton's murder, President McKinley had planned to attend the Nebraska Peace Jubilee Exposition in Omaha, celebrating the successful conclusion of the Spanish-American War. His brother-in-law's funeral was now folded into that junket, and the President was rescheduled to leave Canton for the Exposition after the funeral on Monday. At 7:20 p. m., twenty-five hours after George Saxton's murder, the Presidential funeral party boarded the special car *Campania*, attached to the regular Western Express, at the Pennsylvania Railroad station. Traveling with the President and his wife were his sister Helen, McKinley's friends Webb Hayes (son of ex-President Rutherford Hayes) and Mr. and Mrs. Stewart Bowman. Just before the train left, a carriage pulled up. Out of it came Pina Barber and litter-bearers carrying her son John. A delegation of Cabinet secretaries and aides bade them farewell and the train departed for Pittsburgh, its first stop before Canton.

Cleveland Daily World, October 8, 1898

A Woman Scorned

Meanwhile, it had been a tough day for Annie George. If the rights of accused persons in her era were imperfectly respected by American policemen, such unfortunates had no protection whatsoever from the slanders or defamations of American newspapers. It would later become a cardinal principle of American journalism that newspapers should not prejudge accused persons in their coverage of sensational crimes. There was no such principle operating in 1898, however, and the newspaper coverage of George Saxton's murder unanimously echoed the initial, indeed visceral view of most Cantonians that Annie George had killed him.

First impressions count — and the impressions of Annie presented to Saturday morning newspaper readers were not good ones. "George D. Saxton Shot To Death" screamed the top headline of the Saturday morning *New York Times*. True enough, but scant attention was paid to the fact of the murder in the story below, which focused almost entirely on the history of the troubled relations between Saxton and Annie, her threats to kill him and her known movements on the murder day. Even more damning to Annie were the smaller subheads, spelling out for *Times* readers the identity and fallen nature of the accused:

Brother of the President's Wife Murdered at Canton
The Victim of a Woman
Annie C. George Accused of the Crime and Under Arrest
She is a Dressmaker Divorced From Her Husband,
Who Had Sued Mr. Saxton for
the Alleged Alienation of Her Affection

Other national newspapers, including the *New York World*, *Cincinnati Enquirer* and the *Washington Post*, to name but a few, followed the lead of the *New York Times*, emphasizing Annie's apparent guilt and the sleazy backstory of her seduction and disgrace. More important, however, were that morning's stories about in the murder in the Cleveland newspapers. Few persons in

Stark County, from which Annie's eventual jury would be selected, would have been exposed to the columns of the *Times* or any
large newspapers outside of Cleveland. But the Cleveland newspapers counted in Canton, as the interrogation of Annie's jury
venires would amply demonstrate. Thanks to that city's proximity
to Cleveland and Annie's residence in Cleveland during the 1890s,
many Cleveland newspapermen already knew of the Saxton-
George imbroglio, even if they had previously been relatively
restrained in writing it up for the public. The murder of Saxton
blew that lid off, and Cleveland's four major newspapers immediately vied for the honor of demonstrating which one could more
thoroughly indict Annie for the crime.

First on the streets that morning was the *Cleveland Leader*,
then the most dominant newspaper in northeast Ohio and a
reliable organ of Republican machine politics. Its headlines left no
doubt in the minds of inquiring readers:

MURDERED BY A JEALOUS WOMAN
George D. Saxton, Mrs. McKinley's Brother
Is Killed at Canton

SHOT DOWN WHILE RIDING A WHEEL
Passers-By At Dusk Found Him
Lying Dead on the Sidewalk
Mrs. Annie C. George, Who Was a
Friend of Saxton's In Years Gone By, Is Under Arrest
Charged With His Murder—The Crime Was Committed
By a Woman Shrouded in a Gossamer—
The Motive for the Deed is Said to Have Been Jealousy
of a Woman to Whom Saxton Had Been
Paying Attention of Late and
Revenge for Wrongs

Like the *Times*, the body of the *Leader* account dwelt on the poisonous relations between Saxton and Mrs. George, her threats against him and the fact that she had been unofficially accused of his murder. So, too, did that morning's edition of the *Cleveland Plain Dealer*, a stalwartly Democratic organ and the closest competitor of the dominating *Leader*. First came the damning headlines:

KILLED BY A WOMAN
George D. Saxton,
Brother of Mrs. William McKinley,
Shot Down in the Street At Canton.
Mrs. Annie E. George,
Who Had Threatened His Life,
Arrested and Charged With the Crime.
THE ACCUSED WOMAN MAINTAINS
A STUBBORN SILENCE

The body of the *Plain Dealer* story, apparently written by ubiquitous Canton ex-newspaperman Perry Van Horne, emphasized Annie's threats and public suspicions of her guilt. Van Horne obliquely referenced his jailhouse interview with Mrs. George and then quoted Henry J. Bederman as if the latter were an omniscient eyewitness to the killing:

"I knew what had happened," said Henry J. Bederman, who saw the whole transaction. "As soon as the first shot was fired I said to myself, 'Saxton is getting it.' We had all expected it in this end of the city, and I knew at once that Mrs. George was carrying out the threats she had so often made. She came up just at the side of Saxton. It was rather dark, but I think she clutched as his arm. In a moment there were two flashes of a pistol and two muffled reports, for she was very close to him."

KILLED BY A WOMAN.

George D. Saxton, Brother of Mrs. William McKinley, Shot Down in the Street at Canton.

Mrs. Anna E. George, Who Had Threatened His Life, Arrested and Charged With the Crime.

THE ACCUSED WOMAN MAINTAINS A STUBBORN SILENCE.

CANTON, Oct. 7.—George D. Saxton lies at Shilling's morgue with four bullet holes in his body, cold in death.

He had gone out on Hazlett avenue at 6:15 tonight and was about to enter the home of Mrs. Eva D. Althouse, widow of the late George W. Althouse, No. 319 Lincoln avenue, and had just ascended the steps when a woman in black rushed up behind him and fired two shots, which felled him.

He rolled down on the green sward and two more shots were heard when officers went to the place and found that he was stone dead.

Women at the house stated that a woman had done the work; that she was a tall woman, slender, dressed in black and that she had gone away as soon as the shots were fired.

Mrs. George at Once Suspected.

The woman at the house said Mrs. Althouse was not at home, but that the woman who did the shooting had gone in a direction which they indicated.

Officers were soon on the hunt for the woman and while it was not possible just then to tell who did it, suspicion was strong against a woman with whom Saxton has had dealings and who had promised to kill him. Drs. E. D. and A. C. Brant pronounced Saxton dead after an examination at the morgue. Death must have been instantaneous.

The deceased was a well known figure of the city, and was a brother of Mrs. McKinley, wife of the president, and of Mrs. M. C. Barber.

A hunt was at once made for Mrs. Anna E. George, the divorced wife of Sample C. George, with whom Saxton has had several unsavory lawsuits, leading out of their intimacy.

Had Threatened to Kill Saxton.

Mrs. George had often threatened to kill Saxton. There is ample evidence of that. On one occasion she stated to your correspondent that she would kill him. That was after one of the lawsuits mentioned. So the police thought if they found her they would have the right party.

She has been staying at the residence of Conductor Jake Oberlin, having had a room there. Officers watched the house and at about 9 o'clock she came toward the house, through the weeds and swampy ground, to get in the back way.

The officers at once placed her under arrest. She evidenced no surprise, and did not even inquire why she was being molested. "I will go with you, gentlemen," was all she said. At the police station she was surrounded by a curious crowd, but not for a moment did her nerve fail her.

Kept Silent When Arrested.

Under the most trying circumstances, and with the prosecuting attorney firing questions at her at a furious rate, she did not quail. Her first and only answer was: "Excuse ... sir, but I will not ..."

Cleveland Plain Dealer, October 8, 1898

Van Horne concluded his damning dispatch with a harsh estimate of the accused's unwomanly lack of remorse over what she had done, moralizing, "If Mrs. George suffers any pangs of conscience she does not display them tonight. She is taking things more coolly that the average policeman." Citing the circumstantial evidence against Annie, the *Plain Dealer* account concluded damningly, "With all this evidence at hand, the police can see not the slightest doubt of her guilt."

That afternoon's *Cleveland Evening World* went even further. Aware that Mrs. George had been formally charged with the crime that morning, the *World* took Annie's guilt entirely for granted in its headline summary of the murder:

LOVE AFFAIR ENDS IN MURDER
George D. Saxton,
the President's Brother-in-Law,
Killed by Mrs. George
Shot Dead in the Streets of Canton—
The Accused Woman Appears Unconcerned

Repeating Henry Bederman's quote from the *Plain Dealer* as evidence against Mrs. George, the *World* focused on her troubled relations with Saxton and implied that her motive had been sexual jealousy of Eva Althouse, "the favored one." The *World* was always to be the most "yellow" of the Cleveland newspapers in its coverage of the Saxton murder, and it commenced its more salacious approach with a story chronicling Annie's lurid personal history and her Cleveland connection. Noting that she had been indicted for sending "obscene" material through the mails, it did not stint in describing the physical charms that brought Annie George first to George Saxton's bed and thence to a Canton jail cell:

Striking in appearance and decidedly handsome, is the way Mrs. Annie E. George, who is under arrest in Canton, charged with the Assassination of President McKinley's brother-in-law, is described by her many Cleveland friends. While living in this city she is said to have had many admirers, her flashing black eyes and tall but decidedly shapely figure having made many conquests.

James Rice, Canton Mayor ... and Mrs. George's Attorney
(Cleveland Press, October 10, 1898)

Annie George did not sleep in that Saturday morning. Waking at 5 a.m., she was up and dressed when Marshal Reed brought her breakfast at 9 a.m. Shortly after that, James A. Sterling entered her cell. His arrival indicated that much had been stirring unseen from public view since the discovery of George Saxton's murder. Although Sterling had done legal work for Mrs. George and her ex-husband before, it was Mayor James Rice whom Mrs. George requested as her counsel on the night of her arrest. Only twelve hours later, however, Sterling had joined her defense team and attorney John C. Welty was also soon to come aboard. Both of them had represented Sample C. George in his alienation of affection suit against Saxton. How Mrs. George had secured the two additional lawyers since her arrest is not known. It was a fact, however, that she had been looking for Sterling at his office less than an hour after Saxton's killing. Had she, in fact, been able to track him down sometime in the interval between her visit to the Dannemiller block and her arrest at Cora Oberlin's house? Her circumspect silence following her arrest suggested to observers that she had accessed expert legal advice during that interim. Whatever the truth, Sterling and Welty took charge of Annie's case on Saturday morning, nominally assisted by James Rice.

Rice's assistance was immediately useful, if only in an obstructive way. By early morning prosecutor Pomerene had prepared an affidavit charging Annie George with Saxton's murder. Couched in the usual repetitive and stodgy legalese (richly larded with such archaic terms as "whereas," "saieth" and "aforesaid") it accused Mrs. George of shooting four bullets into Saxton and killing him with "with deliberate and premeditated malice." Pomerene took it first to Marshal Reed, who refused to sign it. So did every other officer on the Canton police force, all of them doubtless aware that their boss, Mayor James Rice, was also serving as Mrs. George's defense counsel. Finally, an exasperated James J. Grant signed it himself. At 10:45 a.m., he and Pomerene took it to Mayor Rice and demanded that he hold an arraignment for Mrs. George immediately. Citing his obvious conflict of interest, Rice refused. After some choice words for Rice's ear, it was agreed that Justice of the Peace Jacob Reigner would assume the role of Acting Mayor to hold the arraignment.

Pomerene's verbal attack on Rice was the first of many conflicts between the prosecution and defense which were obviously staged with an eye to public opinion and the newspapers. Both

Pomerene and Grant had made their unhappiness with the performance of Marshal Reed and Mayor Rice quite public only scant
hours after Saxton's murder. By the next morning, Pomerene,
charging that the Canton police were not cooperating with his
investigation, was demanding public assurances from Mayor Rice
that they would do so. Rice initially refused but eventually decided to make a partial concession to Pomerene, after some negative
newspaper comment appeared in Saturday's newspapers, both
local and national. On Saturday evening he issued a statement,
which was prominently posted in the Canton police station:

> To the police department of the City of Canton: The
> police officers of the above named department are
> hereby instructed that while I have consented to act
> as one of the counsel for the accused in the case of
> the State vs. Annie E. George, my connection with
> said case as such counsel is in no wise to interfere
> with the full performance of your duties as police of-
> ficers with relation to this case. To the contrary you
> are all to exercise the same intelligence in your ser-
> vices to the public and the state that you would ex-
> ercise were I not engaged as counsel. In the event
> the prosecuting attorney appeals to you for assis-
> tance in the capacity of police officers, I desire that
> you promptly respond and render him such services
> as may be in your power so that the final termina-
> tion of this case may be in full accord with the de-
> mands of justice as may be attained.
>   Yours truly, James A. Rice, Mayor, October 8

Rice's concession was insufficient for the *Cleveland Press*,
which offered a stinging critique of his equivocal position:

> The condition is this: A murder has been committed.
> The acting chief of police and officers under his or-

ders will do nothing to bring the criminal to justice, unless appealed to by Prosecuting Attorney Pomerene. Even then, the chief of police is retained to defend a woman charged with having committed murder, instead of being free to use his efforts and the efforts of his policemen to get testimony against her, or evidence that will fasten the crime on someone else, if she is innocent. The officers cannot act without orders from their superior, so they claim. The order issued by Mayor Rice Saturday night asks them to get to work, providing the prosecuting attorney appeals to them for aid. Cantonians are not slow to assert that it is the sworn duty of police officials to ferret out crime without being appealed to, when it is known that murder has been committed by someone.

Pomerene's suspicions about the Canton police would prove to be only too true: during the half-year interval before Mrs. George's trial, Mayor Rice's minions did not unearth a shred of evidence useful to the State's case.

Mrs. George was brought into Justice Reigner's court by Constable Joseph Weilandt about noon Saturday. Still wearing the clothes she was arrested in, she appeared to be the calmest person in the room. Sterling, Welty and Rice showed up shortly afterwards, only to discover that Pomerene had left for lunch. It didn't matter. After hearing the affidavit read aloud in court, Mayor Rice rose and stated that his client was not yet prepared to plead. Justice Reigner immediately granted a delay and the arraignment was rescheduled for Monday, October 11 at 10 a.m. Mrs. George was then removed to what would be her home for the next six months: the Stark County jail, adjacent to the county courthouse on Canton's Public Square.

Although Annie may not have appreciated the irony, it is likely that her jail quarters were more commodious and pleasant than any she had enjoyed since her days as mistress of the Saxton block. With the exception of her first few days, when she shared her cell with a Mrs. Anna Cartia, she remained its sole resident for most of her six-months' incarceration. Although her nominal "cell" was a plain 12 x 12 foot square, there was an identical room next to it which served her as a sitting room. Next to that was a room almost as large, fitted up as a bathroom with a tub and marble washstand. Under Annie's womanly touch, her cell was soon transformed into something looking more like a boudoir, complete with curtains for the window and filled almost to overflowing with fresh flowers sent daily by well-wishers. And although Stark County Sheriff John J. Zaiser provided Annie's daily breakfast, she continued to enjoy her usual diet by having her other meals catered from the Star Restaurant to her cell. Eventually, she dispensed with Zaiser's breakfasts, and restaurant owner Star owner Samuel Kirk personally delivered her three daily meals to her cell.

Annie's jail quarters on the second floor were adjacent to the living quarters of Sheriff Zaiser and his family. It was, perhaps, inevitable, considering Annie's winning ways, that the circumstances of her incarceration progressively improved as Zaiser and his wife got to know their prisoner. After persuading himself that Annie was no threat to escape, Zaiser allowed her frequent access to his home, especially its sewing room and laundry facilities. The sewing room was a particular convenience, as Annie was able to subsidize small luxuries such as her catered meals by selling the products of her jailhouse needlework. It didn't take long before prosecutor Pomerene was complaining that the accused murderess was being treated as Zaiser's indulged, pet prisoner. Pomerene's charges gained some public credibility in December, when Zaiser asked Common Pleas Court Judge Thomas T. McCarty to grant Annie's wish that she be released from jail to do her Christmas shopping in Canton. McCarty's curt denial of Annie's request and his rebuke to Zaiser were well-publicized but Zaiser doggedly defended his partial treatment of Annie to a *Plain Dealer* reporter:

It is not my business as the sheriff to prejudge a prisoner's guilt. Mrs. George is a great deal more intelligent than the average criminal. She is of a higher class of humanity. It is true she has been granted considerable liberty here. She desired it. She has been allowed a great deal more freedom than an ordinary criminal. She is not guilty of murder or any other offense until the jury finds her so.

Annie initially disappointed the newspapermen who dogged her movements that hurried Saturday morning following her arrest. A defense lawyer's dream, she had not given out any information to the police or reporters since the moment of her arrest. She now persisted in her calm silence, telling all questioners that her attorneys had insisted that she remain silent. But there was plenty of good copy still available in the Saxton case. The chief development, both from a journalistic and investigative point of view, was the surfacing of Eva B. Althouse.

Almost as eagerly sought as Annie George, Eva was finally located early Saturday morning at the 811 East Tuscarawas Street home of her mother, Mrs. J. G. Best. Although obviously reluctant to be caught up in this sensational mess, she was willing to expose herself to the extent of allowing herself to be interviewed by a *Canton Repository* reporter. What she told him, and later repeated nearly *verbatim* at the Saxton death inquest, was a story subsequently verified by many witnesses. While clearing up her role in the murder, it only deepened the mystery of George Saxton's death.

Eva, it developed, had been largely absent from her home during the four days before the murder. Her sister-in-law had been gravely ill, and Eva had gone to her brother's house at 1021 North Walnut Street to nurse her on Monday, October 3. Eva had last seen George Saxton that evening. He had bicycled down to meet her at her mother's house and she had told him she needed her bicycle, which was in need of repair. George had volunteered to fix it and she had later met him at 319 Lincoln Avenue and they had bicycled to her brother's house together. Two days later, on Wednesday, October 5, Eva had briefly returned home to feed her canary. She had then stopped off at the Eckroate grocery across the street to leave word that she was going to be absent from her house for a few more days. She had returned by streetcar to her brother's home by 8 p.m. that evening.

Eva, who had reason to be concerned about her already not-too-fragrant reputation, was particularly anxious to clarify public perceptions of her relations with Saxton. Aware that Annie George had long publicly defamed her as George Saxton's Lincoln Avenue strumpet, she primly warbled:

> I wish to say this: that there have been reports circulated that he used to come up to my house, not coming up directly through Tuscarawas Street. This is not so. During the time I have been going with him, he always came right up in a straightforward manner. He has always been very kind to me, and has always used me well. I feel very badly over his death. If I had known that this trouble between Mrs. Saxton and Mrs. George would culminate in this manner, I would not have gone with him. I tried at one time to put an end to it, fearing that she would carry out some of her threats, but he said he knew she would do nothing, so I thought I would be unfair to stop going with him after that. I never dreamed she would really do anything of this kind.

Eva was also at some pains to express her bewilderment as to why George Saxton had met his death on her doorstep. She said that he had known that she was not at home and that she had not arranged to meet him there. True, she admitted that he had a key to the house and at various times in the past had visited it in her absence to feed her bird and water her plants. But there had been no reason for him to show up there on Friday night, much less with a bottle of champagne and a nightshirt. Eva's insistence that George had no reason to be there only fueled public and police suspicions that he had been lured there, most likely by a forged decoy note inviting his presence. No such note was ever found, but there is no reason to doubt the sincerity of Eva Althouse's puzzlement at Saxton's presence at her home on the evening of October 7. Eva also told the *Canton Repository* reporter that George Saxton had been feeling much harassed and depressed of late by his chronic problems with Annie George.

Two hours after Annie entered the county jail, Coroner T. T. McQuate's inquest opened. Much of the testimony heard was a rehash of what had already been retailed in the newspapers, but with some significant differences. Henry J. Bederman was the first witness heard. He repeated his tale about hearing shots and seeing a darkly dressed woman walk up to Saxton's body, shoot it twice more and then flee down the side of the lot by Mrs. Quinn's house. But Bederman now admitted that it had been too dark for him to recognize the shooter or even the victim, until matches were lit. Bederman's wife Frances testified next, but she had little to add, except to echo her husband's assertion that it was too dark to recognize anyone at the murder scene without lighting matches. August Boron, William Glick, Harvey Hoffman and Joseph Schmidt followed on the stand but shed no light on the murder, except to corroborate the obvious confusion and murkiness during the initial minutes following the discovery of Saxton's body. Late Saturday afternoon McQuate adjourned the inquest until Monday morning, October 10.

Saturday, October 8 was an unproductive if not idle day for the Canton police force. Smarting from the criticisms of Pomerene and Grant, Mayor Rice provided a convincing show that his officers were at least active on the Saxton case. And, whatever Rice's equivocal position or any lingering skepticism about the rights of the accused, the sole working assumption behind Canton police efforts was that Annie George had shot George Saxton. So, while one large squad of patrolman noisily searched Eva Althouse's home and the surrounding lots, another painstakingly combed the neighborhood of Cora Oberlin's Tuscarawas Street boarding house. Still another squad went over every inch of Annie's presumed escape route: westward through the lot next to Mrs. Quinn's to Lawn Avenue and then south and east towards downtown Canton. The police were particularly interested in finding the murder weapon, which the autopsy evidence suggested was a .38-caliber revolver. But the day passed without either the revolver or any other important clue coming to light.

With developments in the case awaiting Monday's arraignment and continuing inquest session, Canton's attention now turned to the arrival of the President and his family. After stopping briefly at Pittsburgh at 10:26 a.m., the *Campania* pulled into the Pennsylvania station in Canton at 10:26 a.m., Sunday morning. There was a somber, sympathetic and silent crowd there to greet them. The President and his wife were the first to disembark, greeted as they stepped off by Marshall Barber, U. S. Postmaster General George B. Frease and Ida McKinley's cousin Burt A. Miller The party was immediately taken by carriage to the Barber home at 333 North Market Street, where the President took a nap before dining with the family at 1:30 p.m. He then took a short stroll through nearby streets before returning home to attend to the business at hand.

McKinley's first task was to view George's body, laid out by undertaker Shilling in the north parlor. Shilling had done his work well: the body, reported next day's *New York Times*, was said to look "natural, none of the marks of the tragedy being exposed on the face." Ida and Pina were then excused as the family menfolk conferred on the proper strategy for handling the legal and political fallout from George's murder. Joining them were Stark County Common Pleas judges George Baldwin and Thomas McCarty, prosecutor Atlee Pomerene and James J. Grant.

M'KINLEY'S HOME AT CANTON.
Cleveland Leader, June 17, 1896

The McKinley Family Home in Canton
(Cleveland Leader, June 17, 1896)

The complete details of what was decided at that meeting and a follow-up conference the next morning at the Barber house, will never be known. There was furious speculation that the McKinley family wished to quash any prosecution of Annie E. George, but the President's only public pronouncement on the case, released to the newspapers on Tuesday, October 11, stated that any prosecution of Mrs. George was to be pursued as a routine matter, with no special handling because of the exalted relations of her victim. An unnamed source simply stated that, "the family would not appear as prosecutors of the case, but that they well understood that the officers had a duty to perform, in which they did not intend to interfere." It was further stated that the President's family did not wish a special session of the Stark County grand jury to be called. McKinley's public stance, from the beginning to the end of the case was a consistent one of utter impartiality.

The private feelings of McKinley and his family may have been different. They were willing to go along with having the Democrat Pomerene prosecute the case but they also firmly insisted that he be assisted by the Republican James J. Grant, No one was second to Grant in his nearly feral loathing for Annie George, and his anointing as co-prosecutor by the family served notice that a serious effort would be mounted to put Annie in the electric chair for killing George Saxton.

It is possible, too, that McKinley was simply not sincere in his protestations that the Annie George prosecution would be treated just like any other case. Annie's defense attorneys would later loudly claim that United States government employees of both the Post Office and Secret Service assisted Pomerene and Grant in gathering evidence and investigating and shadowing trial witnesses. On the eve of Annie's trial, *Cleveland Daily World* reporter Arthur Sperry commented that Canton was "lousy with detectives" working for both sides. There is no hard evidence of such assistance, but that may only indicate that McKinley, if disingenuous, was also characteristically discreet.

In her 1959 biography, *In the Days of McKinley*, Margaret Leech, expressed a contrarian view of McKinley's stance on Annie George's trial. Leech, like some Cantonians in 1898, believed that, from the beginning, McKinley and his friends actually may have hoped for Annie George's *acquittal* at her murder trial. George Saxton, after all, had long been the black sheep of his aggrieved family. His misdeeds and sordid behavior had been a festering embarrassment for much of the 1890s — and a trial involving his most notorious and vocal mistress might be even worse. James J. Grant, perhaps the most knowledgeable authority on George Saxton's peccadilloes and the perils of ventilating them further with a vigorous prosecution of Annie George, warned McKinley of the potential dangers in a letter written just before the trial opened. Citing the "possibility of nasty things," even Grant was having second thoughts about his participation in what could become a publicity nightmare for McKinley, then only 18 months away from his reelection campaign.

If Annie George was worried about either the personal or political dangers of her position, she didn't show it. While Canton's Finest searched for a revolver and the McKinley family viewed George's corpse, Annie was cleaning and decorating her county jail cell. As she did so, she had the newspaper accounts of Saxton's murder read aloud to her, making no comment on any of their details or assertions. Her only visitor that day was Mayor Rice, who talked to her briefly about her defense. Presumably, also one of the topics of their conversation was a postcard he had just received. Postmarked 8 p.m. the previous evening at Springfield, Ohio, it read:

> I killed Saxton and am glad of it. Catch me if you can." [Signed] X. Y. Z.

About the same time a *Cleveland Press* reporter caught up with Sample C. George in Alliance. Asked if thought his ex-wife had killed Saxton, Sample replied he had no way of knowing but that the evidence and circumstances in the case were "decidedly" against her. Although severely prompted, he refused to say anything unkind about Annie, except to state that she was "always a good woman up to the time she met Saxton." Bitterly recalling the period of Saxton's seduction, Sample ended the interview by saying he didn't wish to say anymore about it, except that Saxton's fate "may not have been unmerited, if all the facts were known." This comment was not quite so colorful as the remark attributed to him in an unsourced newspaper account: "Served him right. I ought to have done it myself years ago."

And so Sunday passed into Monday, October 10.

Chapter 7   A Chain of Circumstances

As expected, much was clarified on Monday, October 10 for all parties concerned in the Saxton murder. Early that morning, while Mrs. George's elder son Newton visited her in her cell, Sample C. George arrived in Canton and conferred with James A. Sterling at his office. Always careful of at least her personal appearance, Mrs. George was tastefully dressed for her debut performance in a criminal courtroom. No longer wearing her dark garb, she was attired in a blue plaid shirt waist, with standing collar and a blue tie. She was still wearing the sailor hat that she had on when seen on Streetcar No. 21 and at the time of her arrest.

At 10:04 Constable Charles Henry brought Mrs. George into Justice Reigner's courtroom. It was already crowded when she arrived, with perhaps a hundred additional spectators overflowing into the halls and stairway. Many of the curious were women, noted the anonymous correspondent for the *Cleveland Daily World* with disapproval, most of who indicated by their conversation that "their sympathies were with the defendant." Pomerene was busily consulting heavy statute books as Sterling, Welty and Rice filed in and sat down next to their client. A minute later, Grant joined Pomerene and the arraignment commenced. Speaking for the defense, Welty addressed Justice Reigner and stated that they waived the reading of the affidavit and asked that they proceed to the scheduling of the preliminary hearing on the murder charge. Pomerene, determined not to give an inch at the outset, immediately objected, saying, "I understand you have a right to waive the reading of the affidavit, but hardly of the arraignment." Following some desultory bickering over the point, Reigner addressed the prisoner. "Mrs. George, what do you say to the affidavit? Are you guilty or not guilty?" "Not guilty," replied Annie in a firm, clear voice.

More petty argument ensued. Pomerene insisted that the preliminary hearing be delayed until Saturday, claiming that he was tied up in Common Pleas Court all week. Now it was Welty's turn to get huffy. Icily noting that the operative statute specified that the preliminary hearing occur within four days of arraignment, he argued in favor of scheduling it sooner. Pomerene finally conceded the point, and all sides agreed to meet the following afternoon in Justice Reigner's courtroom at 1 p.m.

Shortly after Annie was led back to her cell, the formal obsequies for George Saxton got underway at 2 p.m. Held in the Barber home, they were short and simple, as befitted the scandal of his passing. The officiating minister was the Reverend. O. B. Milligan, pastor of the Saxton family's home church, the First Presbyterian Church of Canton. He was assisted by the Reverend. Dr. O. E. Manchester, pastor of the First Methodist Church, President McKinley's home congregation. Attendance at the rites was restricted to family members and close friends. Milligan, Manchester and a quartet of singers stood in the hall, flanked by the casket in the north parlor and the mourners in the south parlor. After a short hymn sung by Mrs. Elizabeth Frease Smith, Mrs. Herman Kuhns, Captain Herman Kuhns and Mr. Frank Pfirrman, Milligan read a scriptural text and Manchester followed with a prayer. After a final look at the deceased by the mourners, the casket was closed and loaded into the funeral car by pall bearers George Baldwin, William A. Lynch, George B. Frease, J. H. Kenny, David B. Smith and James J. Grant. Carriages containing the funeral party then proceeded to West Lawn Cemetery, watched by a large, silent crowd lining the route. While Ida McKinley remained alone in her carriage at the cemetery, there were more brief prayers graveside at the Saxton family plot. The casket was then lowered into the earth and the mourners left George to commune with his ancestors. The McKinley funeral party returned to the Barber home, where a continuing deluge of sympathetic letters, telegrams and funeral floral gifts awaited their attention.

While Annie comfortably languished in jail and George Saxton was buried, Coroner McQuate's inquest, now almost irrelevant, ground on. Cora Oberlin testified first, relating Mrs.

George's movements on Friday but filling in none of the missing hours between the time she left and returned to Mrs. Oberlin's home. Cora also recalled her Thursday night conversation with Annie in exact detail, recounting Annie's surprise that her ex-husband had remarried and already had another child. Cora remembered asking Annie at the time what Sample C. George looked like. Annie told her he was "a tall man with a sandy mustache and large blue eyes." More helpful to Annie, Cora Oberlin testified that her manner had been calm and cooperative when arrested, with no signs of unusual stress or fatigue. Cora also contradicted the story that Annie had been apprehended while skulking out of a "swamp" at the rear of the Oberlin house; Cora insisted that Annie had come walking down West Tuscarawas Street in plain sight, as was her custom.

Groceryman Joseph Lippert followed Cora Oberlin on the stand. He told of seeing Mrs. George about 8:30 p.m. on Friday night. He had just come out of the store to purchase some celery from a woman in a wagon when he saw her walking "leisurely" along Tuscarawas Street. He recalled his surprise at the time, which he had expressed to the celery seller, remarking, "There goes Mrs. George, the woman who is supposed to have shot George Saxton, and it is kind of funny for her to be coming down this way when everybody is looking for her in the west end." Lippert had noticed nothing else about Annie at the time, except that she was carrying one side of her dress in her hand, presumably to keep it away from burrs and Spanish needles. His son, Frank Lippert, followed him, telling essentially the same story of seeing Annie George pass the store at 8:30 p.m. But Frank also mentioned that it was the "usual" time for her passing by the store, and that her manner was her normal, "quiet" demeanor.

Canton Police officer Aaron Rohn testified next about the circumstances of Annie's arrest. He gave the details of staking out Cora Oberlin's house, Annie's arrest and her circumspect silence afterwards. Rohn added nothing to what had already been printed in the Canton and Cleveland newspapers. But then Russell Hogan took the stand. The thirteen-year-old had already been publicly identified as an eyewitness to the murder and the inquest audience was not disappointed by his testimony. In a calm, clear voice he related how he had just returned from an errand at the drugstore when he heard the sound of two shots. Being a normally curious adolescent, he had begun running immediately north toward the sound of the shots. Just as he came abreast of the Eckroate grocery, across the street from 319 Lincoln Avenue, he heard two more shots. Without obviously embroidering his narrative, Russell now told the rapt inquest spectators what he had seen next:

> I saw a black object; I could not tell what it was. It was right straight across from [Eckroate's grocery] when I saw it. It was either a man or a woman, I could not say which. Whoever it was walked a little ways south and then turned and went back a little way and then returned and came down to the open field and that was the last I saw of it. I went across the street with Mr. Boron and Mr. Bederman. Mr. Boron struck a match and we saw Mr. Saxton lying on the sidewalk. I knew Mr. Saxton when I saw him from having seen him go past the house. I do not think I know Mrs. George; I only saw her once that I knew who she was. I stood in the gutter there a short time when some men told me to go down to Weiss' and send for the patrol and the doctor. I went down and had Mr. Weiss telephone. I then came back when the patrol came.

Russell Hogan's evidence was probably the most important elicited by the inquest. It was clear, it was careful and it was more detailed than that of Henry J. Bederman, the other murder eyewitness. What no one at the inquest knew, however, was that Russell's inquest testimony would be his last word on the subject, unqualified and unchallenged by any contrary testimony or compromising cross-examination.

Eva Althouse took McQuate's stand next. Her testimony, no doubt, was a disappointment to the crowd gathered that Monday afternoon. Her cursory examination, however, may have been deliberate on McQuate's part. Eva had already given an extensive newspaper interview concerning the murder and it was known that she would be called as a witness at Annie's preliminary hearing on Tuesday. So Eva's brief appearance at the inquest was limited to a bland description of her relationship with George Saxton and an accounting of her whereabouts during the week of the murder. Eva did, however, reiterate her bafflement at Saxton's presence in front of her house at the fatal moment. Although admitting that he had a passkey to her home, she could not think of any reason why he would have been there at a time he knew she was absent.

Monday's testimony at the inquest concluded with appearances by city humane officer Charles R. Frazer, Canton city jail turnkey Samuel Becherer and police officer Fred McCloud. Nothing of moment was produced by their testimony and the inquest adjourned for the day.

That night at 9:00 a train pulled into the Canton station with members of President McKinley's Cabinet aboard. Ten minutes later, the *Campania*, containing the President and other family members, was coupled to it and the train left at exactly 9:24 p.m. for Chicago and the Omaha Peace Jubilee. Ida McKinley remained behind at her sister's house; she would leave to join her husband two days later. The McKinleys would not return to Canton until after the conclusion of Annie George's trial in April, 1899. Before leaving, however, the President and his wife were present for the reading of George D. Saxton's will. Filed for probate two days later, the will had been executed six months earlier on April 11, 1898. Like his previous will, it appointed his sister Mary as executrix but differed greatly in its provisions. Saxton's old will had left the income from his estate to his sisters Ida and Mary; the new will left his property, estimated to be worth between $75,000 and $100,000, outright to Mary's children. The actual value of his entire estate was probably somewhere between $175,000 and $250,000.

Sometime that Monday, a persistent newspaper reporter finally tracked down Elizabeth Parks in New York City. The former Elizabeth Frantz of Canton, she had been one of Saxton's alleged paramours during his halcyon playboy years in the 1880s and '90s, and some letters from her to Saxton had been unearthed after Saxton's death. Once married to traveling salesman William F. Parks, later divorced, this single mother of an infant daughter was now working as a cashier at the Hotel Marie Antoinette in New York City. She was in no mood to have intimate or unsavory details of her previous life ventilated but her public comments displayed dismay, tempered with discretion about the past and a becoming loyalty to a dead man unable to defend himself:

> It seems hard that they can't leave the letters of a dead man alone. I have known Mr. Saxton all my life. He was very dear to me. He has always been my friend. I would rather not say anything more.

It was also reported in some newspapers that Mrs. Parks had fainted dead away when she first heard of Saxton's murder, but that may well have been the journalistic license of the day.

As Monday's session came to a close, Canton swirled with wild and often conflicting rumors. Some said that the McKinley family was demanding that the prosecution be dropped. Others insisted that Mrs. George would plead guilty to lesser charges of either second-degree murder, manslaughter or even assault and battery. Still others spread the tale that the reason that the murder eyewitnesses had been unsure of the sex of the killer was because it had been a *man disguised as a woman*

Coroner McQuate resumed his inquest on Tuesday afternoon. But that session and subsequent sessions Wednesday and

Thursday elicited little attention from the newspapers and few spectators. Most Cantonians and other observers were fixated on Annie's preliminary hearing, which got underway on schedule at 1 p.m. Dressed in the same clothes she had worn the day before, she was accompanied to the hearing by her two sons. Perhaps feigning an optimism she did not genuinely feel, Annie told Newton and Howard to wait outside the courtroom for her until the hearing was concluded. Shortly after she entered the door, however, Constable Henry returned and gently told the boys not to expect their mother that day.

Pomerene was already there when Annie arrived. He had brought a   stenographer and Sterling, Rice and Welty had their own when they arrived several minutes later. After Justice Regnier opened the proceedings and the witnesses were sworn, Welty requested and was granted an order separating the witnesses, so that they would not hear each other's testimony. The State then began introducing testimony to buttress its charge of first-degree murder against Annie George.

Dr. Edward Brant testified first. Pomerene's purpose in putting him on the stand was to establish the fact of the murder having been committed. Stating that he had been the first physician to examine Saxton, Brant described the wounds in detail and gave his opinion that death had been almost instantaneous after the so-called "fourth" bullet severed Saxton's iliac artery. Brant also said that he judged Saxton dead when he found him by feeling his pulse and that he might have already been dead for ten to fifteen minutes before Brant examined his body.

Having established the murder, Pomerene now moved to put Annie George at its scene. Streetcar No. 21 motorman Samuel Rittenhouse testified about her presence on his car shortly before 6 p.m. on the murder evening. The morning after the murder he had been reported in the newspapers as saying, "Mrs. George got on my car at the square . . ." and even more unequivocally, "I know it was Mrs. George." Befitting perhaps the fact that he was now under oath, Rittenhouse now carefully hedged his statements.

Noting that it was conductor Shetler who had identified the woman on his car as Annie George, Rittenhouse said he did not know Annie George but that the woman now present in court resembled the woman "identified as Mrs. George" to him by Shetler. Rittenhouse reiterated his prior admission that he had not seen where Mrs. George went after she got off his car at Hazlette Avenue. But he estimated that she had left it at 5:55 p.m., which everyone in the courtroom well knew would have given her ample leisure to walk to 319 Lincoln Avenue by 6:10 p.m.

With Saxton's death and Annie's presence in the vicinity on the record, Pomerene now brought Henry J. Bederman to the stand to identify her directly as the murderess. Bederman repeated his story, already familiar to many in the room from his chatty newspaper interviews and his inquest appearance. He testified that he had known both George Saxton and Annie George for some years and could recognize them by sight. He again described seeing two figures in the darkness by the steps. And while he could not directly identify the shooter as Mrs. George, he insisted that it was a woman, tall and darkly dressed. John C. Welty tried to shake Bederman during his cross-examination but his story remained consistent in its details.

The next two witnesses against Mrs. George were Canton Police officers Fred McCloud and Henry Piero. Pomerene's strategy in putting them on the stand was to establish evidence of Annie's guilt after the murder was committed. His examination therefore focused on the details of Annie's behavior after her arrest and the circumstantial evidence of her personal appearance. McCloud told of the arrest, of Mrs. George's refusal to answer questions and the bodily search conducted by Dr. Pontius at the City Jail. He further stated that although he thought he had smelled gunpowder on her right hand, his examination of her shoes did not reveal any evidence that they were muddy or wet. During cross-examination by Welty, McCloud said that he visited Mrs. George shortly after she was committed to the county jail on Saturday. He had then asked her for the key to her trunk, which she had willingly given him. Welty succeeded in getting McCloud to admit that he had subsequently searched the trunk at Mrs. Oberlin's and found nothing suspicious in it, much less a smoking revolver.

Piero's testimony corroborated McCloud's version of Annie's arrest and her behavior at the police station. But Piero added just the supplementary details Pomerene desired, noting that he had seen Spanish needles and burrs on Mrs. George's dress. Pomerene then drew from Piero the statement that he had searched the area around the Althouse residence and found Spanish needles and burrs growing in profusion there.

Perry Van Horne, the former *Canton News-Democrat* reporter was the last witness at the Tuesday afternoon session. His role was to offer evidence of premeditation in George Saxton's murder and his testimony provided all that Pomerene could have desired. Van Horne told his story of Annie summoning him after she had pulled a revolver on George Saxton and asking him to write it up in his newspaper. He repeated the threat she had made to shoot Saxton during that interview if he did not marry her when Sample C. George's lawsuit was settled. Van Horne related that Annie had also talked about how unsophisticated she was when she first came to Canton and how happily married she had been before meeting Saxton. Van Horne told, too, of visiting Annie in jail on the night of her arrest and her refusal to answer his questions. Interestingly, Van Horne did not mention that it was prosecutor Pomerene who had sent him to that jail cell for the purpose of helping Annie incriminate herself. Welty could do nothing to shake Van Horne's story, except for his eventual admission that he could not remember the exact date of the interview when Annie had threatened Saxton. Judge Regnier adjourned the hearing for the day with Van Horne still on the stand.

The Tuesday inquest testimony continued well into the evening. It must have been at least a nuisance to some of the witnesses, as several of them had already testified or were scheduled to testify at Justice Regnier's preliminary hearing. Officer

Henry Piero testified, as did several of the waitresses from the Star Restaurant and Jesse Taylor. Only Piero offered any information not already known to the general public. According to him, Mrs. George had hardly been the silent sphinx she was reputed to be, at least during her first hour in the city jail cell on Friday night. The policeman testified that she had chatted at some length with him before she fell asleep. Annie had made no reference during their conversation to Saxton's murder or her current predicament. Instead, she talked in a sentimental, even nostalgic manner about her life and her family. She recalled her grim sojourn in South Dakota, telling Piero that she liked the territory there but not as much as Ohio. She talked of other parts of the United States she had seen and then she told Piero of her youth, the early years of her marriage in Hanoverton and her beloved sons. Piero eventually tried to get her to talk about Saxton's shooting but Annie refused to say a word about it.

Star Restaurant waitresses Lena Mauger and Clara Weiser, cook Lucile Monter and proprietor Samuel Kirk followed Piero on the stand. Although convincingly detailed, their testimony only accounted for Annie's movements between 4:45 and 5:15 p.m. on the fateful night.

Coroner McQuate's inquest staggered on into Thursday, October 13, producing progressively less relevant testimony and becoming increasingly upstaged by Justice Regnier's hearing. The diminishing interest in his inquest, however, suited Coroner McQuate just fine. He had been under pressure from James J. Grant and Atlee Pomerene to name Mrs. George as Saxton's shooter from the moment Saxton's body was brought in for the post-mortem. That pressure continued throughout the inquest but McQuate refused to issue an official verdict that Mrs. George was guilty. He informed the prosecutors that he could not in good conscience do so, as not a single inquest witness had conclusively identified Annie George as the shooter. McQuate's caution, it was rumored about Canton, was strengthened by the nervousness of his bondsmen, who did not want to face an expensive lawsuit in the event that a formal murder charge against Mrs. George could not be made to stick. McQuate, an experienced politician, knew when and how to keep a low legal profile, and he waited until April 9, 1899 — five days after Annie George went on trial — before issuing his official verdict. It was the familiar, safe finding that an "unknown hand" had shot George Saxton to death.

Annie George's preliminary hearing resumed on Wednesday morning, October 12 at 1:30. Her sons Newton and Charles remained by her side throughout the day's proceedings. Pomerene got Perry Van Horne to reprise his story about Annie's threats against Saxton and Van Horne's jail visitation. Having established that Mrs. George had threatened Saxton, Pomerene now maneuvered to identify her motive for murder as jealousy evoked by Saxton's attentions to Eva Althouse. So Pomerene asked Van Horne, "Did Mrs. George tell you on that occasion that she had often seen Mrs. Althouse and Saxton occupying her room in the Saxton Block?" "Yes," replied Van Horne, "she said that was the cause of the trouble at the block."

Harry Noble was Pomerene's next witness. His testimony was limited to stating that Mrs. George had visited the Dannemiller block in search of attorney James Sterling at 7:00 p.m. on Friday night, less than an hour after Saxton's murder. Then James Shetler testified that he had seen Mrs. George on Streetcar No. 21 several minutes before the murder and that she had exited the car at Hazlette Avenue.

When Shetler finished his testimony Pomerene told Justice Regnier that the State rested its case. The defense then called its only witness: Eva B. Althouse. Why Annie's lawyers used Eva as a defense witness at the preliminary hearing is a mystery yet to be explained. What Annie obviously needed was a substantial alibi witness, rather than the unpredictable and probably adverse testimony of someone whose life she had threatened and who was more than likely to be hostile to her. But at this point in the case Annie seemingly had no alibi witness, so the probable reasoning of Annie's counsel was that putting the erring Eva on the stand would at least generate sympathy for Annie and at the same time blacken Eva's character in the eyes of the public. Welty and Sterling may also have wanted to shove the prosecution off balance with this unexpected move — and they may, too, have hoped that a brutal grilling might discourage Eva from any future participation in the State's case against Anna George.

There is no reason to believe that Eva's testimony generated any such sympathy for Anna — but her appearance, thanks to Welty's mischievous cross-examination, did constitute a relatively amusing episode amid the grim doings in Justice Regnier's courtroom. It was said by an observer that as Eva took the stand Annie fixed her with a steely gaze of open contempt. Welty then opened the examination by inquiring as to her marital status and where she lived. She told him she lived at 319 Lincoln Avenue and that she was the widow of George W. Althouse. Welty then maneuvered to portray her as the "other woman" in the Saxton-George affair.

"How long have you known Mr. Saxton?"

"Since I remember anything," replied Eva.

"When did you visit him after your husband's death?"

"The first time was at James J. Grant's office when I sold him some brick stock I owned."

"You saw him frequently after that?"

Although Eva was a woman with a past, she was determined to present a demure portrait of her relations with Saxton. She replied, "When I had business I called to see him."

Welty was equal to Eva's imposture of innocence and he replied, no doubt, with just the right tinge of audible irony, "We are assuming it was *all* business." Giving those words a moment to resonate, Welty continued. "After you quit calling to see him on business, he started to see you, did he not?"

"Yes," replied Eva.

"You've been keeping house since, have you?"

"Yes."

"You live alone?"

"Yes."

"During the past year Saxton called upon you almost daily?"

"Yes."

"And he took you bicycle and carriage riding, didn't he?"

"Yes."

"Did you go tandem or each have your own wheel?"

"We each had our own wheel."

"On your return did you stop at his room or at your house?"

"Always at my house. I never stopped at the Block except on business."

Welty was too good a lawyer to smirk but he may have smiled as he replied, "As I said before, we assume it was all *business*." He paused, and then returned to his work of fixing Eva's position in the Saxton-George-Althouse triangle. "Do you know where Mrs. George's room was in the block?"

"I know nothing about it."

"The living rooms of Saxton were next to his office, were they not?"

"I think so."

"Did Saxton have a key to your house?

"He had a pass key that fitted the front door."

"Did he frequently unlock the door?"

"I have known of his going there to water the plants and feed the birds when I was away."

"Were you at home at the time of the shooting?"

"No, I was at my mother's."

"When did you last see Saxton?"

"On Monday evening before the shooting."

"Was he at your house all last Saturday night?"

"No, he was not."

"When was the last time he was there all night?"

"He was never there all night."

"How late did he remain?"

"He never remained later than nine o'clock."

"Were you ever in Saxton's room all night?"

"No, sir, I was not."

Atlee Pomerene had had enough. Annie George was supposed to be the accused at the bar, yet the current dialogue strongly suggested that it was Eva Althouse. He jumped to his feet, objecting, and insisted to Justice Regnier that Welty's line of questioning did not bear upon the phase of the case now before the court. If the defense intended to elicit any testimony with reference to Saxton's murder, Pomerene complained, "they had been at it long enough to get there."

Justice Regnier was initially inclined to agree with the prosecutor. But before ruling on the matter, he asked Welty to justify his interrogation of Mrs. Althouse. And John Welty was ready with his justification. He had recognized from the outset that the key to exonerating his client was to focus on the despicable character and actions of George Saxton and his last paramour. Addressing Justice Regnier, he told him that the actions of George Saxton were central to the case, especially his relations with Eva Althouse and Annie George. These facts would remain relevant, especially if Annie George were tried for Saxton's murder. It was therefore important to find out *why* Saxton had died on Eva's doorstep with a key to her house in his pocket. Regnier was persuaded by Welty's argument and he overruled Pomerene's objection, while also warning Welty to get to the point.

Welty resumed his task of putting Eva Althouse in the pillory of public opinion. At the same time, he hoped that Eva's testimony could be used to undermine the seriousness of Annie's threats against Eva and George Saxton.

"Did you ever receive a letter from Mrs. George?"

"Yes, one."

"Where is it?"

"It was given to George Saxton and delivered to [United States] Post Office Inspector A. P. Owens for use in a Cleveland [court] case."

"Are you certain it was from Mrs. George?"

"I am not certain, as the letter was unsigned."

"Your relations with Saxton continued the same after the receipt of that letter, did they not?"

"Yes, sir."

"She has not killed you yet or attempted to, has she?"

"No, sir."

"Were you and Saxton ever engaged to be married?"

"It had been talked of. He wanted to wait until a business matter was settled."

"He had proposed marriage to you?"

"Yes, but I had not given him an answer."

Welty returned to his ironical tone. "You were holding the matter under advisement, were you?"

"Yes."

"Did Mrs. George ever talk to you when she came around to your house?"

"Yes."

"Was Saxton there?"

"No, sir."

"Was that the time he escaped out the back way?"

"He never escaped out the back way."

"What did she say?"

"She said she would cut my heart out if she caught me with Saxton again. She dared me to come outside, calling me nearly every name in the English language."

"What were the names?" Welty must have been exulting at the possibility of getting Mrs. Althouse to spout smutty words in a public forum. Still, he didn't push it when Eva replied, "Please, is it necessary for me to tell them?" It was common practice in American courts to excuse witnesses, especially female ones, from repeating profane language, and it was also, as Welty knew, a courtesy he might wish extended to his other future witnesses. But he wanted one more shot at Eva's imposture of chaste rectitude in her relations with Saxton.

"What did you do the night she saw you with Saxton, after you returned from a bicycle ride?"

"I dropped my wheel and ran, when I saw her."

"You and Saxton had both been drinking, had you not?"

"I beg your pardon, I had not."

"That was not the night, then?"

"No, nor any other night."

Pomerene's cross-examination elicited further instances of Annie George's hostile behavior to Eva Althouse. The Prosecutor focused on getting Eva to testify that Annie had threatened her by letter and in person, often screaming her threats in obscene language at her very front door. The defense then rested and Justice Regnier called for oral argument from both sides.

Pomerene spoke first, stating that the State was content with the case it had presented and waived its right to further argument. Rice immediately responded, simply telling Judge Regnier that there was no case at all against Mrs. George. Sterling chimed in, asking Pomerene if he really thought he had presented enough evidence to bind Mrs. George over to the grand jury. "I didn't know there was so much humor in Mr. Sterling," bantered Pomerene sarcastically. Rice returned to the evidence, telling Justice Regnier that the testimony presented had not fastened Saxton's murder more clearly upon Mrs. George than any other citizen of Canton. Rice said the fact that she was on the street near the murder scene that night was hardly an extraordinary circumstance and that it meant nothing in the absence of eyewitnesses to the killing.

Sterling vociferously echoed his fellow-counsel's objections. He further argued that first-degree murder was a serious charge, requiring serious evidence—and the evidence Pomerene had presented was not serious. He ended with a plea that the charge be dropped. The Stark County prosecutor was ready with a reasoned rebuttal. Pomerene said he would have expected the same arguments from the defense even if the accused had actually been seen in the act of murder. After all, Pomerene argued, the State's duty was simply to establish that a crime had been committed and that there were reasonable grounds to believe that Mrs. George had committed the crime. And, continued Pomerene, he believed that both points had clearly been established. Mrs. George had been seen to ride past her house on streetcar No. 21. She had been seen getting off the car at Hazlette Avenue just before the murder. Several minutes later a woman was seen near 319 Lincoln Avenue, shots were fired and George Saxton was found dead.

Warming to his subject, Pomerene emphasized the suspiciousness of Mrs. George's behavior from the moment she was arrested by the police. The canny prosecutor no doubt knew that Annie's silence would not and probably could not be held against her if she were to come to trial. So now was the time to exploit that silence, and Pomerene attacked, stating her conduct at police headquarters had spoken "louder than words." He continued, explaining his logical theory of the murder and hurling a challenge at Mrs. George's defense team to produce an adequate alibi:

> If she had been on a legitimate business she could have explained it and would have been released. But she chose to keep her mouth shut. She said she would kill George Saxton, and with almost lightning rapidity she keeps her word. The case was settled Wednesday and on Friday evening George Saxton was a corpse. If I am shown the whereabouts of Mrs. George at that hour on Friday I will oppose any indictment against her.

John Welty finished for the defense. He echoed Rice and Sterling's insistence that there was not enough evidence to connect the accused with Saxton's murder. All he or anybody else knew, concluded Sterling, was that George Saxton had been shot to death by an unknown person. It could have even been, he suggested darkly, an act of self-defense. There was no justification, he pleaded, for holding Mrs. George in jail until the January meeting of the grand jury. As he alluded to the possibility of her remaining in jail, court spectators watched raptly as Anna's face flushed and a solitary tear coursed down her face.

When Welty sat down, Justice Regnier thanked the large audience in the room for its good behavior and read the lengthy indictment out loud again. He then ruled that there was sufficient evidence to hold Mrs. George to a higher court on the first degree murder charge. Aware that the defense attorneys were already frantically scribbling down possible legal exceptions for future appeal, Regnier justified his decision at some length. He acknowledged that the evidence was not complete — but went on to say that it was not necessary that it be so; only in the trial court would evidence be needed to prove guilt. Justice Regnier's court, he explained, was only required to have probable cause to believe that the accused might be guilty. Two or three witnesses might warrant such a belief and were enough to send the accused on to a higher trial. Even if there was conflicting testimony — which there was not in this case — his preliminary court was justified in holding the accused for possible trial. Justice Regnier than reviewed the evidence and stated that there was a "chain of circumstances" linking Mrs. George to the murder. He ended his ruling with the words every lawyer in the room had been expecting: "From all the testimony I am sorry to say that I am compelled to bind her over to await the action of the grand jury."

Mrs. George's lawyers now turned to the more immediate welfare of their client. It was mid-October, and as Pomerene had already vetoed a special session of the grand jury, it appeared that Mrs. George was likely to languish in jail until at least January, and probably well beyond until her trial was concluded. Her lawyers immediately requested bail, although they knew that a charge of first degree murder precluded it. Mrs. George had thus far sat silently and unmoved throughout the hearing, but as John Welty argued that keeping her in jail until January was an unacceptable hardship on her and her sons, another solitary tear appeared on her cheek, to the great edification of the newspaper reporters and spectators present. But the law was the law. Justice Regnier promptly denied bail and Mrs. George was led out of the courtroom, down the street and back to her county jail cell. Throughout her progress she was admired by a large and sympathetic crowd.

Chapter 8   Wanted: One Revolver and Some Witnesses

The six months that passed between Justice Regnier's decision and Annie's trial were deceptively quiet. To many Canton spectators and frustrated journalists, it seemed as though nothing significant in the case was occurring as the months slipped by. But beneath the surface, much was going on. Both sides in the case were preparing for what promised to be an epic legal contest with Annie George's life as the stake. Both sides would later accuse each other of bad faith and bad conduct in their preparations for the trial. Much of what occurred on both sides may never be known, but it is clear that both sides were probably guilty of whatever they charged their opponents with, in what was as much a battle for public opinion as it was to score legal points.

Who were these men who struggled so mightily for the fate of Annie George? Atlee Pomerene, befitting his future prominence, was likely the most ambitious. Born in Holmes County, Ohio in 1863, one of nine children, the 35-year-old Stark County prosecutor was already well up the successful career ladder that would climax with his 12-year tenure in the United States Senate. Golden tongued and distinguished looking, Pomerene's rise in Canton politics had been rapid from the start. After his education at Princeton and the Cincinnati Law School, he settled in Canton and opened a law practice with Charles Russell Miller, a nephew of William McKinley. The very next year he became City Solicitor in 1887 and served four years, followed by a stint on the Canton Board of Education. After building up a successful law practice, he was elected county prosecutor in 1896, the only Democratic official in rock-ribbed Republican Stark County. Respected by all political sides for his eloquence, Pomerene's local nickname was "The Melancholy Democrat," a sobriquet allegedly stemming from the likeness of his somewhat bulging brow to that of Edwin Booth, the most celebrated tragedian in America. A political animal to his core, Pomerene knew that the Annie George trial was the chance of his life, a task which could either make or break his career ambitions. He believed Annie George was guilty of murder and her successful prosecution would be an asset to his political career. At the same time, however, he had to be sensitive to the intense level of public sympathy for Annie in Canton. Pomerene was well aware that to many, whatever her prior sins, Annie was a severely wronged woman, and, however improbable, widely perceived as a damsel in distress. He also had to be circumspect about the ventilation of scandal in the case; as a lonely Stark County Democrat he could not afford to antagonize the McKinley family with too vigorous an exposure of George Saxton's many personal skeletons. It was also said that Pomerene's wife was almost more ambitious for him than he was himself.

James J. Grant, Pomerene's partner in the prosecution, faced some similar obstacles in his conduct of the case. As George Saxton's personal attorney, no one knew better than he what "nasty things" might emerge at Annie George's trial. An even greater obstacle for Grant, as Annie's trial would emphatically demonstrate, was his close personal relationship to the deceased. For Grant, the prosecution of Annie George had long since become a personal vendetta. As he had shown by his conduct on the night of Saxton's murder, his anger against Annie was constant, seething and an almost palpable force to anyone in his presence. Grant was celebrated as one of the most effective and eloquent pleaders in the history of the Stark County bar. It was rumored that he was a candidate for appointment as the federal District Attorney for Northern Ohio, an especially likely outcome if he could secure Annie George's conviction. But could his emotions be held in check as he publicly battled the accused killer of his best friend?

Annie George's defense team was worthy of their illustrious foes. It was clear that a politically compromised James Rice would not stay on the team for long, and John C. Welty assumed complete control of Annie's defense shortly after Justice Regnier

The Prosecution and the Defense:
Atlee Pomerene (Cleveland Daily World, April 6, 1899);
James J. Grant (Cleveland Daily World, April 8, 1899);
John C. Welty and James Sterling
(Cleveland Daily World, April 8, 1899)

committed her to jail. Originally from the Stark County township of Sugar Creek, Welty was considered the best criminal defense attorney in the region. The son of a prosperous farmer, Welty had entered Canton's elite society in the 1870s, hobnobbing with the

same august citizens as George Saxton. Welty, in fact, had originally met George Saxton at the home of Alice Schaefer back then,
and it was George who bestowed on Welty the half-sneering
nickname that clung to him throughout his subsequent career:
"The Duke of Sugar Bush."   Politically almost as ambitious as
Pomerene, Welty had been unsuccessful in his runs as Democratic
candidate for U. S. representative and Ohio governor. But he had
served six years as the Stark County prosecutor, was recognized as
a fearsome courtroom advocate and was not likely to pull any
punches in what promised to be an ugly legal contest.

James A. Sterling, Mrs. George's other lawyer, may have
been the most intriguing of the four advocates, at least in terms of
his personal history. The law was his second career; he had originally been a preacher at the Union Church in Canal Fulton, where
he developed a rhetorical ability to hold an audience spellbound.
Sometime in the mid-1880s, however, he had lost his faith and
occupation, becoming an agnostic. A smooth-shaven man in a
profession dominated by bearded and mustachioed males, Sterling
possessed an ingratiating, persuasive courtroom presence. An
additional asset was his complete personal belief in Annie
George's utter innocence. Next to James J. Grant, Sterling knew as
much about the Saxton-George "backstory" as anyone, having
previously served as lawyer for both Annie and her ex-husband
Sample George. On the other hand, Sterling had never before
participated in a murder case.

Even before the Stark County grand jury met in January,
both sides began to work feverishly on building their cases and
spying on their adversaries. Less is know about the prosecution's
trial preparations than the defense. Prosecutor Pomerene fervently
denied assertions that United States government officials were
helping to construct the State's case against Mrs. George, piously
stating, "It is absolutely untrue, and is done to create sentiment."
But United States Post Office Inspector Alonzo Owens, Secret
Service officer John M. Webb and various unnamed U. S. marshals
were often seen in Canton during the next six months, as was

McKinley intimate H. O. Heistand. Their presence in the city was never convincingly explained and Welty and Sterling were probably correct when they repeatedly charged that Federal officials were acting as ex-officio members of the prosecution. It was also rumored, probably with reason, that celebrated Cleveland private detective Jake Mintz was also working behind the scenes for the prosecution. The chief employment of all these operatives was to dig up dirt on the witnesses for the defense and to learn the background of potential jury candidates. Pomerene and Grant were supplied with complete dossiers on the personal histories of everyone connected with the trial by the time it opened in April. Annie's defense team was also active in pretrial investigations, whatever their outraged public charges of underhanded espionage by the prosecution. Moreover, the defense lawyers' recruitment of amateur detectives to dig for dirt seems to have been more successful than the prosecution's parallel efforts, thanks to widespread public sympathy for Annie George. Chief among defense investigative assets was a woman named Maud ("May") Streeter. From Columbus, Ohio, she was the wife of Albert Streeter, a successful amusement entrepreneur and the originator of the concept of staging the collision of railroad trains for the amusement of paying audiences. Personable, comely, wealthy and blessed with ample leisure, Mrs. Streeter dedicated herself to helping exonerate Annie, whom she had met during the mid-1890s. May's credo was simple and she pursued it single-mindedly in the months before Annie's trial: "I am going to do everything I can to help Mrs. George. I am her friend and I am going to stick to her during her trouble." Mrs. Streeter's strategy was to mingle freely among talkative Canton citizens, collecting useful gossip. She would eventually be credited with unearthing bombshell information about two key prosecution witnesses.

Two other amateur sleuths who proved invaluable to Annie's defense were her son Newton Robert, 17, and his friend Clarence Potter, 18. No one was likely to pay much attention to two unremarkable teenaged boys, and Newton and Clarence made the most of their relative anonymity. Their chief mission was to dog the footsteps of Pomerene and Grant, monitoring their contacts and dealings with probable trial witnesses. Such shadowing by the two boys went on for some months, it seems, without either Grant or Pomerene suspecting a thing.

MRS. GEORGE IN HER CELL.

Mrs. George in her Stark County Jail Cell
(Canton Evening Repository, April 8, 1899)

Meanwhile, Annie waited in her Stark County jail cell. Although her attorneys had originally told her not to talk to anyone, that caution was more and more relaxed as the weeks after her arrest elapsed. One reason was their recognition that Annie was a highly sociable woman and needed contact with other people. Her attorneys could not help but note, too, that Annie's skill at ingratiating herself with other people helped improve the conditions of her incarceration and aided immensely in the battle for public opinion. After Anna was bound over to the grand jury, Stark County Sheriff John J. Zaiser began allowing her visitors, and a flood of friends and well-wishers soon turned Annie's cell into something of a Canton social center. There she received visitors almost daily, stylishly garbed (more often than not in raiment of her own making) and surrounded by fragrant flowers sent by her admirers and sympathizers. Many of them were relatives and longtime friends from Hanoverton. But sometimes Annie entertained more general audiences, as, for example, when she graciously received eight female clerks from the Stark County courthouse on October 28. On such occasions, she would converse pleasantly with all, but always with the stated stipulation that she could not discuss anything directly related to her impending trial. She even joked mildly about her situation, telling the clerks to visit again, as she would always be "at home."

Judging from her behavior, Annie herself recognized from the outset of her legal ordeal that she was her own best asset in the fight for her life. Whether in jail or the courtroom, she remained controlled and disciplined at all times. She never volunteered unnecessary or compromising information and she unfailing presented a demeanor that was pleasant and even demure. Whatever her sins or status as a fallen woman, she was determined to act as though she enjoyed the unchallenged chastity, unsullied reputation and pious virtue of the most irreproachable Canton virgin. Central to this strategy was her unfailing and enthusiastic participation in Sunday night religious services at the county jail. Held every other Sabbath in the lower corridor, the services consisted of an opening hymn, a prayer, a brief talk by a missionary, another hymn or two and then a closing prayer. Mrs. George's high, clear, sweet voice rang out prominently during the hymn portion of these biweekly services and her height, relatively tall for a woman, rendered her even more conspicuous. Her new friend Sheriff Zaiser was quoted as saying that she had the finest singing voice he had yet heard in his two terms as sheriff.

Was Annie's portrayal of herself as a religious person sincere? Perhaps — although it is impossible to see into the inmost heart of anyone, much less a woman as complex as Annie George. During her early life she had been active in the Christian Church of Hanoverton and she had joined a congregation of the same denomination in Canton in 1889. She had never returned to church, however, at least in Canton, after her Dakota sojourn in the early 1890s. She now apparently decided it would be a good idea to highlight her religious identity and, better yet, portray herself as the victim of religious hypocrisy.

After several months of dutiful attendance at the jail services, Annie made her move. Inviting a *Cleveland Daily World* reporter into her cell, she turned the conversation to religion, remarking that she had a reverent regard for the Sabbath day. Indeed, she continued, her piety was so extreme that she refused to talk to her attorneys on Sundays. Finding this outright lie unchallenged, Annie articulated her painful regret that her pastor, the Reverend Clarence Hill of the First Christian Church of Canton, had not called upon her since she had been arrested. "No, not once," she mournfully whimpered to the newspaper reporter, "I have not seen or heard from him at all."

Annie's charge that she had not seen or heard from Hill was true. What she left out of her tearful complaint was that she was hardly a member of Hill's church and that he had no reason to believe she was. In fact she had not attended services there since her return from South Dakota in the early 1890s. As he put in his irritated rebuttal to her published comment:

> I do not think I shall call upon Mrs. George. I never knew her, and did not know until a few days ago that she had been a member of my church. I don't see how she can expect me to visit her. Should she send for me I think I should gladly call upon her. If Mrs. George wanted medical aid she would send for a physician; if she wanted legal advice she would

send for a lawyer; if, under the circumstances, she wants me to give her spiritual aid she should send for me. Had Mrs. George been a member of my church at the time of her arrest, and I had been acquainted with her I believe I would have called on her.

Whatever Annie's pious lament, Hill's records showed she had been dropped from the congregation in 1892 for non-participation.

Annie's grand jury duly met on January 16 and heard three days of testimony from witnesses. These witnesses and their testimony differed in several intriguing respects from the testimony at the coroner's inquest and Annie's preliminary hearing. A key contrast was that the grand jury listened to several new witnesses who had not even been called at the prior proceedings. Three of them were Christina Eckroate and attorneys Nat McLean and W. O. Werntz. Christina was the wife of Joseph Eckroate, who owned the grocery/residence across the street from the murder scene. Although her testimony, like the testimony of all others before the grand jury, was not publicly disclosed, it was soon rumored that she claimed to be an actual eyewitness to the Saxton murder.

The testimony of Werntz and McLean was even more surprising. Both of them had previously represented Mrs. George in her legal entanglements of the early 1890s. It was known that both of them were reluctant to testify, citing their confidential and privileged relationships with the accused. But both attorneys took the stand and testified after two Common Pleas Court judges warned them that the law did not regard communications between client and counsel as privileged if the admissions contained any declaration to commit crime. The compulsion and admission of their testimony did not augur well for Annie George.

JUDGE TAYLOR.

Stark County Common Pleas Court Judge Isaac Taylor
(Cleveland Daily World, April 27, 1899)

On January 19 the grand jury returned to presiding Stark County Common Pleas Judge Isaac Montrose Taylor a true bill charging Annie George with first degree murder. Both Annie and her attorneys tried to show a brave face to the news. Annie retained her impassive calm and returned quietly to her cell, where she was reported to be doing needlework and reading newspapers. Welty proclaimed his optimistic faith to a *Cleveland Press* reporter that the indictment would be quashed on the grounds that Werntz and McLean should not have been allowed to testify against their former client:

> We shall avail ourselves of every right, and will attack the indictment on the ground that a client's statements to counsel are privileged. I think when

this question is brought before the court in the proper way it will be treated fairly, and it will then be decided that the testimony of the attorneys in question was not legal. Should that be shown, of course, the indictment cannot stand. We shall fight the case at every point.

Four days later Annie was brought for her arraignment before Judge Taylor on the first degree murder charge. Her walk from the jail to Taylor's courtroom was the first time she had been outside in the open air since her transfer to the county jail in October. Taylor asked her if she possessed sufficient funds to employ counsel. Annie stated that she did not and requested that he appoint Welty and Sterling as her lawyers. Welty then said that his client was not ready for arraignment and requested more time to study the indictment, especially the supporting testimony of Werntz and McLean. Welty assured Judge Taylor that the defense had no wish to delay the trial and that they would be ready to proceed as soon as possible. Judge Taylor then rescheduled the arraignment for Thursday, January 26.

The newspaper coverage of Annie's abortive arraignment provided an interesting perspective on public perceptions and journalistic preoccupations with respect to accused females. A great deal of space was devoted to descriptions of her dress and her demeanor. This, for example, was the picture given readers of the *Cleveland Leader* the day after Annie was indicted on a capital offense:

Yesterday, she appeared just as she did [last October], except for the jaunty sailor hat she had then sported. She had a dark woolen skirt and a light colored shirt waist, the same as she wears regularly in prison. She wore no hat. Her hair was neat and tastefully arranged as for a reception, her collar and cuffs polished, her skirt free from wrinkles and in every respect she presented the appearance of a well-to-do middle-aged woman to whom neat and tidy dressing was a regular habit and not a special ceremony for state occasions. She was self-possessed in the highest degree when she entered the court room in custody of turnkey, and walked to the table where her attorneys sat with an air of confidence, not to say indifference.

Welty's fight to quash the indictment lasted another week before he capitulated and let it stand. He had filed seventeen exceptions to the indictment, all of which Judge Taylor overruled on February 3. Welty conceded graciously, as well he might: it was now clear that Judge Taylor would likely be the presiding judge at Annie's trial. Both sides now began to prepare for that contest in earnest. On February 24 Mrs. George formally pleaded not guilty to the charge of first degree murder.

Stark County Sheriff John J. Zaiser
(Cleveland Daily World, April 6, 1899)

Another month went by. In late March, 1899, Sheriff Zaiser began serving subpoenas on those called by the prosecution and defense to testify at the trial scheduled for April 4. Over 200 summonses were eventually served, and that total did not include those witnesses who could not be located. Meanwhile, procedural disputes escalated as the rival attorneys jockeyed for advantage. Both sides sought to have depositions taken from out-of-state witnesses, especially those having knowledge of the circumstances of Annie's initial encounters with George Saxton and her Dakota divorce sojourn. Much time was expended and many telegrams sent before both sides could agree on which officials to take the depositions.

A bombshell long in train exploded on March 28, just one week before the scheduled trial opening. It had been known since October that Pomerene's top evidential priority was finding the murder weapon. Much of the Canton police force's activity in the case had been devoted to that search, and it was widely assumed that the missing revolver had been thrown into a creek in the vicinity of Tuscarawas and West Third Streets. That belief was apparently disproved when news came on March 29 that Canton Police Sergeant William J. Hasler had resigned from the force the night before. Hasler's stated reason for leaving the force was that he had found the murder weapon — and that Canton Mayor James Rice (and former lawyer for Annie George) had been the one who had led him to it.

The story was an odd, murky and quite improbable tale. According to Hasler, Mayor Rice had sent for him on Monday, October 10, three days after the murder. Rice, the acting police chief, ordered Hasler to go to the northeast corner of High and South Streets. There, he informed the sergeant, he would find a revolver hidden under the wooden sidewalk. Hasler was to retrieve the revolver and bring it to Rice and he was to tell no one else about it.

Sure enough, Hasler now told newspaper reporters, he had dutifully walked to the corner of South and High Streets that night. He had found the revolver just where Rice said it would be, retrieved it and taken to his own home. If Hasler was telling the truth, his subsequent behavior was even more peculiar. Instead of telling Rice he had found the weapon, he had taken it up to his attic and hidden it there inside an old stocking. His initial motive, Hasler now insisted, had been to protect himself; he suspected that Rice was doing something irregular and he wanted to avoid incriminating himself. So he told Rice he had not found the weapon and he continued to conceal his possession of the revolver for several months, in part because he was a candidate for the city marshal nomination and did not want the episode revealed to potential voters.

After he had lost his bid for the marshal nomination, Hasler said he had taken the revolver to Pomerene on January 10 and told him the whole story. Like Hasler, Pomerene had subsequently concealed the finding of the revolver for his own, unstated motives. Then, on March 24, less than two weeks before the trial, Pomerene had sent Hasler to call upon Mrs. George in her county jail cell. Visiting her that same day, Hasler abruptly said to her, "What shall I do with that revolver which you hid under the culvert and which Rice sent me after?" All Annie had said in answer to him was, "See Welty and then I will see you again."

Hasler's disclosures about the revolver left Cantonians more confused than ever. When queried by newspaper reporters, Pomerene admitted having the revolver but would say nothing about how he had obtained it. Hasler was soon sidetracked by a verbose and nasty public feud with Rice, mainly concerning whether Hasler had resigned or been fired and the reasons for his separation from the police force. Rice, for his part, publicly denounced Hasler's story about the revolver as "ridiculous and absurd."

Even as the reverberations of Hasler's story were beginning, Cantonians were distracted by news that key trial witness Eva B. Althouse had vanished. She had been seen at West Lawn Cemetery on March 19, where she visited both her husband's and

Saxton's graves. Five days later she had been seen there again, ordering a stately marble marker for the late George Althouse. Three days later, even as Zaiser began looking for her, Eva had been seen pedaling her new bicycle down Lincoln Avenue. Eva's relatives all played their parts nicely in this contrived farce, especially her mother, who informed *Cleveland Evening World* reporter Arthur Sperry:

> The last time I set eyes on Eva she was just going out the gate from the house. She had a case with her with a few clothes in it and that is all the baggage she took. I do not know where she went or whether she went to the train or not. She has not been in Canton since, for she would have come to see me if she was. She has friends all over the state and some outside the state.

Eva's disappearance was great copy for the newspapers. They happily reported a dozen supposed locations for her whereabouts, including Cincinnati, Pittsburgh and Wheeling, West Virginia. The truth was that she had apparently fled first to the home of Henry Warren, a friend whose farm was situated just outside West Elizabeth, Pennsylvania, near the Monogahela River. After curious newspaper reporters picked up her trail there, she moved to Perryopolis, Fayette County, Pennsylvania, where she found a more secure haven at the home of friend Aaron Townsend. And there she would stay until the conclusion of the Annie George trial. She let it be known through friends that she only wished to avoid the publicity attendant to a trial and that, anyway, she didn't know a thing about George Saxton's murder.

The unsolved mystery of Eva's whereabouts only stoked the frenzied fires of newspaper speculation about her apparent flight. Most such stories churned unverified rumors of Eva sightings in Canton and various locations around the United States.

More entertaining were baseless insinuations suggesting Eva might have had even graver reasons for avoiding the Annie George trial, such as this choice morsel retailed by Arthur Sperry of the *Cleveland Daily World*:

> Ever since the night of the killing there has been current a report that within half an hour of the time of the tragedy, Mrs. Nighman-Althouse was seen hurrying toward her mother's house with a shawl over her head and a corset rolled up under her arm. Detectives have investigated this story to the fullest extent of their ability, but all they have been able to do was to run the story down to some of the loafers that were hanging about the saloons near the railroad tracks. The evidence of the missing widow at the preliminary investigation of the murder case was to the effect that when Saxton was killed she was at her mother's house, but the rumor that she was witness of the killing from the inside of the house is remarkably persistent.

The corset was a nice touch. Such luridly imaginative details may even have helped distract public attention from the embarrassment of Stark County officials over Eva's flight. As several of them admitted off the record, her legal position was an impregnable one, whatever her motives or whereabouts. Even if she were hiding in her Lincoln Avenue house, she could not be forced out of it until she was served with a subpoena. She was not charged with a crime and no summons had been served on her. Nor could she be accused of aiding a criminal to escape, as it had not yet been proven whether that had occurred. And she could not be arrested for contempt of court until she formally refused to accept a subpoena and the one dollar witness fee. It was useless, moreover, to even ask her for the favor of a deposition, as Ohio law forbade the use of a deposition as evidence in a murder trial if it were taken after the trial commenced.

It seems more than likely that neither the prosecution nor the defense were unduly upset by Eva's absence. Although both sides accused the other of conspiring in her flight and knowing her exact whereabouts, all four lawyers quickly and docilely accepted her absence and agreed that the trial could proceed without her. And while it was probable that Welty and Sterling regretted her absence more than Pomerene and Grant, all of them suspected that Eva's testimony was only of marginal importance to the trial. True, she might have been useful in generating sympathy for Mrs. George and helping to furnish more evidence of George Saxton's caddishness — but Welty and Sterling knew they already enjoyed a surfeit of such material. In fact, it is highly probable that Welty had deliberately *provoked* Mrs. Althouse's flight by his belligerent examination of her at Annie's preliminary hearing. Eva had been visibly mortified by his coarsely sarcastic innuendoes about her nocturnal activities and alleged imbibing with Saxton, and she must have known that there would be a lot more of the same if Welty ever got a chance to cross-examine her during a full-blown trial.

Eva wasn't the only one to take a powder as Annie's trial loomed during the last week of March. Even as Sheriff Zaiser reported his failure to find her, the prosecution learned that Russell Hogan, one of the State's key eyewitnesses, had also vanished. Pomerene immediately called in Russell's father, Canton city councilman Martin Hogan, and demanded an explanation. Martin blandly told Pomerene, and later Judge Isaac Taylor, that he had no idea where his 14-year-old son was or when he was likely to return to Canton. That same eventful week it was reported that Mrs. Elizabeth Parks, George Saxton's reputed former fiancée, had been subpoenaed by the defense, who hoped her testimony would portray Saxton in the blackest hues. But deputies sent to serve her subpoena had been unable to locate her; it was said that she was holed up in a New York town near the Canadian border, ready at a moment's notice to flee to seek foreign sanctuary, rather than endure the notoriety of the impending trial.

As the month of April opened, Canton was bustling with preparations for Annie's trial, which promised to be by far the most sensational in Stark County history. Down at the county courthouse, the bailiffs were renovating Courtroom No. 2 so as to accommodate the largest number of spectators and representatives of the local and national press. Additional chairs were brought in from Courtroom No. 3, the courtroom fixtures were squeezed closer together and a rope was stretched across the floor to separate spectators from the jury and trial participants. An irony not missed by Cantonians was the fact that the trial of George Saxton's accused murderer was taking place in the Stark County courthouse. The building, although probably the most stately and ornate Ohio county courthouse was something of a local scandal. Saxton was one of the prominent Canton boosters who had long agitated for a new county courthouse. As Ohio law prohibited financing county courthouses over a certain cost without voter approval, the proponents of a new courthouse had long been frustrated by frugal Stark County voters, who refused to approve their costly plans. So the courthouse backers resorted to a cunning subterfuge: they demolished all but a ten-by-two-foot section of the existing courthouse and then spent $250,000 of the public's money to accomplish a "renovation" which incorporated the surviving remnant into a splendid new judicial edifice. It was, some ironic souls thought, a most appropriate monument to the dead Saxton.

All Canton was agog with excitement as Annie's trial finally opened on the morning of April 4. Its citizens were well aware that their city was the cynosure of national attention, with reporters and sketch artists (their drawings would not be supplanted by photographs in American newspapers for several years) from a dozen major cities there to report every detail of the trial. But, whatever her true feelings, Annie George continued her public pose as the most serene person in Canton. Two days before the trial, she celebrated Easter Sunday in jail with friends and family, her cell gaily resplendent with flowers, decorations and Easter eggs. The report of her friends was that no one would have guessed from her behavior that she was about to go on trial for her life.

Stark County Court House, Judge Taylor's Court Room, Where George Case Is Being Tried Is Just Over the Portico on the Right (Market Street) Side Of the Building
Canton Sunday Repository, April 16, 1899

Stark County Courthouse
(Canton Sunday Repository, April 16, 1899)

Mrs. George in Court
(Cleveland Sunday World, April 9, 1899)

Annie George awoke at 6 a.m. on Tuesday, April 4 and ate breakfast in her cell. She was not the first one up that morning; dozens of eager persons had been already been waiting in line for some hours to secure one of the coveted courtroom seats set aside for the public. Aware that she was about to give the performance of her life, Annie dressed with elaborate care. Her gown was of serge fabric in the shade known as blue storm. Her bodice, a lighter shade of blue, was made of pleated taffeta silk. With a feather boa stylishly encircling her neck, her head was adorned with an Easter hat of black lace, topped with two high wings and decorated with white violets and small steel ornaments. Her hands were sheathed in brown kid gloves. Annie had long known she was a "handsome" woman, and she surely looked the part that spring morning: a female of above-average height, her 152 pounds of full-figured curves attractively set off by her dark brown (almost black) eyes and gray-flecked brown hair. Whatever her age (she was 40) and whatever her troubles, it was easy to see that spring morning what had enchanted George Saxton a decade before. And although some of her upper teeth were false, it was rumored that one of them was stylishly inlaid with a quarter-carat diamond.

Judge Taylor's courtroom was already packed to capacity at 8:30 a.m., the scheduled time for Annie's trial. It took the efforts of the four bailiffs present to maintain order as the crowd jostled for admission. It was remarked by many observers that there were only five females in the excited crowd of over 200 persons. The proceedings were delayed past 10:00 a.m. because the train from Alliance, containing members of the jury venire, was late that morning. The crowd was briefly titillated by a glimpse of Sample C. George, who flitted through the courtroom and then disappeared for the rest of the day. Finally, about 10:15, a door behind Judge Taylor's bench opened and Annie George stepped through it. Accompanied by her son Newton and Sarah Siddinger, a friend since her Hanoverton childhood, Annie walked to the defense table and sat down next to Sterling and Welty. Seated near her were Mrs. Brown, her mother's sister, and several friends from Hanoverton. A minute later, Judge Taylor entered the room and the trial got underway.

Neither side in the case had yet given a hint of their trial strategy. Although pressed by newspaper reporters to reveal their plans on the eve of the trial, both Pomerene and Welty would only say that they were fully ready for the trial and confident that justice would prevail. The list of witnesses subpoenaed by both sides suggested that neither side would be shy about exposing the dark sides of George Saxton and Annie George. But Welty now tipped his hand, indicating by his first actions that every iota of his client's case would be fought with utter ferocity to the bitter end. Judge Taylor had barely called the court to order when Welty arose to state that the defense was not ready. His objection to proceeding, he revealed, was the absence of Russell Hogan, without whose testimony, he insisted, the trial could not proceed. The defense was willing, however, Welty told Judge Taylor, to accept Hogan's inquest testimony in lieu of his appearance at the trial. Pomerene fiercely objected, claiming that the State could not accept Hogan's inquest testimony because it was at variance with his testimony before the grand jury which indicted Annie George. Pomerene and Welty wrangled back and forth in conference with Judge Taylor for some minutes before Pomerene reversed himself and agreed to have Hogan's inquest testimony read into the court record in case he didn't show up to testify. Welty, too, now reversed himself, stating that Hogan's actual trial testimony was vital to the defense's case. But Judge Taylor quickly overruled him and ordered that jury selection proceed.

Welty had only begun to fight. He immediately challenged the first jury venire of forty men. [Until the passage of the 19th Amendment to the U. S. Constitution in 1920, women could not serve on juries in Ohio and many other states].This was not an unusual tactic at many criminal trials and Judge Taylor listened patiently as Welty objected to the jury pool on technical grounds, arguing that it had not been selected and submitted in the manner prescribed by Ohio statute law. Sterling elaborated on Welty's objections and their challenge consumed the remainder of the morning. Finally, Judge Taylor reviewed the arguments about the jury and overruled the defense. Sterling noted an exception to his ruling for possible later appeal.

Jury selection can be a tedious process. It took almost four days to complete Annie George's jury and the examination of 92 possible candidates before both sides pronounced themselves satisfied with the panel. The lengthy duration of the process was due to several factors. One was the sheer gravity of the task at hand: to decide, possibly, whether a woman should be sent to the electric chair. Ohio law, then as now, was crafted to protect the rights of accused persons on trial, especially those with their life at risk. Hence the disparity in the number of preemptory challenges respectively afforded the two sides in the case: two for the prosecution and sixteen for the defense. The glacial pace of the jury

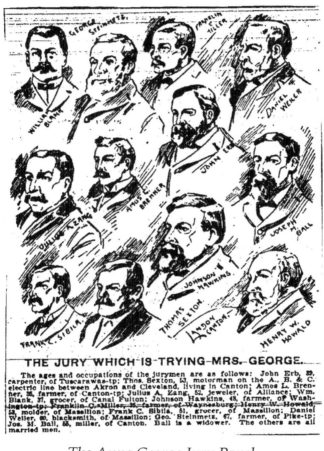

THE JURY WHICH IS TRYING MRS. GEORGE.

The ages and occupations of the jurymen are as follows: John Erb, 39, carpenter, of Tuscarawas-tp; Thos. Sexton, 53, motorman on the A., B. & C. electric line between Akron and Cleveland, living in Canton; Amos L. Brenner, 35, farmer, of Canton-tp; Julius A. Zang, 52, jeweler, of Alliance; Wm. Blank, 37, grocer, of Canal Fulton; Johnson Hawkins, 43, farmer, of Washington-tp; Franklin C. Miller, 35, farmer, of Waynesburg; Henry W. Howald, 53, molder, of Massillon; Frank C. Sibila, 51, grocer, of Massillon; Daniel Weiler, 60, blacksmith, of Massillon; Geo. Steinmetz, 67, farmer, of Pike-tp; Jos. M. Ball, 55, miller, of Canton. Ball is a widower. The others are all married men.

The Anna George Jury Panel
(Cleveland Press, April 8, 1899)

selection process also, however, reflected the shrewd thought and assiduous research that both sides had invested in their preparation of the case. Both sides made it their business to learn the background of potential jury members: their characters, opinions, prejudices, political leanings and all available particulars of their personal histories. The defense did a better job than the prosecution in this respect, and not the least of their assets was Annie George. From the beginning of the trial she took an active role in the case, whispering suggestions to Welty and Sterling and studying the papers in the case — especially the inquest, preliminary hearing and grand jury stenographic transcripts — as aids to formulating cross-examination strategy. And it was clear from their courtroom manner with her and their comments to reporters that Annie's attorneys highly valued her shrewd counsel, her common-sense instincts about people, her profound knowledge of her fellow Cantonians and her flawless public demeanor. Mrs. Sarah Sinclair, Anna's sister, a regular attendee at the trial, was also an asset to her defense team. Enjoying a wide acquaintance in the districts from which the jury venires were drawn, she often whispered her judgments concerning prospective jurors to Welty and Sterling.

Over the first four days of the trial virtually all of the prospective jurors were asked the same questions. Had they formed an opinion about the case? Had they talked to anyone about the case? Had they read newspapers accounts about the case? Which newspapers? Did they believe in capital punishment? Would they be willing to convict in a capital case on the basis of circumstantial evidence? Would they be willing to vote a death verdict for a woman? Some additional questions reflected the concerns, both real and feigned, of the particular sides to the case. Welty and Sterling asked all prospective jurors whether they had been approached by agents of the United States government, specifically by Alonzo P. Owens, John M. Webb or Deputy Marshal John J. Keeley. Pomerene and Grant, in the same vein asked some of the prospective jurors whether they had talked to Andrew Weilandt, a Canton private detective alleged to be working for the defense. The fact that not a single prospective juror had apparently talked to any of the specified government officials did not discourage the defense lawyers, who were content to create the mere impression — regardless of the reality — that the entire resources of the puissant United States government were arrayed against a lone, friendless and discarded woman. Sterling and Welty must have been ecstatic when they learned that Alonzo P. Owens had been goaded into angry denials by their repeated accusations that he had been tampering with potential George jury members. His exasperation boiled over in an interview with a *Cleveland Evening World* reporter, to whom Owens spluttered:

> It is an outrage against me and against the other officers of the government against whom the imputations are made to suggest anything of the kind. It is an outrage against the government itself. I state positively that the imputations made by the lawyers for the defense are false.

Weilandt, Webb and Marshal Keeley made similar denials to no avail, as Welty and Sterling cheerfully continued their interrogations. When asked by a *Cleveland Evening World* reporter about such allegations, James Grant sourly commented, "The only tangible evidence so far as the examination has gone touching any attempt to tamper with the jury comes from Wielandt, the admitted agent of the defense." In fact, the only testimony elicited during the examination of the prospective jurors that their views had been canvassed by agents for either side of the case was William H. Penrose's admission that Wielandt had solicited his opinions about it. This disclosure eventually led Pomerene to exercise one of his two peremptory challenges to eject Penrose from the George jury.

The reasons for rejecting potential jury candidates were almost as numerous as the population of the combined jury venires. The first to be rejected was Lafayette Swigart of Lafayette Township. Pomerene used one of his precious preemptory challenges to excuse him, believing he was a close personal friend of James Sterling. The prosecutor had wanted to husband his two challenges until the defense began its own winnowing but Judge Taylor ruled that the State had to exercise its challenge first, so out came Swigart. It is fortunate for the historical record that Swigart was ejected, as his ensuing comments shed much light on the seething partisanship aroused by the George murder trial in Stark County and the intense lobbying of both sides by operatives of the prosecution and defense. Speaking even before jury selection was completed, Swigart told a *Cleveland Evening World* reporter:

> From my experience, I have no doubt that every juror drawn has been approached. Saturday I was over in Summit County and a man who was one of the richest residents of Canton till he moved away told me I ought to let Mrs. George go free. Dozens of relatives and friends of Saxton have come to me and tried to influence me. I made no promises. Some of the members of the Saxton family have told me they hoped Mrs. George would go free. Most of the Saxton people want her executed for murder. Nobody knows what influences are being brought to bear in this case.

Perhaps Pomerene knew what he was about in his challenge of Swigart, as the chatty farmer also opined to the *World* reporter his prediction that Mrs. George would only be punished with a prison term.

Rejections for personal reasons were an obvious potential problem in an area as small and close-knit as Stark County. H. H. Everhard was excused because he was a relative of the murder victim in the fourth degree. (His first cousin, Mrs. Maria S. Saxton, was the aunt by marriage to the late George D. Saxton.) Josiah Shively of Canton was excused because he had been the bailiff at the grand jury session which had indicted Annie George and had, not surprisingly, formed a strong opinion about the case. David Warstler was excused after he said that Judge William R. Day had served as his legal counsel. George C. Lindsay was peremptorily challenged by the defense—but it was Prosecutor Pomerene who noted that John Welty had recently purchased his horse harnesses from Lindsay. John W. Reese was excused because he had served upon a jury in a case that involved James J. Grant within the past year. Thomas Seeman was rejected because he acknowledged that he was a personal friend of George Saxton's. The examination of Eli Miller on Friday afternoon nicely showcased the almost claustrophobic closeness of Canton society. Pomerene asked the 68-year-old Miller whether he had any prejudice against any of the counsel in the case. "Not especially," replied Miller, "although Mr. Grant and I, both heavy weights, pass on the street and never speak." Grant interrupted, "We cannot challenge on that ground." Pomerene tried again. "Would your lack of friendly relations with Mr. Grant prejudice you in the case?" "It certainly would not," retorted Miller. "When I get as small as that I want to leave town." Miller did not make it onto the Annie George jury.

Most of the more than 80 jurors rejected were weeded out by the standard questions asked all jurors. Nelson S. Miller, 50, a farmer, was successfully challenged by the prosecution and excused after he said he opposed convicting a prisoner on circumstantial evidence. Peter F. Koontz, Henry W. Elsass and W. C. Jacobs of Massillon were excused because they had formed opinions about the guilt or innocence of the accused, as was Matthias Eartle. Edward J. Hamill of Massillon was excused because he was partially deaf. Henry Herr and John C. Bohecker of Alliance were excused because they were opposed to capital punishment. John Bartley, 72, of Alliance was excused on account of age. W. Edward Brons and Frank Bollinger were excused because they were opposed to conviction on purely circumstantial evidence in murder cases. J. H. Dalzell, a slate roofer of Alliance was excused because he had "an opinion about her innocence but none about her guilt." Adam Gibb successfully claimed exemption on the grounds that he had been a member of the Canton volunteer fire department for five years.

The line between what was considered acceptable in a juror at times seemed almost indistinguishable from what was unacceptable. While a number of jurors were excused because they had formed opinions about the case, Canton butcher August Barchfield was accepted after he stated that he had formed opinions but that they would not prevent him from rendering a fair verdict in the case. David Weiler, a 59-year-old retired blacksmith, was accepted even though he was partially deaf, while Edward J. Hamill was rejected for the same reason. A *Cleveland Plain Dealer* writer offered a cynical analysis of the increasing difficulties faced by the court as it worked its way through its series of increasingly reluctant prospective jurors:

> [Jurors] are not so easy to get now. Men taken from their business without a chance to prepare for a prolonged absence are likely to be possessed of opinions on one thing or another that will disqualify them. Besides, they have read the questions propounded to others and are learning how to proceed when they want to get off the jury.

Judge Taylor's early ruling that the prosecution's two peremptory challenges had to be exercised as soon as a juror as admitted to the panel was a victory for the defense. Pomerene soon used both of them, while Welty and Sterling still had seven peremptory challenges left when the panel was completed on the afternoon of Friday, April 7.

If a post-verdict analysis of the jury selection process published in the possibly partisan *Canton News-Democrat* is to be credited, Annie and her defense team did a better job than the prosecution in recruiting potentially favorable jurors and weeding out hostile candidates. Defense sleuths devoted much effort to learning the political leanings of all potential jurymen. During the jury selection process James Sterling remarked aloud that he did not "want anyone on this jury who worships McKinley instead of God." Any venireman with known or suspected Republican sympathies was excluded, as was anyone with ties to the McKinley family or known reader of the *Cleveland Leader*, the most vehemently Republican Ohio newspaper. At the same time, unbeknownst to the prosecution, the defense managed to secure the placement of a Democratic juror who had been fired from his postmaster's job at the onset of the McKinley administration in 1897. They also placed a juror whose nephew had been hanged for murder in 1880, their hope being that the juror was no enthusiast for capital punishment.

Who were these twelve men of Stark County who sat in judgment on Annie George? It is difficult to make generalizations but it seems clear they were predominately middle-class, middle-aged and married. John Erb, 39, was a carpenter and slater in Tuscarawas Township. Six months before, about the time of Saxton's murder, he had fallen 30 feet while working on a house. The 225-lb. Erb had landed on a wagon below, smashing it to pieces and suffering little injury. Thomas Sexton, 53, lived in Canton and was a motorman on the Akron, Bedford & Canton interurban rail line. Sexton was the only member of the jury who was considered "working-class" by his peers and the press.

Amos L. Bonenner, 35, was a farmer in Canton Township. He attracted the most initial attention from the courtroom crowd when he chose to affirm rather than to take an oath as a juryman. [United States law, both federal and state, has traditionally allowed persons having religious objections to swearing oaths "before God" to simply "affirm" the truth of their testimony]. Julius A. Zang of Alliance was 52 years old and a jeweler. He would become Mrs. George's most implacable foe on her jury. William Blank, 37, was a grocer in Canal Fulton. He had the greatest distance to travel of any juror. Johnson Hawkins of Washington Township, 48, was a farmer, as was Franklin C. Miller, 35, of Sandy Township. Iron moulder Henry W. Howald, 53, was jocularly described by *Cleveland Leader* reporter as "a moulder for a living, a Socialist for amusement and a resident of Massillon." Frank C. Sibila, 51, was a grocer in Massillon. He was one of the more reluctant jurors; when asked if he could try the prisoner fairly and impartially, he replied, "I guess I could, but I would rather not."

Fifty-nine-year-old blacksmith David Weiler's partial deafness seemed a handicap to his jury qualifications. But after Judge Taylor himself tested his hearing, asking him various questions at various levels of volume, he was accepted by both sides to the case. George Steinmetz, 67, a farmer of Pike Township and Joseph M. Ball, 55, a retired miller of Canton, rounded out Mrs. George's jury. Ball, the last juror chosen, was the only unmarried man on the jury, having become a widower two years before. Pomerene fought hard to keep Ball off the jury, after he stated during his examination that he had formerly employed Welty as counsel and expressed some reservations about the weight of circumstantial evidence. But Judge Taylor overruled Pomerene's challenge for cause and the prosecutor, with no peremptory challenges left, saw Ball take his seat on the jury.

Like all theaters of the human comedy, the jury selection process offered unscripted scenes of droll humor. Some of it was provided by Judge Taylor. A veteran of ten years on the Common Pleas bench, he was noted for fairness, impartiality and no little wit. Taking part in the examination of prospective jurors, Judge Taylor asked jury candidate Lewis Lind on Wednesday afternoon whether he had ever employed any of the four attorneys in the case. Lind replied that he didn't remember ever doing so. "Well," riposted Judge Taylor, "if you had ever employed any of these gentlemen, you would remember it." Judge Taylor wasn't the only comedian in the room, as he discovered during the examination of Abraham Fasnacht on Wednesday afternoon. When Grant asked Fasnacht how old he was, the Perry Township farmer replied mischievously, "How old do you think?" "Well, how old are you?' persisted Grant. "Guess, and I'll tell you!" teased Fasnacht.

After the crowd laughter died down Judge Taylor ordered Fasnacht to answer the question. Fasnacht admitted to 66 years and was accepted by both sides, only to be rejected by the defense later in the afternoon.

The jury was finally filled at 3:30 p.m. After they were sworn in by Clerk of Courts Thomas C. Casselman, prosecutor Pomerene rose to make his opening statement. He had waited six months for this moment and his oratory was charged with the fervor and rhetorical force expected by his eager audience. Picking up a copy of the murder indictment, he began slowly and calmly. "Gentlemen of the Jury, this indictment charges Annie E. George with murder in the first degree." Pomerene then read the long and graphic charge contained in the six-count indictment, using several hundred words to describe the paths and effects of the four bullets that had killed George Saxton.

Having established Saxton's death, Pomerene turned to the scene of the murder, using a chart prepared by Stark County surveyor John S. Hoover to describe the dwellings and terrain on Lincoln Avenue. Pointing to the diagram of the steps in front of the Althouse residence, Pomerene turned to glare at Annie George and snapped, "There! There are the steps where this George Saxton was killed by this defendant!" If Pomerene intended to shake Annie with this dramatic accusation, he failed: although her eyes nearly closed as he shouted at her, she managed to maintain her unruffled calm. Returning to Hoover's chart, Pomerene pointed out the Eckroate grocery and the streetlamp at the corner of West Third Street and Lincoln Avenue. Acknowledging that the leaves on adjacent trees might have compromised a clear view of the murder scene, the prosecutor nonetheless claimed that sufficient light "streamed" from the grocery store window and the streetlamp to provide ample illumination of the Althouse steps at the moment of Saxton's murder.

Now it was time to put Annie George into the picture and Pomerene did a masterful job at presenting the State's scenario of her actions on the fatal evening of October 7:

146

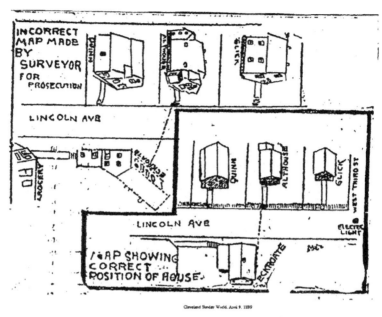

Stark County Surveyor John S. Hoover's Misleading Map
(Cleveland Press, April 13, 1899)

We expect to show you, gentlemen of the jury, that on the night of the tragedy, about twenty minutes past five o'clock, the defendant left the restaurant where she had taken her supper, and went west on Tuscarawas Street. We expect to show you that George D. Saxton, about the same time, went west-wardly on his wheel; the two were on that street at the same time. We expect to show you that on this very night at about that time the defendant was on the hunt for her victim. She got on the street car westward bound about ten or fifteen minutes before the hour of six. She passed the place where she lived

147

or where she had rooms, known as the Oberlin house, which is the first house on the south side of Tuscarawas Street, west of the bridge. She did not stop there, but went across the bridge and got off the car at Hazlette Avenue. The testimony will show that as she got off the car she went in the direction of the Althouse residence. When she got to that place the people in the neighborhood were generally at their evening meal. The first thing to disturb the quiet was the quick report, twice in succession, of a revolver.

The testimony will show you that Saxton got off his wheel right there in front of the Althouse residence; that this woman approached him and fired twice almost as quick as you could count. After she had fired two shots she started away. There was a call as if for help. She turned around, walked deliberately back to Saxton's body, and fired two more shots. She was not content yet. There was a moan. She went back, stooped down over the body to satisfy herself that it was beyond mortal help, and then she ran away. She went down the sidewalk to one of the vacant lots, the second one south of the Althouse residence. There is a crosswalk over this vacant lot to the alley, and it was across this walk that she disappeared in the darkness. Within a few minutes after the firing a report was sent to police headquarters and search was begun, but the woman was not then about her usual haunts. The testimony will convince you that she took perhaps the course down Dueber Avenue to South Street, and the next thing that is seen of her after leaving that street, she appears at Mr. Sterling's office. This is within an hour after the crime was committed. She then took a course along Fifth Street, finally she went into Tuscarawas Street in the direction of her home, which at that time was at the Oberlin residence. The officers were waiting there for her. They approached her and she was put under arrest, but not a word was uttered by her. She did not ask what she was arrested for, nor anything else. At the time she was laboring under suppressed excitement, and she was perspiring freely. She was then taken to the city prison. On the way to the prison, different questions were asked her but she made no reply. She went to the prison and was there inquired of by myself. I will not detail the questions which were asked, but I think the testimony will show that the questions were asked in no unkind spirit, but for the purpose only of eliciting the truth. There was no reply, except perhaps to one question, in which she said she would talk when the time came. It was noticed that evening that her right hand was discolored by burned powder, the forefinger and the thumb particularly; that the conduct of this woman from the time that the crime was committed was that of a woman who was conscious of her guilt.

Pomerene had established the murder, Annie's presence in the area and her suspicious and uncooperative behavior afterwards. He now turned to the most important elements in making his charge of first degree murder stick: malice and premeditation. Pomerene was well aware of public sympathy for Annie and he must have known this was his first and best opportunity to paint her as a cold-blooded, scheming and cunning murderess:

The testimony will further show as leading up to the tragedy, that for a couple of years prior to it and right up to the very day that this offense was committed, and on the day that she killed Saxton, that

she repeatedly threatened that she would kill him.
There will be no question when the proof is in, that
this is the woman who did the deed. That she had
thoroughly canvassed the situation; that she had
adroitly laid her plans to do it; that she laid these
plans before different persons, that she did not care
what the consequences were to herself, but that she
was determined to kill this man; that she went even
into details as to what she would do with the revolver after the crime was committed; that there was
deliberation, premeditation, that there was malice,
and there will be no doubt in your minds when you
have heard this case. A malice not born of legitimate
disappointment, but malice that can only lurk in the
bosom of an adventuress!

Pomerene also knew well that the greatest weakness in his
case was the character of George Saxton. He now hammered home
the State's key argument that that Saxton's behavior to Annie,
however beastly, could not have justified murder:

It will be contended on the part of the defense, no
doubt, that improper relations existed between Saxton and the prisoner. I care not what the testimony
will be on that point, suffice it to say that the position of the State is that whatever may have occurred
there was no justification for this crime; there
was not even a legitimate provocation.

In closing, Pomerene appealed for justice to the victim:

The testimony will show further, and I recognize
that the State will be handicapped somewhat by the
fact that one of the parties to the tragedy is silent in
his grave. The testimony will show, I think, to your

satisfaction, that whatever may have been their relations, that this woman by her conduct forfeited every confidence which he or any other living man
could have in a woman. There is no question, when
the proof is all in, that it will be established that this
woman did the deed.

Pomerene didn't finish his oration until 3:30 p.m. Informed
by Welty that his opening statement would be a lengthy one,
Judge Taylor decided to recess court until Saturday morning and
announced that because of the delay in completing the jury, all of
the defense witnesses would be excused until Thursday morning,
April 13. Although Saturday sessions were uncommon in Common
Pleas trials, there were several motives to accelerate what was
obviously going to be a lengthy trial. With 158 witnesses already
subpoenaed, it was a hardship for so many persons to have their
lives disrupted for several weeks and the delay caused by a late
train on the first morning highlighted the potential logistical
pitfalls of this unprecedented trial. There was also the problem of
costs. With witness fees at $1 a day and the county liable for the
fees of Sterling, Welty, Grant and three extra bailiffs, the total costs
of the Annie George trial were already expected to amount to at
least $10,000 — and would increase with every additional trial day.
If Pomerene and Grant secured a conviction of Anna George the
costs would be paid by the state — but if they failed, by the taxpayers of Stark County. $10,000 was a lot of money for a largely rural
area like Stark County, and its judicial budget was already so
strained when Annie's trial commenced that it was announced
that the witness fees would not be paid until the June tax receipts
came in. Any public official perceived as inflating these expenses
would be an unpopular man. In this respect, the pressure was
greatest on Atlee Pomerene. He might have to endure something
worse than losing the case of a lifetime: if the jury could not agree,
he was the one most likely to be held accountable for the expense
of a second trial.

PROSECUTOR POMERENE ARGUES OUT AN OBJECTION.

*Prosecutor Pomerene Argues Out an Objection
(Cleveland Daily World, April 24, 1899)*

Chapter 10   "Putty in His Hands"

Prosecutor Pomerene had made a powerful opening argument. Whatever its deficiencies — which would become manifest — he had presented a strong narrative of a resolute, brazen killer stalking her victim to his death on Lincoln Avenue. He had shown motive: a lengthy, toxic relationship which, after multiple and very specific threats, culminated in cold-blooded murder on a public street. He had shown opportunity: Annie passing by her home and alighting from a streetcar just two blocks from the fatal rendezvous at 319 Lincoln Avenue. True, he hadn't mentioned the means — not once in his opening statement had Pomerene alluded to the gun used to kill Saxton. Nor had he tried to connect the presumed murder weapon to Mrs. George. This was odd enough, considering the publicity Sergeant Hasler's alleged discovery of the murder revolver had occasioned only a week before. Odder still was the fact that Pomerene's omission did not immediately provoke comment by either Annie's defense team or the score of newspapermen avidly speculating on every aspect of the trial.

However impressive Pomerene's opening assault, Annie's lawyers had reason to be pleased as the first day of the trial proper came to an end. Like all experienced practitioners of the law, Sterling and Welty knew that their case would not be decided strictly on the evidence. They were well aware that Annie's twelve jurors were flesh and blood human beings who would evaluate and weigh the personalities of the victim and the accused. How Annie came across to the jury would greatly determine her fate — and her performance that first week left nothing to be desired.

The copious pretrial publicity and Pomerene's opening oration had presented Annie as a hard-boiled, cunning, "fallen woman." But the image of soft and melting female rectitude Ann presented in her courtroom demeanor went far to modify, if not quite obliterate the negative portrait of the prosecution and press. Whatever their pretrial assumptions, what the jurors saw was a still beautiful woman, tastefully dressed, calmly observant and surrounded at all times by a solicitous cast of family and friends. Her eldest son Newton was with Annie that first morning in court and he remained in a chair behind her most of the days that followed. Nearby sat loyal Mrs. Siddinger from Hanoverton and various relatives — mostly aunts and cousins — and other friends from childhood days and her Cleveland and Canton sojourns. This sentimentally human context was further visually reinforced with flowers. Beginning on the morning of the trial's second day, Annie's arrivals in court were punctuated by her being presented with bouquets of flowers from family, friends and admirers. Annie's first nosegay that Wednesday had been picked early that very morning in Hanoverton by her childhood friend V. T. Norris. Better still, it was handed to her by her son Newton and all the circumstances of their origin and procurement were assiduously broadcast to courtroom spectators and the press by Annie and her supporters. Such tableaux of unwavering support by Annie's family and friends continuously set before the jury, press and public countervailing images of this notorious woman as "mother," "family member" and "beloved friend."

Mrs. George holds the testimony given by the witnesses during the preliminary hearing in her hand continually. When a witness varies she is quick to see it and calls the attention of one of her attorneys to it.

Mrs. George Consults with Her Attorney in Court
(Cleveland Daily World, April 13, 1899)

Annie reinforced the impact of such ritual scenes with her unvaryingly proper demeanor in court. Always the perfect lady there, she often smiled, even during Pomerene and Grant's most blistering vilifications of her character and conduct. Occasionally, as when Pomerene shouted at her in his opening speech, accusing her of shooting Saxton, her eyes might flicker or her head momentarily bow. But her occasional tears and highly becoming blushes were seemingly rationed for appropriate tactical occasions.

Annie's public stance as a suffering, persecuted and patient Madonna was perfectly projected during her *Cleveland Evening World* interview with Arthur Sperry after the court adjourned on April 5, the second day of jury selection. Commenting that her health was better than she expected it to be after six months in jail, Annie warbled:

> The prospect of the end of my troubles cheers me. I have the most absolute confidence in the court and in the jury so far as chosen. They seem, most of them, elderly, and all intelligent and careful men. Judge Taylor seems determined to have the utmost fairness, and the beginning of my trial is as fair and right as anything could be. I have the most absolute confidence of the outcome in view of this spirit of fairness that is manifested. I have been asked by my lawyers not to talk about the case and it is only right that I should not. But I do wish to thank my friends for their interest and sympathy and assure them that it is very comforting to me.

Annie was wise to charm the susceptible Sperry. With the exception of the copious — and surprisingly neutral--coverage appearing in the *Canton Evening Repository*, Sperry's coverage was the most detailed, most personal and, taken as a whole, the most sympathetic version of Annie George presented to newspaper readers. The fact that his coverage of Annie's trial was widely syndicated throughout the United States no doubt helped to increase the already widespread public sympathy for her. It seems obvious, too, that Sperry was somewhat personally smitten by Annie from the beginning of his contact with her. He was particularly infatuated with her eyes and face, which had always been the most celebrated features in her arsenal of personal attractions. Writing of them while jury selection plodded on, he described what he saw as Annie watched the marathon parade of candidates:

> Her great brown eyes were wide open and her famous dimples came and went in her cheeks, which seemed smooth and firm, though a little drawn by her jailing.

Just two days later, Sperry had succumbed so much further to Annie's seductive orbs that he could rhapsodize in such head-over-heels prose as this front-page sample:

> Hard, ardent, intellectual, fascinating, all of these adjectives are applied to the eyes of Mrs. Annie E. George, the woman they are trying to make out a murderess in Canton. Perhaps they are all of these in turn. When a questioned jury talesman says he is in favor of capital punishment and looks at the prisoner as he says it, the eyes are apt to have the hard look as they gaze, unflinchingly, back into his. Intelligence speaks in them as she follows the intricate points of the argument of some knotty legal technicality. They are always fascinating. There is the charm in them that must have glowed in Cleopatra's eyes and kept Antony from Rome. No one ever looks deep into those eyes without feeling their power. But it is when the beautiful prisoner looks at her son, as she does often these days, that they are

ardent. Their expression changes momentarily, so that there is often a mingling of these expressions in them and back of all there is the thought of that electric chair in Columbus whose first woman occupant they are trying to make her. They are handsome eyes, too. No one who has looked into them will forget them. They are large, brown and perfect. They have the quality that is called magnetic.

Sperry's prose-poem to Annie's sterling orbs was accompanied by a sketch artist's understandably inadequate attempt to reproduce Annie's mesmerizing eyes.

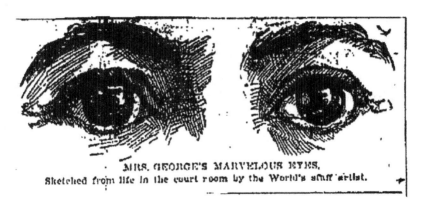

MRS. GEORGE'S MARVELOUS EYES.
Sketched from life in the court room by the World's staff artist.

The Eyes of Anna George
(Cleveland Daily World, April 7, 1899)

If Annie's behavior was a defense attorney's rapture, Welty and Sterling's handling of the newspaper media was expert and proactive, keeping the prosecution constantly off base. Sensational contemporary trials of recent years, such as those of O. J. Simpson, Michael Jackson and Scott Peterson, have highlighted the "spin control" skills of criminal defense lawyers like Johnnie Cochran and Barry Sheck. But Welty and Sterling could have given textbook lessons to such modern masters of media manipulation. Both in court and out, they constantly needled the prosecution, frequently provoking them to needless and blustering public denials of irrelevant but embarrassing facets of the case. At every opportunity the two defense lawyers repeated the charge, unsupported by proof, that agents of the Federal government were working surreptitiously in Canton to aid the prosecution. In vain did Atlee Pomerene deny the charge, stating, "It is absolutely untrue and is done to create sentiment." Pomerene and Grant also endlessly repelled the charge that they knew the whereabouts of Eva Althouse and had conspired to keep her away from Canton. Every denial by Pomerene or Grant served only to echo such charges.

Continued insinuations by the defense that the State was employing agents to influence potential jurors provoked an eruption at the trial on Friday afternoon, when Sterling asked a jury candidate whether he had been approached by Charles C. Upham. Upham, a personal friend of George Saxton's, had been publicly vociferous in his opinion that Mrs. George should be convicted and electrocuted. The juror replied that he had not. After court recessed for the day, an enraged Upham confronted Welty, warning him that if he repeated such an insinuation he would file a lawsuit against him. Aware that their confrontation was being observed by members of the press, Welty responded in kind, ending with a jeer that Annie George would outlive Upham.

Sterling and Welty also worked effectively at spreading beneficial, if often fanciful rumors through cooperative reporters. Their most startling and oft-repeated item was the rumor, first whispered during the weekend after the murder, that George Saxton's killer had been a woman disguised as a man. The two defense lawyers had been nurturing this theory for months, and Sterling contrived further elaborations of it as the trial commenced. He told reporters on the second day of that trial that just that very morning he had been approached by a "well-known" citizen of Canton. This man had told him, Sterling proclaimed to the scribbling newsmen, that several residents in the area where Saxton had been shot had told him that they had seen a man dressed in woman's clothing skulking about for several days before the murder. And, Sterling informed the reporters, the cross-dressing figure had not been seen since Saxton's assassination. Sterling embroidered this tale nicely, telling reporters that detectives working for the defense were investigating this angle round the clock. Sterling further hinted that the apparent transvestite was doubtless one of the many outraged husbands that George Saxton had provoked during his career of unrestrained sexual havoc.

The defense finally got its chance to make Mrs. George's case on Saturday, April 6. So far, in the six months since Saxton's death, hardly a word had been said in Annie's defense. All the official events of the Saxton case — her arrest, her interrogation, the inquest, her preliminary hearing, the grand jury session and Pomerene's opening statement — had been almost entirely devoted to asserting that Annie George had cold-bloodedly shot down George Saxton after threatening and planning to do so for years. Annie had been passively complicit in this one-sided case, first choosing silence herself and then maintaining it at her attorneys' insistence. Now it was her turn, and John C. Welty was expected to make the most of his task. Anticipating a burst of powerful oratory, a crowd of several hundred persons, many of them women, besieged the courtroom doors early Saturday morning. After one bailiff was knocked off his feet by the surging mob, officials temporarily closed the doors and then reopened them to admit one person at a time. It was noted that the crowd included a large contingent of lawyers, anxious to hear one of their own at the top of his game.

Welty began slowly and calmly. He first complimented the jury, noting that his client was satisfied to leave her "life and her liberty" in their hands. Indeed, he continued, it was strong evidence of her confidence in their impartiality that the defense had not exercised seven of its preemptory challenges. He then addressed the presumption of Annie's guilt, emphasizing that Annie had maintained her innocence from the start and that it was their sacred civic duty to consider her as not guilty until they heard the evidence and testimony. The State, said Welty, had charged Annie with first-degree murder. It was a charge that required proof beyond a reasonable doubt. The State had no such proof, he contended, and would be unable to present enough evidence to convict Annie on any one of the five possible guilty verdicts: first-degree murder, second-degree murder, manslaughter, assault and battery, or just plain assault.

Welty then turned to demolishing Pomerene's portrait of Annie as a libidinous but cold-blooded and calculating adventuress. It was a touching, sentimental narrative, and Mrs. George, flanked by her two sons, contributed to the lachrymose effect of the tale by clutching a handkerchief to her eyes during the more affecting passages of Welty's tale.

Once upon a time, Welty told the jury, there was a beautiful, innocent and young girl from a little Ohio town. Her name was Annie Ehrhart and she grew to sweet, blossoming maidenhood in a loving family of spotless repute and stainless rectitude. Reaching womanhood, pure Annie, the belle of Columbiana County, fell in love with Sample C. George, an honest, hard-working young carpenter from her home town. They married, were blessed with children and passed the idyllic years of their early conjugal bliss in uncorrupted, bucolic Hanoverton. Then, in 1886, economic hardship caused them to move to Canton.

Here Welty's narrative turned darker. As all American rural dwellers of the 19th century knew, cities were notorious corrupters of the innocent, replete as they were with the most powerful temptations, hideous vices and most depraved scoundrels of humanity. And poor, pure, artless Annie, Welty now related, soon fell victim to the practiced wiles of the vile seducer Saxton. "When she came here," Welty throbbed, "she was as pure, upright and virtuous as any woman that ever lived—and was until she met this man Saxton." Indeed, Welty marveled, Annie had been so unsophisticated that she had never taken a train ride until her removal to Canton.

Having established Annie's pre-Saxton purity, Welty now turned to the narrative of her ruin that began in the Goldberg brothers' store:

> It was while she was shopping one day that he saw her. That was the fatal day. He had marked her as his own. In 1886, the George family moved into the Saxton block. Until that time Mrs. George did not know Saxton. He was no novice in the matters that led to their later relations. Saxton visited that home in 1886 and 1887, while they lived in his block. Gradually he portrayed to Mrs. George the humble position she occupied. He said she was entitled to a higher station. Rather than the wife of a carpenter, she should be the wife of the owner of a block.

Pomerene had heard enough. He knew that the battle over the respective moral reputations of George D. Saxton and Annie George was a zero-sum game. Every word besmirching Saxton's character elevated Annie's image by contrast, and he could see that Welty was determined to turn the trial into a simple referendum on Saxton's character and misdeeds. Jumping to his feet, he shouted, "I object to this statement! This has nothing to do with the murder of George Saxton!" Pomerene went on to tell Judge Taylor that Saxton's sexual behavior was irrelevant to his murder. But it was too late. As Judge Taylor noted, while overruling the prosecutor's objection, it was the State that had previously "opened the door wide enough to let the statement in." It was Pomerene who had brought up Annie's alleged moral laxity with his sneer that she had "forfeited every confidence which [Saxton] or any other living man, could have in woman." The door was now open to a no-holds-barred scrutiny of Saxton's affair with Annie, and Welty rushed happily through it. After Pomerene sat down, Welty concluded the story of Annie's ruin:

Saxton made advances. He was scornfully refused. To escape his attentions, the George family removed from the block. He followed Mrs. George, until 1889, when she unfortunately agreed to accept his advances. Afterward he induced her to separate from her husband. Then, at his own cost, he induced her to get a divorce. They went to a hotel in Dakota, and Saxton registered, with his own hand, 'George D. Saxton and Wife, Canton.' At his request, she afterward lived in his block, He had won her affection. She was willing at all times to do his bidding. She was as putty in his hands. She opened a pretended [dressmaking] establishment. Saxton provided her living. He was in her rooms more than in his own. After their return from Dakota, they removed to Cleveland, Mrs. George living there and Saxton visiting her frequently. He delayed the fulfillment of his promise on the ground that George's suit against him for damages should first be settled. Her desire was to become his wife. His desire was only lust. He tired of her, and turned her an outcast into the world. Then came her breach of promise suit. After she had brought the suit, Saxton sought her again. For a conference they went to Allegheny. That was in 1896. He registered this woman as his wife. The register was 'George B. Smith and wife, Toledo.' At that conference their differences were healed. He renewed his promise to make her his wife.

So far, Welty had done a superb job of placing the lion's share of the blame for the affair on Saxton. Annie had been a pure woman until he seduced her; it was he, therefore, who was to blame for all that followed. Now it was time to stand Annie's adultery on its head: by emphasizing Annie's subsequent and unstinted loyalty to Saxton, Welty could present her as the injured party, whose emotional threats against Saxton were but harmless symptoms of her unquenchable passion for him:

> He had won her love and affection. However unkind his treatment, she never wavered in her regard for him. She believed him when he said again that he would make her his wife. She believed him because she loved him, and he was the only man she loved. She dismissed her suit. She even delivered letters to him. I say to you, not only did Mrs. George never commit a crime against Saxton, but her heart always went out to him. When Mrs. George dismissed her suit, Saxton did not keep his part of their agreement. He kept in force the injunction restraining her from entering his block. She saw him only to plead that he keep faith with her. She asked him, at times, for money, with which to pay for a night's lodging. There were times when she suffered cold and hunger. There were times when she did not even have covering to keep her warm. She suffered everything but death. The prosecutor says Mrs. George threatened the life of Saxton. When you hear those threats, with all the conversation and circumstances attending them, you will understand the threats. They cannot be given the construction sought to be placed on them by the prosecutor. This woman has loved and suffered, but she has committed no offense. She is not guilty. Saxton ruined her, separated her from her family and her home. We ask the jury to look at the case only in the light of justice.

After talking for fifty minutes, Welty sat down. The general feeling when he finished was that he had made a good impression on the jury. True, his emotional presentation had avoided the facts of the murder itself, focusing instead on the scoundrelly conduct of George D. Saxton. But, as Welty knew, it was the prosecution's job to prove Annie murdered Saxton; his easier task was merely to prove that she couldn't have because she loved the reprobate.

Welty wasn't the only one who made a good impression. Annie continued her conquest of the spectators and press, moving her besotted fan Arthur Sperry to compose new hymns celebrating her attractions and demeanor. Sperry had characterized her reception of Pomerene's assault as "like listening to a piece of music that she did not like." What a contrast to the rapt attention she gave to Welty's peroration:

> Before, even while Prosecutor Pomerene was delivering his awful arraignment of the prisoner to the jury, she sat erect, open-eyed, seemingly unfeeling. But when her lawyer told the story of her life romance, the story told the readers of the *World*, her attitude changed. She leaned forward in her chair with her elbow resting on the table before her, her handkerchief pressed to her lips by her neatly gloved hand. Her wonderful eyes, before wide open and alert with their light of intelligence and self-possession, were now hidden under her dropped lashes till they seemed almost shut. Her head bent forward, too, losing its queenly erectness. In this position she sat almost motionless during the whole time her defender talked to the jury.

When Welty finished, prosecutor Pomerene called his first witness to the stand. Stark County surveyor John S. Hoover brought with him his chart, which Pomerene had already flourished before the jury. It purported to be an accurate birdseye view of the murder scene. It proved to be something less than that as Hoover patiently interpreted it to the jury and then endured Welty's blistering cross-examination. Hoover was particularly at pains to show that there was ample lighting at the scene and that there was a direct, clear view of the Althouse front steps from a rear window of the Eckroate residence-grocery across the street. But despite Hoover's reluctance to admit inaccuracies in his chart, Welty's merciless cross-examination exposed its major defect: the rear windows of the Eckroate residence did *not*, as shown, face the steps in a direct line of sight, but faced them nearly at right angles. This discrepancy was a major embarrassment for the prosecution, as it was rumored to have a witness ready to testify that she had witnessed the murder from one of those very rear windows. Any such witness, Welty assured the jury, would have had to open one of those windows and lean very far out to see across the street to the Althouse steps, which would most likely have been obscured in darkness. Hoover was more successful in demonstrating to the jury how easily Mrs. George could have fled from the murder scene to High and South Streets, where the alleged murder weapon had allegedly been found by Sergeant Hasler.

Satisfied with his examination of a squirming Hoover, Welty tired of the game after an hour and made a formal objection to the surveyor's chart being introduced as evidence in the case. After interrogating Hoover himself, Judge Taylor made his inevitable ruling, "It seems that this map does not in all parts present things as they are and it will not be admitted in evidence." Swallowing his mortification, Pomerene tried to salvage something from his failure by requesting that the jury tour the murder scene and see its features for themselves. Judge Taylor and the defense acquiesced and the jury departed at 10:45 a.m.

While the jury and the newspaper reporters waited for a streetcar, Annie, Sheriff Zaiser and Stark County turnkey Charles Doll rode to Lincoln Avenue in a carriage. There, while Annie sat quietly in her carriage seat, just six feet from the fatal steps, Canton resident Edward C. Baumberger explained the neighborhood and terrain to the jury. For a good half hour they all walked around the Althouse house and up and down the street, not neglecting to examine the numerous side lots and lines of sight. Newspaper reporters at the scene could not agree later as to

Annie's behavior there. Some wrote that she sat stolidly in her carriage, not even deigning to gaze at the famous Althouse murder steps. Others insisted that she got out of the carriage and gaily conversed with Sheriff Zaiser and turnkey Doll. *Cleveland Evening World* reporter Arthur Sperry, never able to resist the purple patch, remarked that "she could have opened the carriage window, stretched out her arm and dropped a flower on the spot where murdered George Saxton fell dead in his tracks." When they had completed their examination the jury returned to the courtroom. After Judge Taylor cautioned them not talk to anyone or listen to anyone talking about the case, he dismissed them until Monday, April 10. Judge Taylor had intended to hold a Saturday afternoon session but decided to adjourn for the weekend after learning that prominent Canton citizen Lewis. V. Bockius was gravely ill and probably dying. Here was another index of Canton's small sphere: Bockius was both Pomerene's father-in-law, the husband of John Welty's wife's aunt, and also father-in-law to prosecution witness Dr. Edward Brant.

It had been a great day for the defense. Sterling and Welty's goal was to put the late George Saxton on trial, rather than his accused killer--and Judge Taylor's unexpected ruling to admit testimony concerning the personal relations of Saxton and Annie George would allow them to do exactly that. Added to this strategic victory was the surprise bonus of Hoover's botched map, a blunder which made the prosecution appear sloppy at best and sneaky at worst.

Never dropping out of character, Annie continued burnishing her image of perfect female rectitude through the weekend break. After arising late Sunday morning, she received a *New York Herald* reporter in her cell. Pointedly apologizing for her spartan hospitality, she was nonetheless careful to thank Sheriff Zaiser fulsomely for his efforts to render her jail sojourn "pleasant." She then took occasion to mourn her lack of religious amenities, polishing her new-found image as an innocent church girl lost in the sinfully secular toils of big-city Canton:

Pose for Miss Williams During the Trial.

MRS. ANNA E. GEORGE SKETCHED FROM LIFE.

Courtroom Sketch of Anna George by Miss M.B. Williams
(Canton Evening Repository, April 28, 1899)

Now you know, I cannot talk with you of my case. That would not be wise and, moreover, I do not wish to get my mind fixed upon my troubles on the Sabbath. I try to keep this day apart from the remainder of the week. I was brought up in a strict school and have never departed from my early teachings. I have even made it a custom not to see my attorneys on Sunday and, though I know the coming week is to be an important one to me, I told Mr. Welty and Mr. Sterling that I would prefer not to see them today.

In case the interviewer missed the point, Annie recurred to her religious preoccupations a minute later:

How have I spent the day? Much as I have other Sundays since last October. Unfortunately, religious services are held here only once a fortnight, and this is an off day. I enjoy the Bible reading, the singing and the spiritual consolation. Today I had my two precious boys, Newton and Howard, with me during the morning and we spent several hours reading the Bible and praying together. They are a great consolation to me, and help me to bear up under my burden of trouble.

Alluding anew to her alleged abandonment by Pastor Hill of the First Christian Church of Canton, Annie made it clear, at least to *New York Herald* readers, who the real Christians were in Canton:

Perhaps my name has been erased from the church rolls, but as I read the Bible that does not make my case hopeless. It makes me sad to know that those who have expressed the greatest charity for me have been those who knew me not in church.

The seemingly confident Annie also took the occasion of this interview to praise her jury and her own contribution to the selection process:

My lawyers allowed me to say whether I was satisfied with each of them as he had chosen, and as you know, we only used nine of the 16 preemptory challenges allowed by law. I was guided in my selection of the jurymen by their faces. Some of the men called for the jury seemed to have cruel faces, and some seemed unintelligent and ignorant. I would not have them on the jury and they were excused by my lawyers.

Her cup of blessings running over, Mrs. George also shared a sample of the hundreds of letters and telegrams of support daily pouring into the Stark county jail. A typical such missive, from an unidentified New York couple, read:

Dear Mrs. George: We saw your story in one of the New York papers last Sunday and we wish, both of us, to extend to you our sincere sympathy in your grief, and we earnestly hope that your life will soon brighten and that you may really obtain deep peace from the court proceedings. We feel that you have been deeply and dreadfully wronged, but we fervently hope that you may yet feel that life has yet much joy in store for you. Earnestly hoping that you may soon again be at liberty and that, looking at the past, you may feel that it was not all failure, we remain in spirit and truth, very kindly yours . . .

Chapter 11   "A Frog on a Wet Clay Bank"

The second day of testimony opened at 10 a.m. on Monday, April 10. Arriving early, Annie was attired in a blue brocade satin shirt-waist and black skirt. The shirt-waist was of light figured silk with stripes of a pale, blue flowered silk alternating with darker blue strips and finished with satin. Around her neck was a blue chiffon collar she had worn the previous week. Still wearing her stylish feather boa and hat, she had slightly altered the wings on the latter. As ever, she maintained a completely unruffled expression on her face. There was another large crowd on hand when the bailiffs opened the courtroom doors. Many spectators were so anxious about missing any juicy testimony that they stayed in their seats through the lunch recess.

Adhering to the script of Pomerene's opening statement, James J. Grant commenced the prosecution's first task, which was to prove that the death of Saxton had occurred. His first witness was Charles R. Frazer, the Canton city humane agent who had accompanied the police wagon to the murder scene. Once again, Frazer told in great detail of finding the body at the scene and how he had then notified Marshall Barber of his brother-in-law's death. Although a State witness, Frazer's testimony did not help its case. James Sterling had no interest in the crude facts of Saxton's death and his skilled cross-examination of Frazer zeroed in on the weather and visibility at the time Saxton's body was discovered. Frazer could not remember whether it was rainy or foggy but he did recall that it was very dark by the Althouse steps during those first minutes after he arrived at the murder scene. Pomerene and Hoover had emphasized the ample amount of light there and Sterling pressed Frazer to contradict their assertions:

"Could you recognize the features of the dead man without the aid of light other than that from the electric lamp and from the buildings?"

Frazer replied, "No, sir."

"When were you able to discern the features?"

Frazer replied, "When a match was struck. We recognized that it was Saxton when matches were lighted. Afterward someone brought a lantern. Most of the light in the street came from the grocery across the street."

Grant objected at this point. He was painfully aware that if the jury were persuaded that Saxton's face could not be easily recognized by witnesses standing over him, they were unlikely to accept eyewitness identifications of his alleged murderess from witnesses standing across the street or perched at a distant window. Judge Taylor overruled his objection, however, and so during his redirect examination of Frazer, Grant attempted to suggest that Frazer's testimony about having to light matches was irrelevant because his view of the available illumination was blocked by the crowd gathered around Saxton's body. Welty objected to this ploy and, after consideration Judge Taylor sustained the defense, stating that it was Grant himself who had initially elicited Frazer's testimony about the matches in his direct examination. "I presume," Taylor dryly concluded, "he struck matches because it was *dark*." It was another early setback for the prosecution, and the admission of Frazer's testimony allowed the defense to elicit similar testimony about the poor visibility at the murder scene from many subsequent witnesses.

Dr. Edward D. Brant testified next. He told Pomerene he had been with the first police squad that viewed the body and he had examined Saxton's corpse on the spot. He described what he saw at the scene and produced in court the bullet that he had found on Saxton's body. Brant then testified on the probable sequence of Saxton's bullet wounds, what caliber of bullet had caused them and how long he had been dead when Brant saw his body. Once again, the defense scored off the State's sloppy preparation of the case. The first count of its indictment had described the so-called "first bullet" as causing a six inch-deep wound. Under Sterling's skillful cross-examination, however, Brant was forced to admit that there was no such wound, the "first" wound being far more superficial. This made little technical difference to the case; there were still five valid murder counts remaining, any one of which could send Mrs. George to the electric chair. Inexorably, Sterling pressed on, eventually making Brant admit that his opinions on the sequence of the wounds, the caliber of the bullets and how long Saxton had been dead when he arrived were just that—opinions, not facts. Better yet for the defense, John Welty then took over the cross-examination and got Brant to describe again for the jury the spectacle of the observers at the scene lighting matches so as to identify the corpse. Welty also got Brant to admit that Saxton's autopsy physicians had been unable to find the so-called "fourth bullet," which was assumed to be the most fatal slug. Even more importantly, Welty succeeded in eliciting from Brant his opinion that the first two wounds might have been caused by spent bullets, as if fired from some distance. This was a critical issue, as the State was insisting that Saxton's killer had fired all four bullets at close range. And as for their caliber, Brant was forced to admit that the size of holes made by bullets might vary, depending on the range at which they were fired. The only point lost by the defense was when Welty, hoping to burnish Saxton's credentials as a practiced roué, asked Brant if he had heard that there was a satchel found at the murder scene. Pomerene immediately objected, and Judge Taylor properly ruled out the question as involving hearsay.

The examination of Brant extended into the Monday afternoon court session. During his graphic description of Saxton's autopsy, Pomerene had the dead man's clothes brought into the room for the jury to see. As the garments were handed to Brant one by one, Mrs. George looked away with studiously downcast eyes. After examining the powder-burned dark-worsted coat, shirt, suspenders and vest Brant stated that he thought there were more holes in the garments than he had noticed the night of Saxton's postmortem. The vest, with four apparent bullet holes in it, seemed particularly questionable, and Welty and Sterling examined it carefully and then objected to it as evidence. Judge Taylor sustained them and it was excluded.

Everyone in the courtroom could see that there was still a wilted flower in the lapel of Saxton's suit coat. One wonders if it were a carnation, well known to be President McKinley's favorite flower.

Dr. Alonzo B. Walker followed Brant on the stand. He described Saxton's wounds in even greater detail, as he had been the physician assigned to take notes during the autopsy. It was his opinion that the "fourth" bullet had caused death and that all four wounds had been caused by bullets of the same caliber. Walker thought Saxton had fallen in his tracks by the steps, dying almost instantaneously after the fourth bullet hit him. Before he stepped down, Welty got Walker to state his opinion that the first two bullets had probably been spent by the time they hit Saxton.

A Curious Crowd at Mrs. George's Trial
(Cleveland Press, April 10, 1899)

Coroner T. T McQuate testified next. Shown Saxton's clothing—minus the vest—he told of how he had taken the clothing and the items found in Saxton's pockets from Shilling's morgue on the night of the murder and carefully locked them in a vault at the county treasurer's office. He read a list of the items found on Saxton's person and in his pockets: one gold watch and chain, some inconsequential letters, two memorandum books, a diamond ring, a diamond collar button and two bunches of keys, holding about 30 keys altogether. For reasons still obscure, Welty now decided to pick a fight over Saxton's keys. Already knowing the answer, he asked McQuate whether he could produce Saxton's keys in court. Acknowledging that he had turned them over to Marshall Barber after the autopsy, McQuate hedged, saying he didn't know whether he could or not. Welty pressed McQuate until Judge Taylor interrupted him, saying, "The defense can obtain the keys by due legal process." "We have tried legal process," retorted Welty, "and we are met by the statement that the person having the keys is sick. There is one particular key that we wish to inquire about." "You *say* there is," shot back Grant. "There is nobody sick either." Grant was right on both counts. The reference to a sick person pertained to Mary Barber, who was currently battling defense attempts to subpoena her as a witness in court. And Welty probably didn't care about the possible content of Mary Barber's testimony, any more than he did about Saxton's keys. But the keys were yet another opportunity to paint the prosecution as obstructionist and uncooperative, and Welty made the most of it until Judge Taylor suggested they move on to a more fruitful topic. Perhaps more intriguing, no one in the courtroom brought up McQuate's equivocal inquest verdict, discreetly issued the same day as his testimony at Annie's trial.

Drs. Austin C. Brant and A. H. Gaus followed McQuate on the stand. Like his medical colleagues, Brant had strong opinions on the order of Saxton's bullet wounds but neither he nor Gaus offered anything new to the already prolix and graphic medical descriptions.

Pomerene then called Wrought Iron Bridge Company treasurer Frank Wyant to the stand. Wyant told of seeing both Saxton and Mrs. George on West Tuscarawas Street about 5:30 p. m. on October 7. He recalled that Annie was dressed in black and carried a black cape. Cross-examined by Sterling, Wyant could not remember the color of her hat. But he stated he noticed nothing unusual in her appearance. He was certain she was walking westward but he couldn't say how far she had gone in that direction.

With the appearance of the next witness, Wrought Iron Bridge Company president, Edward J. Landor, Pomerene once again embarrassed the State's case. Landor, a passenger on streetcar No. 21, was able to testify that he had seen a woman getting on the car at High Street as he got off it about 5:45 p.m. on October 7. But he was unable to identify the accused as that woman and he admitted that he did not know Mrs. George by sight. Cross-examined by Welty, Landor disclosed that he had only recalled the woman who got off the car when conductor Henry Stauffer jogged his memory during a conversation the morning after Saxton's murder. Following a defense objection to Landor's conversation with Henry Stauffer as hearsay, Judge Taylor ordered it stricken from the trial record.

Conductor James Shetler, the next witness, compounded Pomerene's tactical error with Landor. Shetler did not recall when Mrs. George had gotten on the streetcar, and when he stated that she had boarded it somewhere west of Canton's Public Square, Welty objected, arguing that Shetler hadn't seen her board the streetcar and that her doing so was not grounds for suspicion of murder. Judge Taylor listened to both Pomerene and Welty and made his ruling in favor of the defense, stating his view as a rhetorical question: "Shall suspicion be cast on a person for boarding a street car because three or four street car men talk about her?" The reference to Annie's boarding the car was stricken from the record.

Shetler must have thought *he* was on trial before Welty concluded his vigorous cross-examination of the streetcar conductor. Indeed, the wily lawyer got him so confused in his testimony that he finally confessed that he didn't remember "much about anything." Contradicting his previous assertions, he couldn't even be sure that Annie had exited the streetcar at Hazlette Avenue. Contrary to all previous witnesses at the inquest, preliminary hearing and grand jury sessions, however, Shetler insisted that Annie George had not been dressed in black when he saw her. He recalled her clothing as dark but definitely not black. Shetler was also unsure just how close to 6 p.m. it was when Annie exited streetcar No. 21. Capitalizing on his gains, Welty drew from Shetler the additional information that Annie's failure to get off the streetcar before it passed the Oberlin house might have been due to the fact that motorman Rittenhouse was the lone operator on the car. It was possible, Shetler conceded under Welty's relentless prodding, that Rittenhouse had not been aware of her desire to make an earlier exit.

Late Monday afternoon William Choffin took the stand. The Grand Opera House treasurer told the jury of seeing Saxton mount his bicycle and pedal away north on Market Street at about 5:40 p.m. on October 7. The last witness of the day was John Shanafelt, secretary-treasurer of the Canton Steel Roofing Company. He told Pomerene that he had seen Mrs. George on streetcar No. 21 and that he thought she had gotten off the car at Hazlette Avenue about 6 p.m. At first he said he thought she was dressed in black and was carrying some sort of black wrap in her arms. But by the time Welty finished his grueling cross-examination, Shanafelt confessed he was now uncertain about the color of her garments, even though he had seen her later that same evening as she was marched down Tuscarawas Street by her police escort. Judge Taylor recessed court at 4:30 p.m. with Shanafelt still on the stand.

It had not been a good day for the State. As the next morning's *Plain Dealer* noted, two days of detailed testimony for the State had established just three meager facts:

1. George Saxton was found dead with four bullet wounds.

2. Annie George was seen traveling in the direction of the area where his body was found.

3. Annie George was seen getting off a streetcar two blocks from the murder scene just before it occurred.

After Monday's sessions ended, more than one trial observer commented that it was going to take stronger evidence to convict Annie than Pomerene had thus far provided. Pomerene, aware that he needed to do some spin control, obliging chatted with reporters about the case. Narrowing in on the State's failure to produce any eyewitness tracing Mrs. George from the streetcar stop at Hazlette Avenue through the two blocks to 319 Lincoln Avenue, Pomerene promised that he would soon put just such witnesses on the stand.

The biggest crowd yet packed Judge Taylor's courtroom as the trial resumed at 8:30 a.m. on Tuesday morning, April 11. After John Shanafelt finished his testimony without further damaging the State's case, Pomerene called Jesse C. Taylor to testify. The streetcar barn employee simply stated that he had seen Annie George board streetcar No. 21 at High Street on October 7. Taylor had been a passenger on the car and he recalled that it had left the Public Square about 5:45 p.m. and made a few stops before arriving at High Street. He said that Annie was wearing a dark dress, light sailor hat, and carrying a dark cape. But Taylor had gotten off the car before it was blocked by the Valley Railroad train and couldn't say where Mrs. George had exited the car. He had later seen Annie opposite Holwick's Shoe Store on Tuscarawas Street, about five minutes before she was arrested at Mrs. Oberlin's house.

Streetcar motorman Samuel Howenstine testified next. He told Pomerene he had known Mrs. George since she had lived at Cora Oberlin's house and he had seen her on Rittenhouse's streetcar as it passed by the car barns on Tuscarawas Street about 6 p.m. on October 7. But during cross-examination Welty wrung from

Howenstine the admission that his time estimate could be off by as much as fifteen minutes either way. Such testimony was not helpful to Pomerene's goal of placing Annie definitely in the murder locale no later than 6 p.m. And, unlike previous witnesses, Howenstine insisted that it was not very dark and not very wet. Indeed, contrary to all prior testimony, he couldn't even recall it raining on Saxton's murder day.

Howenstine was followed by Charles Rittenhouse. Repeating his testimony at the preliminary hearing, Rittenhouse said he had been the motorman on streetcar No. 21 and he had seen Annie board the car at High Street and alight from it at Hazlette Avenue. More precise in his estimates of time than most witnesses, Rittenhouse thought Annie had gotten off the car at 5:55 p.m. He had also seen someone else get off at the same time but he could not say who it was, nor did he know in which direction Annie had proceeded after she exited the streetcar.

When Rittenhouse left the stand, Pomerene sprang his first surprise with the appearance of Stark County Common Pleas Court judge Thomas McCarty as a prosecution witness. At least it was a surprise to the jury, press and spectators; Judge Taylor and the prosecution and defense lawyers had known since January that McCarty would be an important State witness but had kept the fact secret in deference to McCarty's desire for privacy. McCarty's secret involvement in the George case was also the reason, only now disclosed, that Judge Taylor — who was not the senior Common Pleas judge — was presiding over Annie's trial. McCarty now took the stand and told of his two personal contacts with Mrs. George. The first was in 1896 when he had granted the injunction barring her from the Saxton block. The second was her conversation with him at his home, little more than a half-hour before Saxton's murder. McCarty now testified that on the latter occasion Annie had asked for permission to try and see Saxton in his block and that he had sternly counseled her to "leave Saxton alone."

McCarty was supposed to be a devastating witness against Annie George. Pomerene particularly valued his testimony as showing that Annie had been anxiously seeking Saxton just minutes before he was murdered. The effect of McCarty's testimony, however, was just the opposite. Prodded by Welty during his cross-examination, McCarty said that there was "nothing unusual" or agitated in Annie's manner when he talked to her on the fatal Friday evening. And, as the defense lawyers would subsequently argue to Annie's jury, the very fact that she had calmly asked Judge McCarty's permission to enter the Saxton block was quite at odds with the State's portrait of her as an angry, reckless and relentless killer. Could the law-abiding, deferential woman who said to McCarty, "I will not go, I do not want to disobey any of the rules of the court," be the same person who committed a carefully planned murder just thirty minutes afterwards? And the fact that Annie had been seeking access to the Saxton block implied that she thought he was there, not in the vicinity of the Althouse residence.

Harry Noble, the Dannemiller block janitor, testified after McCarty. He told the jury of Mrs. George's unsuccessful attempt to visit James Sterling there about an hour after Saxton's murder. He was not cross-examined by the defense, nor was his wife Virginia, who testified shortly after Harry and corroborated his memory of Annie's visit. Both of the Nobles remembered that Annie had worn a dark dress, a light hat and carried a dark cape.

Sandwiched in between the testimony of the two Nobles came Martin J. Hogan's appearance on the stand. Denying first — presumably with a straight face — that he knew the whereabouts of his son Russell, Hogan recounted his memories of the evening of October 7. He had been sick at home, he said, when he heard the first two shots at 6:10; he had noted the time by a clock in the room where he was sitting at 216 Lincoln Avenue. He told the jury that he thought the reports sounded like a shotgun and that they seemed to be coming from the north. After a brief interval, he had heard two more shots. Hogan said he knew nothing more about the shooting and had no idea where his son Russell had been when it occurred.

James J. Grant now moved decisively to incriminate Annie George with testimony about her post-murder behavior. Calling Canton Police officer Henry Piero to the stand, he led him through a detailed narrative of his actions the night Annie George was arrested at Cora Oberlin's house. One of the key moments of the trial arrived when Piero told of officer Fred McCloud asking Annie why she had come in the side door of the Oberlin house. When Grant asked him, "What did she say in answer to that?" Welty shouted out his objection to Judge Taylor. It was not the law of Ohio, he thundered, that the silence of an accused person could be held against her as evidence of guilt. "This raises a question of importance," responded Judge Taylor. "It involves a proposition as to whether an accused shall be convicted by silence." He then invited opposing counsel to argue the point.

The four lawyers now proceeded to wrangle ferociously over the legal point upon which they knew the trial might very well turn. Appealing to Judge Taylor, Pomerene asserted that the State had the right to show the conduct of the prisoner. It was legally entitled, he continued, to show her refusal to reply to questions as a circumstance "tending to show that the defendant is not wholly innocent."

Sterling responded with equal force, noting that silence was not equal to guilt before the law and that *nothing* Mrs. George had said or not said after her arrest could be used against her because she had repeatedly been denied counsel until the morning after her arrest. Warming to his theme, the former preacher painted a poignant word picture of his fair client at the mercy of the thuggish minions of the law:

> There can be no force in the conduct of the prisoner
> under the circumstances in which she was placed.
> Where a defendant is in the hands of the law, under
> duress of officers, silence is not to be taken as evi-

dence of guilt. The prisoner was in the hands of four stalwart officers. They began at once an inquisition. No warning was given her that her statements might be used against her. It will be shown that the effort was renewed, afterward, and her request that that she be allowed to send for counsel was denied. A confession could not be used unless it was made voluntarily. That being so, no conduct of hers and no words, if she had uttered any, could be used, because she was under duress.

After a break for lunch, Sterling resumed his impassioned plea at 1 p.m. He was followed by Grant, Welty and Pomerene,, all of them citing a plethora of supportive legal citations for their views. Finally, just before 2 p.m., Judge Taylor issued his ruling in favor of the defense. Stating that Annie's arresting officers had acted as a *de facto* extralegal court of law, he ruled that no testimony about her behavior between her arrest and her access to legal counsel could be admitted. Judge Taylor explained:

There is a statute in Ohio which says a person accused of a crime cannot be compelled to go on the stand and if the accused does not go on the stand the fact cannot be used against the defendant. It is equally true that officers are not to be permitted to constitute themselves a trial court, put the accused on the rack and force him, or her, to tell why he did this; why did he do that; where did you get mud on your shoes; where these burrs. It cannot not be done in an improvised, self constitututed court of policemen, opened on a street car or a street corner. It does not appear to the court that such is the law, and the objection is sustained.

Notwithstanding Judge Taylor's firm ruling, Pomerene and Grant made repeated attempts to introduce just such barred testimony throughout the rest of that Tuesday afternoon. Finally, after again sustaining yet another of the defense objections to such testimony, Judge Taylor wearily admonished Pomerene, "The matter has already been decided and it is useless to waste time trying to force it in." Moreover, after Welty forced Pomerene to admit in court that he had willfully ignored Mrs. George's request for an attorney during his Friday night interrogation, Judge Taylor ruled any testimony about Pomerene's own dealings with her that night out of evidence.

Pomerene's luck turned for the better when he resumed his examination of officer Piero at 2 p.m. While previous witnesses had described Mrs. George as calm and collected at the time of her arrest, Piero asserted that she was perspiring copiously and visibly "excited" when arrested at the Oberlin house. Pomerene led Piero through the narrative of her arrest, focusing on the physical details of what he had witnessed. When Piero told of sniffing the residue scraped from Annie's discolored right hand by Dr. Pontius, Welty erupted, "I object to the *smelling!*" Pomerene appealed to Judge Taylor, who sustained him, noting, "If he can state what the material scraped from the fingers smelled like, it is admissible. In so ruling I do not mean to say I hold that the previous questions not objected to by the defense are admissible." This was Judge Taylor's polite but pointed way of telling Welty and Sterling that he thought they *should* have objected to some of Pomerene's previous questions about Annie's physical examination. Piero was then allowed to state that Annie's hand smelled like gunpowder. Queried by Grant as to his qualifications as a gunpowder smeller, Piero stated that he had served in the army and was familiar with guns.

Pomerene's examination of Piero now turned to burrs and Spanish needles. This was considered an important facet of the prosecution's case: the vacant lot through which Saxton's killer had supposedly fled was rife with them and quantities of both had been found adhering to Mrs. George's dress when she was examined at the Canton police headquarters. Pomerene then produced the envelope containing the burrs and Spanish needles scraped off Annie's dress and it was entered into evidence. Piero further testified that he had searched the vacant lot near the Althouse residence right after the murder and found just such flora in the lot and an adjacent alley.

Welty's cross-examination of Piero once again revealed his careful preparation and forensic skill. Retracing the route of Mrs. George's Friday night progress eastward down Tuscarawas Street in Piero's company, Welty drew from him the admission that most of the burrs and needles on her dress had been found on the side nearest to him as he walked beside her down the street. Piero admitted that some of this vegetation could have migrated from his clothing to hers and that it was a remarkable circumstance that none had been found on her shoes. Contradicting some previous witnesses, Piero insisted there had been no rain on the day of Saxton's murder. He thought there was no moon on the night of October 7 but remembered some starlight. He recalled Mrs. George's shoes were "dusty." He thought she was dressed in black and carrying a dark cape.

Piero's lengthy cross-examination also allowed Welty to again paint the prosecution as a tribe of brutish, insensitive bullies. Leading Piero up through the events at the Canton police headquarters, Welty sprang his trap:

"After you got Mrs. George to the police headquarters, you sent for Mrs. Pontius to search her?

"Yes."

"Did you *stay* in the room?"

"Yes."

The audience in the courtroom laughed. But it was clearly nervous laughter, and Welty continued his shrewd maneuver to elicit sympathy for his client:

"Did the other three braves stay in the room?"

"Yes."

"Did you help?"

"No, sir."

"What did you do?"

"Stood back and watched."

It was not a seemly picture of the prosecution that had emerged by the time Officer Piero stepped down the witness chair.

Adams Express Company delivery clerk Ed Bour testified after Piero. He told of passing George Saxton on his bicycle on Tuscarawas Street at about 5:45 p. m. on October 7. Bour was not cross-examined. He was followed by Canton Police patrolman Fred McCloud. He corroborated many details of Piero's testimony but was repeatedly blocked by Judge Taylor from testifying about Annie's behavior after her arrest. And when, during Sterling's grueling cross-examination, he stated his opinion that Mrs. George's right hand smelled like gunpowder, Sterling barked sarcastically, "Gunpowder or face powder?" Notwithstanding Judge Taylor's ruling, Pomerene again tried to force in some testimony about his police station interrogation of Mrs. George, asking McCloud, "Describe my manner as I talked to her." Once again, Judge Taylor sustained the defense's objection to the question but the wily Pomerene noted an exception and stated that he had only wished to offer evidence that his manner then to Mrs. George was "mild, quiet and not at all threatening or violent." Police officer Aaron Rohn, a member of Anna's arresting party, followed McCloud on the stand but did not add any admissible testimony to that of his fellow officers and was still testifying when the afternoon session came to a close at 4:30 p.m.

It had been a great day for Annie's defense team and their growing confidence was manifest to the reporters covering the trial. When one of them challenged Welty with a report that the State was going to present an unimpeachable eyewitness to Saxton's murder, Welty laughed it off, promising that the defense had "a surprise up the sleeve" for any such witness. Pomerene tried to put on a brave face for the State. Emphasizing how McCarty's unexpected testimony proved Annie had been looking for Saxton to kill him, he pooh-poohed the effect of Judge Taylor's ruling on the evidence of Annie's post-arrest behavior, insisting, "We will get along all right without that." Perhaps taking a leaf from the defense playbook, Pomerene tried to change the subject by fulminating about an alleged attempt to intimidate a State witness. The unnamed female witness, Pomerene charged in high dudgeon, had been approached by a Stark County court official and threatened with "trouble" if she gave testimony damaging to Mrs. George. In fact, Pomerene never pursued this charge judicially, although he would repeatedly use it for rhetorical effect throughout the trial. The official — if he existed — was never identified.

That Tuesday evening the uneven progress of the State's case thus far was best characterized by an unnamed Stark County courthouse wag, who put it this way:

> It's like the frog that tried to jump up a wet clay bank. Every time the frog would jump two feet he would slip back three. That's the way with the prosecution in this case. Every time they put a witness on the stand to prove something against Mrs. George he proves something else better in her favor.

Chapter 12   Unprivileged Communications

Wednesday, April 12 was only a half-day court session, owing to the funeral that afternoon of Lewis Bockius, attended by many persons involved in Annie George's trial. But the morning session offered sufficient excitement for the large crowd in attendance. Officer Aaron Rohn resumed his testimony, most of it consumed by John Welty's painstaking cross-examination. Although Welty got Rohn to admit that there were plenty of Spanish needles and burrs growing in the area around Cora Oberlin's house, Rohn insisted that they grew in greater profusion in the famous vacant lot on Lincoln Avenue. Rohn said that they grew so thickly in the lot that he could see them in the dark on the moonless night of October 7. What's more, the sidewalk between Mrs. Oberlin's house and the police station was so wide — from five to six feet — as to preclude Annie's having picked up the burrs and needles there. Welty then suggested to Rohn that perhaps the burrs and needles on Mrs. George's dress had come from his uniform as he helped steer her down Tuscarawas Street to the police station. But Rohn adamantly denied this, insisting that he had noticed a lot of burrs and needles on the back of her dress at the time she was first accosted by the policemen at the Oberlin house. Then Welty scored for the defense when he pressed Rohn as to the actual visibility that night. Rohn tried to evade a direct answer and was eventually rescued by Pomerene, who blustered, "The question has been answered by the witness." "I beg your pardon," intervened an annoyed Judge Taylor, "the question has *not* been answered and the witness *will* answer." A minute later, Welty got Rohn to admit that it had been an exceptionally dark night. Worse yet for the State, he stated that the light coming from the window of the Eckroate grocery window was "not enough to benefit you any on the street."

The appearance of former Canton police officer Charles Dickerhoff, the State's next witness, was much anticipated by the crowd present that morning. His testimony was considered crucial to proving the prosecution's assertion that Annie George had been looking for George Saxton with homicidal intent on the night before his murder. Pomerene's examination therefore led Dickerhoff through the tediously detailed itinerary of his Thursday night jaunt with Annie around and around the Saxton block. Dickerhoff recalled their nocturnal quest for Saxton perfectly, detailing their vain search for signs of Saxton through the maze of streets and alleys surrounding his downtown Canton lair.

To the surprise of all, most especially Pomerene, the totality of Dickerhoff's testimony proved yet another setback for the State's case. Annie was used to confiding in sympathetic persons and she had chosen Dickerhoff as her escort because she was already comfortable with him. It was therefore not surprising that she had poured out her heart to him during their 90-minute circuit of the Saxton block. As usual, she had chanted the litany of Saxton's many wrongs against her, most especially the chronic violation of his promise to marry her. More importantly, Dickerhoff now told a chagrined Pomerene, she had said she had requested a police escort because she feared Saxton would commit violence against *her*. Before completing his direct examination of Dickerhoff, Pomerene made things worse for himself by asking, "Why did Mrs. George not go into the Saxton block?" "She said she was not allowed to enter the building," replied the policeman, reinforcing the weight of Judge McCarty's testimony that Anna was scrupulously careful to obey the terms of the restraining order.

Sterling happily drove these points home in his cross-examination. It offered him a chance to emphasize Annie's peacefulness and Saxton's potential for violence simultaneously:

"Did she say she wanted to see Saxton because he had promised to marry her, after the suit brought by Sample C. George had been settled?

"Yes," replied Dickerhoff.

"Was she calm?"

"Yes."

"No trace of excitement or ill feeling?"

"None."

"Did she say she was afraid of Saxton?"

"Yes."

"Didn't she tell you she was afraid to go and see Saxton because he had kicked her down stairs the last time she called?"

"Yes, she did," replied Dickerhoff.

"Didn't she tell you Saxton had abused her and threatened her with violence?"

"She did."

"Didn't she say that she asked the mayor to have you go with her to protect her from such attacks?"

"That is about what she told me."

"What was her manner?" asked Sterling.

"About as I had seen her before."

"She was calm and gentler, wasn't she? She talked of no harm or violence to Saxton?"

"She did not."

"Did Mrs. George tell you to stop Saxton if you saw him?"

"No, sir; she told me to let her know."

An incensed Atlee Pomerene now took on Dickerhoff in re-direct examination. Dickerhoff had appeared before Annie's grand jury and conferred repeatedly with Pomerene and Grant before his trial appearance. Pomerene had counted on the weight of his testimony and he now wanted to know why this unexpected abyss had opened below the feet of the prosecution.

"Mr. Dickerhoff, you testified before the grand jury and talked of the case with Mr. Grant and myself. Did you at either of these times tell that Mrs. George had said Saxton kicked her down stairs?"

Dickerhoff never got a chance to answer the question. Welty immediately objected, telling Judge Taylor that court procedural rules on criminal evidence precluded Pomerene from eliciting further testimony on matters he had not brought up in his direct examination of Dickerhoff. After mulling it over, Judge

Taylor sustained the objection, stating that "the rule as to surprise [testimony] was not broad enough to drag in what had not previously been said, although it did allow the introduction of what had previously been testified to." The courtroom audience may not have understood the technical grounds for Judge Taylor's ruling, but it was clear to all observers that it was yet another victory for the defense. Once again, the words of a key State witness had become a serendipitous weapon in the hands of the defense. In shifting the focus of Dickerhoff's testimony from Annie's search for Saxton to her fears of his violence, the defense, abetted by the prosecution's ineptness in handling Dickerhoff, was effectively maintaining its strategy of putting George Saxton, not Annie George, on trial.

Stove and tin merchant E. J. Rex testified after Dickerhoff. His store was located in the Saxton block, and he told of how he had watched curiously on the night of October 6 as Annie and patrolman Dickerhoff, both of whom he knew by sight, searched for Saxton in the vicinity. Oyster merchant Monroe M. Herbst followed Rex on the stand. His store was next to Rex's and he corroborated Rex's story about seeing Dickerhoff and a woman walking through the neighborhood on the night before Saxton's murder. When Herbst was finished testifying, Welty asked Judge Taylor to strike his testimony from the record. His argument was that Herbst, by his own admission, did not know the identity of the woman accompanied by Dickerhoff. Judge Taylor quickly overruled, stating that Herbst's testimony was admissible because it directly corroborated Rex's recollections.

William F. Cook now took the stand. The import of his testimony had been kept under wraps and it came as an unpleasant shock to the defense. Now a baker in Mansfield, Ohio, Cook had lived in a flat in the Saxton block from the latter part of 1895 until the spring of 1897. Owing to his severe deafness, his appearance in court was a lengthy and frustrating ordeal for all concerned. At times, his hearing was so defective that the examining lawyers were forced to submit their questions to him in writing. It was immediately evident, however, that his testimony was bad news for Annie George. Thus far the State had been unable to put the murder weapon in Annie George's hands; it now settled for an opportunity to put *a* weapon in her hands.

James J. Grant led Cook through his narrative, sometimes shouting, other times scribbling questions with a pencil and shoving them at the deaf witness. The highlight of Cook's testimony was his recollection of the night after Thanksgiving in 1896. That evening, he told Grant and the jury, he had returned to his room in the Saxton block after attending a theatrical performance at the Grand Opera House. As he entered the hallway by the staircase to the second floor, he saw Mrs. George at the top of the stairs. She was standing opposite the radiator next to the door of Saxton's living quarters, holding a revolver in her hand, and appeared to be tinkering with it in some fashion. Catching sight of Cook, Annie hastily shoved the revolver under her cape. Cook passed her without saying a word and did not see her again that night. Sometime the following spring he had again seen her standing in the second floor hallway by Saxton's rooms, this time without a revolver. Although it was late in the evening, all the hall lights were out and again Cook passed by her without exchanging a word. He now testified that he had later told Saxton about the two incidents and also related them to his own lawyer.

A THREAT TO KILL SAXTON·

Witness Says He Saw Mrs. George With a Revolver.

Had It in Her Hand in the Dead of Night in the Saxton Block—Defense Says It Will Tear His Testimony to Pieces—She Was at the Block the Night Before the Murder.

A Threat to Kill Saxton
(Cleveland Daily World, April 12, 1899)

There was more. The prosecutors wished to persuade Annie's jury that Annie had been stalking George Saxton for some time before his murder. Cook now provided the testimony they sought, telling of his visit to the Meyer's Lake resort during the summer evening of 1897. As he sat there under the trees near the lake, he suddenly noticed Annie George nearby. She was standing behind a tree, and it soon became clear to Cook that she was furtively watching and stalking George Saxton and Eva Althouse, who were sitting on a bench near the lake shore. After a while, the two moved onto to another bench and Cook watched as Annie shifted to another clandestine observation site. Annie watched the couple for another half hour until they mounted their bicycles and pedaled away. Cook estimated that Annie stayed within 25 or 30 feet of them, while he was situated about 40 feet away from her throughout the incident.

Welty and Sterling fought hard to blunt the impact of Cook's testimony. When he told of seeing Annie with a gun by Saxton's room, Welty objected to the story, saying it was too remote in time to constitute evidence of Annie's threats against Saxton. Pomerene responded quickly, "We expect to show that the threats beginning then continued through a long period up to the time of the death." After thinking it over, Judge Taylor tentatively agreed to allow Cook's testimony into the record, stating, "I will take your professional word that you will offer such testimony. I do not expect you to make your whole case by one witness."

Cook fared better than some previous State witnesses in cross-examination. He was quite emphatic and consistent in reiterating the details of his two sightings of Annie in the Saxton block and at Meyer's Lake. But Welty caught him in a serious error when he got him to state that Annie had lived in the Saxton block at a specific period during 1895. The date did not jibe with the known record, and it seemed likely, too, that Cook's memory of the Meyer's Lake incident was off by a year, probably occurring not in 1897 but 1898. Aware of Cook's confusion, Grant fought hard but unsuccessfully to have Cook's misdating struck from the record. After that failed, Welty moved to capitalize on the suggestion that Cook's memory might be faulty, asking him if he had ever seen Mrs. Elizabeth Parks, Miss Corinne Smith or Miss Emma Saltzman in the Saxton building. Cook had already testified that he had seen Saxton with other women there. The clear implication was that these three women had, like Annie, lived with Saxton during the time of Cook's residency in the building. After showing Cook photographs of the three women, Welty was happy to have the jury draw its own conclusions when Cook confessed that he had never even heard their names. He also drew from Cook the admission that he actually did not know whether Annie had been living at Saxton's block during his own residence there. The morning session ended with Cook still on the stand and court recessed until Thursday morning.

All in all, it had been another good day for the defense. Dickerhoff and Rohn's testimony had unexpectedly helped the defense more than the prosecution. So Judge Taylor's gavel had barely rapped adjournment when a happy John Sterling began spinning the day's events for reporters in the courtroom. Commenting to Arthur Sperry, he stated that at the rate the State was presenting its numerous witnesses the trial was likely to last until at least June. And he gleefully gloated about the gaps in the State's direct evidence against his client:

> They have got Mrs. George within two blocks of the scene of the crime some 15 minutes before it happened, and they have a witness who says he saw her, in the dark, with a revolver in her hand one night two years before the crime is alleged to have been committed. It has taken them about three days to do that. How long will it take them to prove something connecting her with the alleged murder?

That same afternoon an unnamed Canton lawyer offered Sperry a bleak assessment of the State's copious but incomplete circumstantial evidence:

> There is in this case the finest example of circumstantial evidence that I ever knew of. They have proved that Mr. Saxton was killed by a bullet that inflicted certain injuries, but that bullet has not been found. So far as circumstantial evidence goes, that fatal bullet was fired by the same person that fired the three bullets that made the three other wounds. If they found the fatal bullet and fitted it to a revolver in the hands of a certain person, that would be direct evidence. That not being done, it is only circumstantial evidence to prove that the other bullets were fired by a certain person.

Meanwhile, the funeral of Lewis Bockius proceeded, followed by his interment at West Lawn Cemetery. Many of the hundreds gathered there for his final obsequies gawked at the nearby grave of George Saxton. That evening, nine of the correspondents reporting Annie's trial held a private dinner at a Canton hotel. At its conclusion they took an informal vote on the likely verdict at the trial. Three reporters voted for acquittal. One voted for manslaughter. Three voted for a hung jury and the remaining two plumped for a second-degree murder conviction. Not a single one of them voted for a conviction of first-degree murder.

Thursday's morning session opened promptly at 8:30, the packed courtroom containing many female spectators. Following the ritual that by now had become routine, Annie was presented with a stunning bouquet of roses by an admirer, Carrie Bancroft Fell, a well-known Cleveland "recitationist."

Irritated by the increasing disruption caused by spectators leaving the courtroom before adjournment, Judge Taylor warned those present not to do so in the future. Sterling was present in the courtroom but deferred the day's work to Welty, saying that he did not feel well. He probably wasn't the only one. The poor ventilation in Judge Taylor's courtroom, already overtaxed by the large crowds, was further aggravated by unseasonable high temperatures for mid-April.

Welty resumed his cross-examination of William Cook but could not get him to alter his testimony of the previous day. Altogether, Cook's dogged performance was something of a setback to the defense, clearly nullifying Sterling's boast of the previous day that the defense would "tear him all to pieces." Canton lawyer Lorin C. Wise was next in the witness box and told of his ride on streetcar No. 21 on the evening of October 7. He said he had seen Mrs. George get on the car at High Street and get off it at Hazlette Avenue. Wise thought she had exited the car at 5:55 p.m., giving her plenty of time to get to Lincoln Avenue by 6:10 p.m. Wise also remembered that Mrs. George had been wearing dark clothing but he could not describe it or specify its color. Nor could he recall whether anyone else had gotten off the car at the same time she did.

As Wise stepped down, the defense braced itself for the State's most dangerous witness thus far: W. O. Werntz. Werntz, formerly James Sterling's law partner, had been Annie's attorney and had handled much of her legal business during her last tumultuous decade, including her fight against Saxton's injunction, her breach-of-promise suit, her obscene mail indictment and an attachment suit filed by her former landlady Mary Finley. It had been expected since his original, unwilling appearance before Annie's grand jury that Werntz would testify that, sometime before Saxton's murder, Annie had consulted him about the best way to kill him. It was rumored in Canton that clients were beginning to shun Werntz in anticipation of his expected testimony against Mrs. George. It was also said, with a similar lack of evidence, that Werntz was testifying only because of a falling out with his former law partner. The bald truth was simply that

Werntz was testifying because he had been forced to by a subpoena.

Pomerene took his time with Werntz, savoring each moment of an examination he hoped would decisively reverse the negative momentum of the State's case. Werntz first stated that he had known Mrs. George about three years and gave a general catalog of the legal business he had handled for her. Then came the moment Pomerene had been waiting for:

"Mr. Werntz, did you have a conversation with Mrs. George on the Monday prior to Saxton's death?"

It is Damaging to Mrs. George
(Cleveland Daily World, April 14, 1899)

"I claim a privilege," replied Werntz. "My conversation with Mrs. George was of a privileged character and I refuse to testify as to the conversation unless ordered to do so by the court." The words were barely out of the lawyer's mouth when Welty chimed in with his own objection. Addressing Judge Taylor, he insisted that any conversations between Annie and Werntz be excluded, as they enjoyed the protected character of such conversations between attorney and client. Providing the most contentious moments of the trial so far, Pomerene joined the free-for-all, insisting that the lawyer-client privilege did not cover any conversation pertaining to a homicide about to be committed.

Judge Taylor motioned to Pomerene and the two stepped out of the hearing of the jury. "Just what do you expect to prove by Werntz's testimony?" he asked the prosecutor. Two things, replied the confident Pomerene. He said he expected Werntz to testify that Mrs. George had asked his opinion as to whether it was a good idea to go out to Mrs. Althouse's home and "raise hell" with Saxton. This would be evidence consistent with the State's claim of a pattern of threats by Mrs. George against Saxton. Pomerene added that he also expected Werntz to say that Mrs. George had asked him if it was a good plan to kill Saxton and then throw down a revolver beside him to make it appear she shot him in self-defense. Judge Taylor replied that there still remained some doubt about the admissibility of some of the testimony Pomerene had described. But he deferred decisions on specific content for later and requested that the four attorneys make their arguments as to the general admissibility of Werntz's testimony. Most of the morning was consumed in their citation-laden pleas and they were still arguing when court recessed for lunch.

At 1:50 that afternoon, after hearing over two hours of oral arguments, not omitting their copious legal citations, Judge Taylor issued his ruling overruling Welty's objection and rejecting Werntz's claim of lawyer-client privilege. Judge Taylor's ruling was a lengthy one but he stated its crux quite plainly, focusing on the criminality of Annie's alleged conversations with Werntz:

One about to commit a crime cannot employ an attorney to get his advice as to how it should be committed, because it is against public policy. Public policy demands such communications shall not be privileged when they have for their object the commission of crime. The privilege to the defendant is denied.

Experienced lawyers in the courtroom were acutely aware that Judge Taylor had just made Ohio legal history with his ruling. Although Iowa and Michigan courts had ruled in similar cases that conversations about the committal of intended crimes were not protected, the point had never been passed upon by an Ohio court.

Pomerene now returned to his happy task.

"Mr. Werntz, did you have a conversation with Mrs. George on the Monday prior to Saxton's death?"

"I did, at her room in West Tuscarawas Street, sometime in the forenoon."

"What conversation, aside from that on litigation in which you were interested, did you have with her?"

"We talked about the Althouse case. She said she was going out to the Althouse house to raise hell with Saxton. I told her not to go, and she said she wouldn't go."

"What else was said about Saxton?" continued Pomerene.

"She asked what she could do to get her household goods back from Saxton."

Welty objected here that the last remark was irrelevant and Judge Taylor ordered it stricken from the record.

"How long were you at the house?" asked Pomerene.

"I could not tell how long I was at the house, probably half an hour."

"What was said about a revolver?"

"She said she had a .38-caliber revolver in her trunk; she had bought it in Chicago. She did not say what she was going to do with it. She didn't say what she paid for it."

Pomerene then turned to Werntz's second meeting, several hours later that same Monday.

"Did you have another conversation with Mrs. George?"

"I had another conversation with her in my office the afternoon of that day. She said, 'When the suit of Sample C. George is settled there will be a funeral or a wedding.' She asked me what effect it would have on the suit if she killed Saxton. I told her the result might be the same, but if she was going to kill him she had better wait until the case was settled. She said if she shot him she would make a good job of it; she would give him all the balls she had."

"What did she say she would do with the revolver?"

"She asked if it would be a good plan to have two revolvers, throw one at his feet and shoot him with the other. I told her in view of the threats she had made against Saxton, no one would believe she killed him in self-defense."

Welty objected to Werntz testifying about his responses and this last remark was stricken from the record. Pomerene modified his question slightly and Werntz replied, "She asked me how it would do to shoot him in the back and throw the revolver away."

"What did you say?"

Welty again objected and the question was stricken from the record.

Pomerene tried again. "What did you advise her?"

"I told her she had better let Saxton alone. I told her she had two bright boys, and if she had no respect for Saxton she ought to have for her family." Welty was satisfied with that answer and let it stand. But when Pomerene tried to elicit from Werntz whether Annie had made threats to both Mrs. Althouse and Saxton in his presence, Welty objected and all such testimony was ruled out by Judge Taylor. Pomerene took one last shot at Werntz, asking the attorney if Mrs. George had used profanity during her Monday conferences with him. Scrupulously understated to the last, Werntz dryly replied, "She used a few adjectives." Welty objected to the comment and Judge Taylor ruled it out.

When Pomerene had finished with the reluctant Werntz, John Welty took over the cross-examination. There was little he could do to negate Werntz's devastating testimony against his client. But Welty was determined, if he could, to subtly modify the context of Mrs. George's conversations. He also wanted to put George Saxton back on trial and his quizzing of Werntz accomplished both goals. Referring to Annie's comment about a "funeral or a wedding," he asked Werntz a series of rapid-fire questions that became increasingly rhetorical; Annie herself could hardly have improved on the detailed enumeration of her woes that the clever Welty now led the State's witness to confirm:

"Did she tell you Saxton promised to marry her as soon as she got a divorce?"

"Yes."

"And that he had abandoned her?"

"Yes."

"And was persecuting her?"

"Yes."

"Did she say she was without a home?"

"Yes."

"That Saxton had induced her to leave her husband, had paid the expense of her divorce in Dakota?"

"Yes," replied Werntz.

Welty returned to her first Monday conversation with Werntz.

"What were you talking about when she spoke at her house about raising hell?"

"She referred to the peace proceedings pending in the probate court. She was enraged and indignant. She went over the whole story."

"Did she say Saxton had kicked her out of the building?"

"Yes. She asked whether she could begin suit to recover goods locked in a room in the Saxton block by George Saxton. A sewing machine was included and she said part of the goods had been given to her by her mother. She said Saxton and Mrs. Althouse passed and repassed her house every day on their wheels. She never showed me a revolver. At my office on that afternoon she practically repeated the story of the morning about his ill-treatment and broken promises. She said Saxton was the only living man she loved. That she loved her husband once, but Saxton had alienated her affections."

"She was crying that afternoon, was she not?"

"Yes, I think she was."

"What she said was 'more in sorrow than in anger'?"

"Object!" shouted Pomerene and Grant simultaneously. It was bad enough that Werntz had turned into a runaway witness; now Welty was brazenly baiting the prosecution with quotations from Shakespeare's *Hamlet*. "I don't want any poetry at this stage of the game," snarled Grant to Judge Taylor. His objection was sustained. Before releasing Werntz, Welty decided to put him through one more inventory of Annie's sufferings and degradations at the hands of the beast Saxton.

"She was crying?" prompted Welty.

"Yes. She said Saxton had been after her for years before she had consented to follow him."

"She told you of the places where they had stopped together?"

"Yes, sir. Mrs. George told me that during two years she lived in the Saxton block, Saxton spent most of the time in her rooms. She said Saxton had given her presents and that he attempted to persuade her to leave her husband from the day they moved into the Saxton block, and that finally at Meyers Lake casino in 1889, he accomplished her ruin. At the conference in Allegheny in 1896 Mrs. George said Saxton had promised to support her until their marriage and that he would give her two sons a property in Canton worth $3,000."

"What was Mrs. George's manner when talking about Saxton?"

"Sometimes she was kind and sometimes she was not; sometimes she showed anger. She asked me one time about the penalty for murder. She said that if she did not get more than ten years in the penitentiary she would kill him or shoot him; I can't remember just what term she used."

When Welty relinquished Werntz, Pomerene had another go at him in redirect examination. He was unable to extract any additional useful information about the attorney's meetings with Annie. When he was finished, Welty couldn't resist the opportunity of one more crack at arraigning Saxton's behavior towards his client. During re-cross-examination Werntz repeated Annie's statement to him about Saxton being the only man she loved. Her tender assertion served as a sharply invidious contrast to Werntz's retelling of the story she had told him about her arrest at a Massillon resort of ill repute. Every circumstance of Saxton's vile machinations and Annie's mortifications at his hands was exposed — yet again by a witness upon whom the State had counted heavily. And Annie's threats against Saxton lost yet a little more force when it emerged from Werntz's testimony that he was mistaken about the date of his two conversations with Annie George. If they had actually occurred, as he said, on the date Mary Finley's attachment suit was decided in Mrs. George's favor, than it was Monday, September 19, not October 3, as originally thought. This altered the timing of Annie's last threat again Saxton to Werntz from four days before the murder to more than two weeks.

The net effect of Welty's brilliant cross-examination of Werntz was a triumph for Anna's defense. The unidentified reporter covering the trial for the *Canton Evening Repository* astutely analyzed how Welty had transformed the menacing litany of her threats into a powerful narrative of her sufferings at the hands of Saxton:

Once the witness was on the stand and open to cross-examination . . . the defense used him to detail Mrs. George's version of her relations with Saxton and her alleged wrongs at Saxton's hands. This story followed closely the statement made by Mr. Welty in opening the case. Being presented in cross-examination the examining attorney was practically permitted to frame the language of the testimony. That is, he put the questions in the form of a narrative of the incident or language to be described, preceded by "Didn't she," etc., or other words to that effect. Had the same evidence been introduced by a witness for the defense in direct examination, the questions would have had to be free from suggestion and the answers confined to the language of the witness.

Mary Finley was the last State witness of the day. Her testimony was expected to be particularly hostile to Annie George. Annie had once been friends with Finley and had roomed from 1896 to 1898 in her house at 536 South Walnut Street. Finley had even appeared as a character witness at the peace proceedings instituted against Annie by Eva Althouse. Then, Finley had testified that Annie was a peaceable woman who wouldn't hurt anyone. But there had been some unexplained falling out since, a breach exacerbated by Finley filing an attachment suit against Annie for non-payment of rent. Finley had lost that suit shortly before Saxton was killed, and courtroom observers expected a battle royal when she took the stand.

They weren't disappointed. It was apparent from the moment Finley took the stand that Pomerene had carefully coached a witness he considered crucial to providing evidence of Annie's premeditation and malice. His questions drew from Finley her recollections of Annie's threats against Saxton. Some of them were at least two years old, but all of Finley's memories seemed quite precise. She recalled the first time Annie ever uttered a threat about Saxton to her, in the fall of 1897:

> Just wait till the case of Sample C. George and Saxton is settled; I will see Saxton. I am going to ask Mayor Rice to go with me to Saxton's office. I am going to ask Saxton what he will do for me, and if he does nothing I will shoot him so full of lead that he will stand still.

Finley likewise recalled her sober remonstrance to Mrs. George, warning her she would go to prison if she shot Saxton. "Only a few years if I do," sneered Annie, "and what of that?" Finley then inquired, "Will you shoot yourself then?" When Anna riposted, "No," Finley couldn't refrain from adding, "That's customary." Finley further testified that Annie had made similar threats in early 1898 and given her a detailed account of how she pulled a revolver on Saxton at the Althouse residence. Finley also recalled Annie bragging to her about what a "dandy letter" she had written to Mrs. Althouse.

Welty's cross-examination of Finley began harshly and never faltered in its ferocity:

"Are you married, Mrs. Finley?"

Hesitating for a moment, Finley replied, "Yes, sir, I was married."

"But you haven't been married for a long while past?" An obviously flustered Finley made no answer. Welty then asked her if she were angry with Mrs. George. Finley denied it. With deepening sarcasm, Welty asked her if she knew that George Saxton was actually the one paying Annie's rent when the latter roomed with her. Finley primly denied it. "Who did he come to see, then— *you?*" jeered Welty. "Yes," blurted out Finley nervously. After a few more questions, Welty wheeled on Finley and shouted at her, "You know your story is all a fabrication, don't you?"

"No!"

Here Grant interrupted, saying, "I don't think the witness knows what fabrication means." Following another burst of laughter from the court room spectators, Welty continued his merciless attack:

"You told James Lavin [a friend of Mrs. George] you did not know anything about this, didn't you?"

"No!"

"Did anybody write down your testimony for you?"

"No!"

Under further badgering, Finley admitted that she had "talked over" her testimony with James Grant the night before. She said he had asked her questions about the case and she had tried to answer them. As she became more rattled and confused by Welty's questions, she began looking nervously at Grant. That was just what Welty wanted, and he shouted, "Look at the jury! What is the matter with you? Don't keep looking at Mr. Grant!" Finally, Grant took pity on her and began interrupting Welty so that Finley could regain her equilibrium. When that didn't help, he stood behind Welty, where he couldn't see him, making the courtroom spectators laugh. This aroused the long-patient Judge Taylor, who threatened to clear the courtroom. He then put both sides on notice that he had had enough of their unprofessional posing, bickering and baiting, warning, "We are not going to have so much of this byplay between counsel. It must be stopped." He then adjourned court with Mary Finley still on Welty's hot seat.

Finley's testimony was another setback for the prosecution. It wasn't so much the deficiencies in her testimony, which constituted distinct and detailed recollections of Annie's repeated threats to take George Saxton's life. That itself was half the prosecution's problem: her story was *too* detailed, *too* precise, especially as to dates. It was apparent to everyone in the courtroom that Finley had been rigorously rehearsed — indeed, over-rehearsed — by Pomerene or Grant before taking the stand. The result, wrote correspondent Arthur Sperry, was that she "sounded like a phonograph." That was all right as long as she stuck to the script. But when Welty got her rattled enough to go off script, she couldn't remember much of anything. The other half of the problem was simply Finley's personality. Whenever she veered from her rehearsed answers, it was obvious she was a stupid, unattractive woman with a pronounced, comically difficult German accent. She perspired visibly, she wept frequently and her animus against Annie George seemed a palpable presence in the courtroom. It even led her past the brink of outright perjury, as when she baldly denied recalling that she had testified to Mrs. George's pacific disposition at Justice Robertson's peace proceedings. By the time Judge Taylor's adjournment interrupted her testimony it seemed almost cruel to prolong her ordeal another day.

Chapter 13   Sister Morphine

Another large crowd jammed the courtroom as Welty resumed Mary Finley's cross-examination on Friday morning, April 14 at 8:30 a.m. Emboldened by his success the previous afternoon, Welty picked up where he had left off, badgering Finley anew into a state of quaking, stuttering and tearful incoherence. Once again, James J. Grant tried to intervene, and increasingly acrid sniping flared between the two feisty attorneys. Periodically, Judge Taylor would caution them to cease their negative byplay and it would subside for awhile. But it would soon break out again; Welty had found the combative tone he wanted for Annie's trial and he skillfully maintained it until its conclusion.

As soon as Finley resumed her testimony, Welty demanded to know where she had been the previous night. At her neighbor Mrs. Mary Nauman's house, from 7 to 9 p.m., replied Finley. "Did you have any visitors?" persisted Welty. A few questions later Mary reluctantly admitted that James J. Grant had met with her the same evening. Once again, the defense's superb espionage work had paid dividends, for now Mary accused Newton George of snooping around her house while Grant was there. Welty then led Finley back to her memories of the April 1898 peace proceedings brought against Annie by Mrs. Althouse. Again, Welty provoked Finley to deny her favorable testimony for Annie on that occasion, conceding only that she had signed Mrs. George's peace bond. She also denied recently telling State witness Mary Grable in the witness waiting room that Grant had told her what to say on the stand. She likewise denied that she and Grable had agreed to date their shared conversations with Mrs. George so that they aligned perfectly. Before Finley stepped down, more bickering broke out between the defense and the prosecution teams on the subject of coaching witnesses. Welty averred piously that it might be a good idea for Judge Taylor to issue an order prohibiting counsel for the State from conferring with prosecution witnesses between trial sessions. Pomerene shot back, snarling that if the other side "would let *their* witnesses alone there would be less trouble and more progress in the case." A weary Judge Taylor tartly remarked that there was no law preventing such conferences and suggested that the four attorneys proceed with the case.

Mrs. Mary Nauman
(Canton Evening Repository, April 15, 1899)

Mary Nauman, another former friend of Mrs. George, testi-fied next. She had lived on South Walnut Street, just three houses away from Mrs. Finley's home and often visited her and Annie while the latter boarded there. In response to Pomerene's ques-tions, Nauman related a damning chronicle of threats against George Saxton that Annie had made in her presence. Nauman's most vivid such recollection was the quilting bee at her home in February, 1897, where Annie swore that if George Saxton did not marry her "he will not walk the streets of Canton another day." That was the occasion when she boasted that if she were sent to the penitentiary, she would "knock everybody's eyes out." Nauman said that Annie had also confided in her how she had pulled a gun on Saxton and forced him to walk with her. Annie had boasted that she could have easily killed Saxton then but she wanted her ex-husband to get some money from Saxton first. Annie had also bragged to her about the obscene, threatening letter she sent to Eva Althouse, "Let them prove who did it!" was her rejoinder to Nauman's remonstrance at the time. Seeking evidence of premeditated malice, Pomerene drew Nauman out on Annie's mood when talking about the obscene letter:

"What was her manner?"

"She clenched her fists."

"What did she do?"

"She used profane language," replied Nauman.

Knowing her answer in advance, Pomerene asked Nauman to repeat Annie's words. When she demurred, Judge Taylor ruled that she did not have to repeat profane or obscene language if she did not wish to.

Sterling's initial strategy in his cross-examination of Mary Nauman was a subtle variation on John Welty's successful attempt to stigmatize Finley as an Annie George hater. His opening gambit was an attempt to show that Nauman and Mrs. George had once been great friends. But it soon became clear that his real purpose was to persuade Annie's jury that the now hostile Nauman had once encouraged Annie to rant about Saxton and had been a virtual accomplice and abettor in Annie's tirades against him and Eva Althouse.

"You were once friends with the accused?" began Sterling.

"Yes."

"You sometimes saw Mrs. George at Mrs. Finley's house?"

"Yes"

"You sometimes sent tea cakes?"

"Yes."

"And other delicacies?"

"No. Only the tea cakes."

"You sometimes sat on the porch with Mrs. George?"

"Yes."

"You sometimes gave Mrs. George presents?"

"No."

"You gave Mrs. George a handkerchief as a Christmas present in 1896?"

"No."

Sterling then led Nauman through her version of what Annie had allegedly told her about pulling the revolver on Saxton. He quibbled with every detail of her recollection of the conversation, repeatedly forcing her to lose her composure:

"You say she said she could have "done" him on the Tuscarawas Street bridge? Don't you know she said Saxton had picked up her pistol and put it in his pocket?"

"That's what she said."

"Don't you know they didn't cross the Tuscarawas Street bridge at all?"

"I don't know anything about it. I'm only telling what she told me!"

Sterling cheerfully continued his skeptical barrage, accusing Nauman of complicity in Annie's obscene letter campaign:

"Did you advise Mrs. George to write a letter to scare Mrs. Althouse?"

"No."

"Did you tell her what to put in the letter?"

"No."

"Did you give her the paper and envelope?"

"No."

"When the United States marshal came after her, didn't you tell her to come to your home and hide?"

"No sir; I wouldn't have her!"

"Didn't she take dinner with you that day?

"No; she was in hiding for three or four days. When she came back she came to our house about noon and we asked her to eat with us."

Having thoroughly rattled Nauman, Sterling adopted Welty's favorite tactic, accusing the prosecutors of assiduously coaching Nauman before her appearance in the witness box:

"You saw Grant last night?"

"Suppose I did?" retorted Nauman defensively.

"You fixed dates to be used in your testimony?"

"No, sir!"

Before their colloquy was over, Sterling forced Nauman to admit that she had talked to both prosecutors the previous night and that Pomerene might have written down part of what she now said on the stand.

Taken as a whole, Nauman's testimony was another reverse for the State's case. Like Mary Finley, she became a nervous, incoherent and cranky wreck as soon as she departed from the script of the testimony that Pomerene and Grant had rehearsed with her. And, like William Cook, she was wildly inaccurate as to dates; her recollections of some of the incidents recounted were obviously off by as much as several years.

Nettie McAllister testified after Mary Nauman. A handsome, middle-aged woman, this South Cherry Street resident had once been part of the Annie George-Mary Finley-Mary Nauman social sorority. Like Nauman and Finley, she had since fallen out with Annie. But McAllister, too, had once been a willing auditor of Annie's impassioned and imprudent confidences. In addition to hearing some of Mrs. George's vows to shoot Saxton, Nauman had also been present when Annie bragged about a letter to him in which she had promised to "fix" him and "cut out Eva's heart and hang it on a telephone pole." Indeed, Nettie now told Pomerene and the jury, Annie had asked her to write some of her letters to Saxton and Eva, so as to prevent her handwriting from being recognized. Nettie had virtuously refused. After her arrest on the

Mrs. Nettie McAllister
(Cleveland Daily World, April 15, 1899)

obscene mail charge, Annie had asked Nettie to write an anonymous letter to Marshal John J. Keeley in Cleveland. This task, too,
she declined, Nettie now testified. She also repeated details Annie
had told her about her 1896 conference with Saxton at the Hotel
Federal in Allegheny.

When Pomerene was finished with her, John Welty wasted
no time trying to disprove the facts of McAllister's recollected
conversations with the accused. They were specific, credible, and
McAllister was a lot more careful about dates than Finley or
Nauman. So Welty, well briefed on the biographies of all the
witnesses, attacked her character instead:

"Mrs. McAllister, are you married?"

"Yes."

"Where is your husband?"

"He left for parts unknown."

After softening her up with a few more personal questions, Welty returned to her conversations with Annie. As he probed the subjects of those talks, it became clear to his audience that most of Annie's conversations with McAllister — like most of her conversations with others — had been devoted to emotional catalogues of Saxton's wrongs, rather than threats of what she might do to him. Before letting McAllister go, Welty signaled his intention to increase the level of cross-examination nastiness by querying McAllister as to whether she spent the greater part of her leisure time in an Eighth Street saloon. She piously denied the charge. Grant then used his redirect examination of McAllister to chip away at the defense portrait of the pre-Saxton Anna as a dewy-eyed, happily married innocent:

"What did Mrs. George tell you about her husband?"

"She said she never cared for him."

"What else?"

"She said she never liked him from the day she married him."

However contrary such testimony was to the idyllic defense portrait of Annie's pre-Saxton marriage days, Pomerene's decision to have McAllister recount her jailhouse conversations with Annie may have boomeranged with the jury and the courtroom spectators. Welty had previously pushed McAllister to admit that she was now hostile to the accused. Why then, except probably at the instigation of Prosecutor Pomerene, had McAllister bothered to repeatedly visit Mrs. George in jail? Once again, Pomerene looked sneaky, as he had in his kindred attempts to entrap Mrs. George in staged jailhouse conversations with Perry Van Horne and William Hasler.

John L. Jackson, the janitor of the Davis block, next took the stand. His testimony was a mixed blessing for the State. Jackson was quite precise about his last meeting with Mrs. George on the morning of October 7. He recalled in great detail exactly what she had said to him, especially her frustration at Saxton's failure to marry her and her prediction that he would get his reward in "hell or eternity." But Pomerene wanted a more specific threat, and he prodded Jackson hard to recall a previous meeting with Annie, several weeks before Saxton's murder. Jackson did remember the meeting, and he eventually recalled Annie making threats and using profane language against Saxton and Mrs. Althouse, calling the latter a "hussy" and still viler names. But Pomerene couldn't pin him down as to the precise language of Annie's threats: Jackson persisted in making vague generalizations about her statements, merely reiterating that "she swore vengeance."

John L. Jackson
(Cleveland Daily World, April 15, 1899)

Jackson was still on the stand when Judge Taylor announced a recess for lunch. Growing more aggressive with every witness, Welty celebrated the break by again taunting the prosecution. In the hearing of the jury he asked Judge Taylor to issue an order preventing Jackson from conferring with the State's counsel during the recess. Pomerene barked back, "There had better be an order preventing *you* from seeing *our* witnesses!" James Grant chimed in, "If you let witnesses alone after the evening adjournments, the noon adjournments will take care of themselves." Judge Taylor's only response was a repeated, "I have no such jurisdiction."

It was probably little consolation to Pomerene and Grant that Sterling had little more success with Jackson during his cross-examination after lunch. Sterling's focus was on Mrs. George's avowals of love for Saxton and her recitation of Saxton's wrongs, rather than her threats against Saxton and Althouse. But Jackson merely repeated his euphemisms and obfuscations and Welty finally gave up on him. For whatever unknown reasons, Jackson proved to be the most elusive of the more than one hundred witnesses who testified at Anna's trial.

Dr. Maria Pontius now took the stand. She stated that she had been a practicing physician for fourteen years and had been the police physician on duty at the Canton city jail the night Saxton was murdered. There had been rumors prior to the trial that she had changed her mind about the events of October 7 but nothing certain was known as to the character of her testimony. Pomerene now led her through her physical examination of Mrs. George to the critical moment:

"What did you find when you examined her hands?"

"I found her right hand not so clean as the left. The first and second finger and thumb were blackening. I scraped the cuticle of the right hand and saved the preserved scrapings on a clean piece of white writing paper. A very small amount of the scrapings was all I could get. There was just enough to know that it was on the paper. I sealed the scrapings up in an envelope."

"Is this the envelope?" said Pomerene, handing it to Pontius.

"Yes, I see by what is written on the envelope I gave this to you at my office the 30th of November. It is my writing on the envelope."

Welty's cross-examination of Pontius was brief, polite and devastatingly effective. Pomerene had emphasized the gunpowder on Annie's hand during his opening statement and reiterated its importance during his examination of officer Henry Piero. His careful preparation now came undone.

"Was there any smell of gunpowder about Mrs. George's hands?

"No sir."

"The scrapings from Mrs. George's cuticle; was it a large quantity?"

"The amount was so small that you could scarcely see it on white paper. I think it was too small to stand a chemical analysis." After getting Pontius to make the further damaging disclosure that she had searched Mrs. George before she had secured counsel, Welty relinquished the physician to Pomerene.

The chief prosecutor was tired of having his witnesses self-destruct on the stand. When Pontius reiterated her denial that she had smelled gunpowder on Mrs. George's hand, Pomerene exploded with obvious anger:

"Did you not say to me, two or three days ago in my office, that you did not know how gun powder smelled?".

The courtroom audience laughed.

"*Burnt* gunpowder?" Pomerene pressed. The crowd laughed even louder.

"I said I did not have as much experience as gentlemen had with gun powder and I say it was not gunpowder to the best of my knowledge."

Dr. Alfred B. Smith, a professor and chemist at the Case School of Applied Science in Cleveland, followed Pontius on the stand. Pomerene had sent the scrapings from Mrs. George's right hand to Smith for chemical analysis. Smith had performed a rigorous analysis and he was ready to testify that the scrapings contained the elements commonly found in gunpowder: sulphate of potassium, carbonate of potassium and carbon. He was also ready to state his opinion that the stain on Mrs. George's hand was caused by a defective, "leaky" revolver.

Smith never got the chance. Pomerene handed him the envelope and Smith identified it as the one that had contained the cuticle scrapings, explaining that they had been consumed in the process of his analysis. As soon as Pomerene asked Smith to give the results of his analysis, Welty rose to make two objections to his testimony. The first was that there was no proof that there had been enough material from the scrapings to insure an accurate chemical analysis. The second was that the scrapings were illegally obtained from the accused, who was under duress and without counsel at the time they were taken from her person.

Pomerene fought savagely for the admission of the scrapings and Smith's testimony about his analysis. It was the only solid physical evidence he had that connected Annie to any firearm, much less the actual murder weapon. The chief prosecutor cited criminal cases in which matter had been scraped from under the fingernails of accused persons, analyzed and then used in evidence against them.

After listening courteously to the arguments of both the State and defense lawyers, Judge Taylor ruled out Smith's testimony. Judge Taylor's reasoning was what while Smith might be allowed to draw speculative conclusions from his chemical analysis, the whole matter was rendered inadmissible by Annie's legal predicament at the time she was searched by Dr. Pontius:

> The way the scrapings were obtained is even more important [than Smith's analysis]. The right to search prisoners is ordinarily confined to the right to search for weapons or for property that may have been stolen. The right of search does not go far enough to enable the state to cut off a lock of hair or take out a set of false teeth to search for evidence.
> The prisoner was under duress at the time, without counsel and it rested upon the State to prove that the

substance was obtained as a voluntary act of the accused. The objection is sustained.

Although he did not say so at the time, Judge Taylor later privately explained to reporters that the decisive factor in his exclusion of the evidence was Dr. Pontius's opinion that the scrapings were too negligible in quantity for analysis. He conceded his ruling might be reversed by a higher court but stated he did not care to run the risk of having human blood on his hands on the basis of such evidence.

Pomerene wasn't ready to give up. Judge Taylor had hardly finished stating his ruling when Pomerene renewed his argument, citing the case of "Frenchy," a Jack-the-Ripper style killer in New York City. Frenchy, as Pomerene now informed Judge Taylor, had unwillingly had the skin under his fingernails scraped and the blood of his victim found under them was used to convict him. (The Frenchy precedent had just been helpfully fed to Pomerene by a *New York Herald* reporter present in the courtroom). Judge Taylor wasn't pleased. He chastised Pomerene in as severe a tone as he had yet used during the trial, stating icily, "I did not expect you to make an argument after the decision on the objection. The objection is sustained."

Charles Lloyd followed Professor Smith on the stand. The *Canton Evening Repository* reporter had known Mrs. George for four years and she had cultivated him as a sympathetic listener and potential channel for getting her side of her troubles into his newspaper. Lloyd now recalled various threats she had made against Saxton in his presence, especially one made at her home, probably in mid-1897. Like most of her other threats, it was a specific threat to kill Saxton *if* he failed to marry her after Sample George's lawsuit was settled. Lloyd added that a man named Adam Jackman had also been present when that threat was uttered. Lloyd said he had once seen a revolver lying on a stand in her room and that Annie had once told him that she had sewn a special pocket in her dress for concealing a pistol.

John Welty's cross-examination diminished some of the impact of Lloyd's revelations. It turned out he had not actually seen the revolver pocket in Mrs. George's dress. Nor had she claimed to Lloyd that she actually possessed a revolver or carried one. Lloyd's chief recollections of her conversations, as Annie had intended, were Annie's repetitive complaints about the wrongs of George Saxton.

Ex-*Canton News-Democrat* reporter Perry Van Horne came next. Like Lloyd, his testimony was mainly comprised of conversations in which Mrs. George had complained to him about Saxton's treatment of her. Van Horne's recollections of his interviews with Annie included her versions of the Hotel Federal reconciliation and her pulling a revolver on Saxton in front of Eva's house. Van Horne also testified that Annie had repeatedly threatened to kill Saxton, but always making the act conditional on his not marrying her after Sample's suit was settled. Before letting Van Horne leave the stand, however, Pomerene made sure that the jury heard an allusion to the ex-reporter's jailhouse interview with Annie, when he had mentioned her previous threat to kill Saxton.

It was John Welty's turn to pounce. He'd been waiting to make Pomerene pay for the murder night missteps in his treatment of Annie George and Welty's cross-examination focused on the disingenuous circumstances of Van Horne's jailhouse interview with Annie on the night she was arrested for murder:

"This [interview] was at the instance of the Prosecuting Attorney?"

"Yes sir."

"You were to report to him?"

"Yes sir."

Welty's stress on the Van Horne interview paid a handsome dividend when Pomerene conducted his redirect examination of the reporter. Returning to the theme that Annie's behavior that night had incriminated her, he queried Van Horne closely about it.

But John Welty had baited his trap well and he now sprang it. Leaping to his feet, he noted that it was Pomerene, not he, who had introduced the jailhouse interview, and he vociferously objected to such testimony as inadmissible on the grounds that Annie had been under duress and without counsel at the time. Conferring with Judge Taylor outside of the jury's hearing, Pomerene pleaded that Van Horne be allowed to tell his story, characterizing Annie's demeanor at the time as a silent admission of guilt. But after listening to Pomerene, Judge Taylor ruled it out, telling Pomerene that Annie's constitutional right to silence could not be qualified, especially when she had not been permitted to see a lawyer. Sterling's remaining cross-examination of Van Horne then reverted to his favorite subject of just how badly Saxton had treated Annie and how miserable it had made her feel. It also allowed Welty to embellish the image of Annie's pre-Canton, pre-Saxton innocence:

"Didn't she tell you that when she first came to Canton she was so unsophisticated she would not give the baggage man the check for her trunk because she thought he wanted to steal it?"

"Yes," replied Perry Van Horne.

MRS. GRABLE AND DEFENDER WELTY.

John C. Welty Cross-Examines Mrs. Mary Grable
(Cleveland Daily World, April 15, 1899)

Once again, it had not been a good day for the prosecution. It soon worsened with the appearance of Mary E. Grable, yet another ex-friend of Annie George's. Like Mary Finley, it wasn't so much her actual testimony that caused the State damage. Pomerene's direct examination of Grable focused mainly on two threats Annie had made against George Saxton in her presence. Annie had once rented a room from Grable, and in early 1898 told her she would riddle Saxton with lead unless he kept his promise to marry her. She had repeated essentially the same threat on another occasion. With help from Pomerene, Grable managed to stumble through her two anecdotes, interspersing frequent complaints of her own miseries. Such detours eventually prompted an exasperated Judge Taylor to warn her, "Don't bring in your troubles, too."

Grable's troubles, it soon developed were serious ones. The defense had done its homework and Welty began his demolition without preface as he opened Grable's cross-examination:

"You're an opium-eater, are you not?" he began.

"No sir."

"Don't you buy opium?"

"Yes, as an astringent," primly replied Grable.

"I didn't ask you if you bought it as an astringent. You eat opium?"

"I have taken it."

"How long have you been an opium-eater?"

"I am not an opium-eater!"

"How many years have you been buying opium at Doud's drug store on McKinley Avenue?"

There was a long pause. "About a year."

"Don't you know you have been chewing opium in the witness room all day? You went out to the drug store for it and said it was for another person."

"No, sir! As God is my witness, as true as I sit in this witness chair, you will have to prove that!"

"We'll prove it," said Welty, grimly.

Welty then read another list of Canton drug stores where Grable had bought opium.

"Is it not true that you husband went to the drug store and ordered them not to sell you opium?"

"No, sir!"

"And that since then you have been sending your son for it?"

"I never sent my son for any in my life! I take only tincture of laudanum!"

"How long have you used laudanum?"

"I don't know."

By the time Welty let Grable go she had completely lost her composure. Arthur Sperry summarized the appalling impression Grable's appearance and demeanor made on Annie's jury in the following day's edition of the *Cleveland Evening World*:

> Mrs. Grable seems a pitiful human wreck. Her 'hop voice,' as it would be called in the tenderloin, her evident feebleness and her clothing made what the defense said in cross-examination about her being an opium fiend deeply impressive. She was formerly the wife of a prominent Canton physician.

Pomerene now called Michael Barr to the stand. Barr was the money order clerk at the United States Post Office in Canton and he had been involved in the investigation of Annie's obscene letters to Saxton and Althouse. Specifically, Pomerene wanted him to identify her handwriting on the letter threatening the excision of Mrs. Althouse's heart, insisting that Barr qualified as an expert witness on her handwriting because he had seen letters she had mailed and her application for a money order. But Welty challenged Barr's expertise, and Pomerene was unable to persuade Judge Taylor that Barr was qualified to identify Mrs. George's hand, forcing the prosecution to withdraw him as a witness.

Mattie Grimes, Pomerene's last witness that long Friday, furnished a fitting anticlimax to a tumultuous day. The spinster school teacher testified simply that she had passed Mrs. George on Tuscarawas Street about 8:10 p.m. on the night of Saxton's murder. Grimes recalled that Annie was dressed in dark clothing, carried a dark cape and was walking at a normal gait. At the time Grimes had supposed Eva Althouse was the presumed killer, and she noticed nothing usual about Annie's appearance except that her face was flushed. Grimes was still testifying when Judge Taylor adjourned court at 4:30 p.m.

It had been a disastrous day for the State. Motive enough for several murders had been documented by the testimony of almost all the State's witnesses, particularly the repetitive and often graphic threats narrated by Finley, Nauman, McAllister and Grable. But the testimony of all these women was heavily discounted by their admitted bias against Mrs. George and their unreliability when straying from their rehearsed testimony. Pomerene, moreover, had put an actual drug addict on the stand to support the State's case. Worse yet, he had lost every important legal argument of the day. With the barring of Pontius and Smith's testimony about the suspicious stain on Mrs. George's hand and Van Horne's testimony about his jailhouse interview, the State was unable to present any evidence about Mrs. George's behavior or the evidence of her person from the moment of her arrest until she fell asleep in her cell early the next morning. Adding insult to injury, Judge Taylor had even prohibited Barr's testimony about the obscene letter — a documented misdeed for which the accused had actually been indicted (but not prosecuted or convicted).

Friday's revelations were a depressing spectacle, too, for respectable Cantonians. The acute Arthur Sperry articulated the exposure of the seamy underside of their community in a long feature article headlined:

Chapter 13   Sister Morphine

CANTON ALL AGHAST AT SENSATIONAL TESTIMONY
IN THE GEORGE CASE
SUGGESTIONS OF DEPRAVITY
IN THE EVIDENCE ARE STARTLING.
Mrs. Grable, An Alleged Opium Fiend,
On The Rack in Court

Sperry went on to wring his hands in feigned shock at what had been heard in court that day:

> What is making Canton gasp is the revelation of the social depravity of which they are trying to show Mrs. George was the center. The killing is only a part of it. Every man witness is asked to admit something dishonorable — every woman witness something disgraceful. One man, who had been a newspaper reporter in Canton, told glibly how he had tried to get something out of Mrs. George for the prosecuting attorney as a reporter while she was locked up. He said the prosecuting attorney got him to do this. A woman admitted she had used opium for years. She talked on the witness stand in the peculiar, husky voice of the opium fiend, a hoarseness that is different from any other. It seems to have nothing to do with a cold and to cause its victim no discomfort. It is what in the Tenderloin they call "the hop voice." "Hop" is Chinese slang for opium.

Friday evening Annie entertained a minor celebrity in her cell, Madame De Ovies. De Ovies — whatever her real name — had attended the trial for several days and had quite ingratiated herself with the defendant. Well known to her Cleveland patrons as a professional "clairvoyant," Mme. De Ovies now requested the great liberty of reading Annie's palm. Permission was granted and

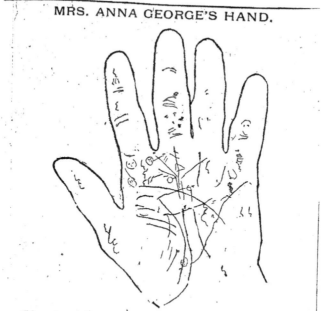

MRS. ANNA GEORGE'S HAND.

Cleveland Psycho-Palmist Discusses Her Fate.

While in her cell at Canton last Friday evening the above impression of the hand of Mrs. Anna George was taken by Mme. De Ovies, a psycho-palmist of this city. The impression is a remarkably plain one and the lines are brought out with great clearness. Not only do the various lines appear, but in many places are indications t likenesses of faces, which Mme De Ovies considers vital points in the make up of the palm. In the above illustration there are emphasized in order to illustrate more clearly at what parts of the palm they appear.

The flatness of the thumb and the long and lucky fate line are, according to Mme. De Ovies, indications that Mrs George will live to an old age. The heart line coming between the two fingers and her thumb denotes faithfulness in love. The head line having a loop running down on the mount of the moon, together with a very thick base of the thumb, shows an emotional tendency and in love uncontrollable. The loop in the headline, in Mme. De Ovies' opinion, suggests that the deep affection was not one of level-headedness.

The island in the fate line between thirty and forty, which appears the same on both hands, indicates some action over which no will power would have control and which fate could not thwart. The triangle on the fate line indicates a legal entanglement. Brevity is expressed in the shortness of the fingers and the little finger shows a natural inclination to language, diplomatic and good business ability. Some of the indications portrayed in the palms Mme. De Ovies refuses to disclose.

Mrs. George's Hand
(Cleveland Plain Dealer, April 21, 1899)

a cast of Annie's palm was successfully taken after some difficulty. Several days later Mme. De Ovies disclosed her analysis of Annie's palm to a *Cleveland Plain Dealer* correspondent. She initially coyly refused to say a word about it, expressing her earnest concern that her interpretation of Annie's character might affect the outcome of her trial. But she was eventually persuaded to unburden herself:

224

Chapter 13 Sister Morphine

When I visited Mrs. George in her cell I found her to be a charming woman and very refined. The thumb of her left hand shows that she comes from good blood. I cannot say very much regarding our interview as she needs protection in her case at this time, and for me to tell everything would be to do her an injustice, which I would no more do than would a lawyer disclose the secrets of his client. However, I would say that Mrs. George is of an artistic nature, with a wonderful ability as a lawyer. This I think is what makes her so cool and collected during the trial. She has an abnormal argumentative power and her fingers, which are short, show brevity. As a politician she has fine wire pulling ability. Her little finger shows her to have to a natural inclination to language, a good business ability and a diplomat. She is talented in art, music and literature. Her heart center line coming between her two fingers and her long thumb shows faithfulness in love, but an island on her fate line between thirty and forty on each hand shows that no will power could thwart fate in some action. Had she been a single woman she would have been in love with a married man and vice versa. She is inspirational; does things on the spur of the moment and her head line having a loop running down on the mount of the moon, together with a very thick base of the thumb, shows an emotional tendency and in love uncontrollable. Otherwise she is cool and calculating and about the only fault I could find portrayed in her hand was that she has an eye for money. By a close scrutiny of the hand one face may be seen showing out at many places. This, I think, proves her devotion to one person and with the loop in the head line this affection could not be a level headed one. Her thumb being flat denotes a lack of lasting revenge and her lucky fate line does not end until eighty years. The rest of the reading I am not at liberty to give out at this time. Mrs. George has the original chart and I do not think it would be justice to her to give out anything else that passed between us.

Chapter 14   The Unsmoking Gun

MRS. GEORGE APPEARS IN "A NEW HAT:

Mrs. George Appears in a New Hat
(Cleveland Daily World, April 19, 1899)

Mrs. George was observed to be in a cheerful mood when she entered the courtroom just before court opened on Saturday, April 15 at 8:30 a.m. Perhaps it was the bouquet of tea roses, a gift from Canton clairvoyant Madame Alma, handed to her by her friend Florence B. Klingler as she made her entrance. Just maybe, however, it was some foreknowledge of what was about to occur in Judge Taylor's courtroom.

The day began uneventfully enough with the remainder of Mattie Grimes' testimony. Nothing new was gained from Welty's cross-examination and the school teacher stepped down. Next up was Canton police officer E. E. Willis. He had guarded Mrs. George's cell on the morning after her arrest and Pomerene wanted him to testify about her behavior. The prosecutor also wished Willis to talk about Mrs. George's legal consultation with Mayor

Rice that same morning. Judge Taylor immediately ordered the reference to Mayor Rice stricken from the record, ruling that it was covered by the lawyer-client privilege. He did allow Willis to testify about how he had read newspaper accounts of the murder to Annie, and how she had asked him to skip over the descriptions of Saxton's wounds. But before Willis stepped down, Judge Taylor cautioned the jury directly that Annie's alleged comments constituted neither a "confession or even the semblance of a confession." Taylor then ordered virtually all of Willis' testimony stricken from the record.

Cora Oberlin, Annie's last landlady, entered the witness box. She told the jury about the circumstances of Annie's living in her home and her last conversation with her on the night before Saxton's murder. When she testified that there was nothing unusual about Annie's demeanor as she left the house the next morning, Pomerene decided her testimony needed some tweaking. He kept pushing Mrs. Oberlin to say that Annie was unusually quiet and thoughtful on the morning of Saxton's murder. Prompted by Welty's objections to such prodding, Judge Taylor intervened, demanding to know what the State was trying to prove with its questions. After listening to Pomerene's explanation, Judge Taylor sustained the objection, testily telling the prosecutor: "You are permitted to show that the accused was excited and all that sort of thing, but I never knew the rule to be stretched as far as you desire." Mrs. Oberlin was then allowed to restate her testimony that there was nothing unusual about Annie that day. She then stepped down from the stand.

"The State calls Mrs. Christina Eckroate to the stand." All heads in Judge Taylor's courtroom craned to see the woman who now trudged to the witness chair. Looking older than her 56 years, she was a stout woman, sharp-featured, pale and quite frail looking for all her bulk. Her voice was weak, high-pitched and tentative but her rapt audience hung on every word. Everyone present knew that the State's hopes in the George case now rested on the uncertain shoulders of this trembling old lady. Rumors had been percolating since her grand jury appearance that Mrs. Eckroate was the "mystery" eyewitness to the Saxton murder. It was said, moreover, that her husband Joseph might be the person Pomerene had accused of attempting to intimidate a State witness—her. Every ear in the courtroom strained to listen as Mrs. Eckroate began her testimony. It was often difficult to hear what she was saying, and Judge Taylor frequently had to request her to speak louder.

Speaking gently, Pomerene drew Mrs. Eckroate out, having her explain how she had come to be present near the scene of Saxton's death. She told the jury that she lived with her husband in their home across the street from Eva Althouse's residence. Joseph ran the grocery there with his son-in-law August Boron, and August and his wife Mary lived with the Eckroates. Mrs. Eckroate's stepdaughter, Mrs. Loretta Huwig of Cleveland, had also been present in the house that night.

Having established the setting, Pomerene now brought Annie George into the picture. Mrs. Eckroate explained that she known George Saxton and Mrs. Althouse by sight for some time before his murder. She had learned to recognize Mrs. George during Annie's campaign of harassment against Eva in early 1898. As she told the jury:

> I commenced to know her by sight at the time of the peace proceeding. I saw her about the Althouse home very often; several times after dark. I saw her once go to the door of the Althouse residence, rap on the door and call, "George, are you not through; will you not come out?" She would walk up and down in front of the Althouse residence when Saxton was there; then she would call for Mr. Saxton. Before the peace proceeding brought by Mrs. Althouse, I saw her out there a dozen times or more; one time I heard her talk to Mrs. Althouse and call her a bad name. I saw Mrs. George at Squire Robertson's office

at the time of the peace proceeding. I saw her after
that at the Althouse place.

The decisive moment had come, and Pomerene asked the
questions everyone had been waiting for:

"Where were you the night of Saxton's death?"

"I was at my home in the east side of the house. My daughter, Mrs. Boron lives in the house with us. I heard four shots."

"Where were you when you heard the first report?"

"At the supper table, in the east part of the house."

"Where were you when you heard the second?"

"In my bedroom."

"Where is your bedroom?"

"On the first floor, on the north side of the house.

"What did you see?"

"I took the screen out of the window and leaned out. I saw
a person stooping forward and saw two flashes of a revolver, fired
by the stooping figure. The shots seemed to be fired towards the
ground. The person walked slowly away. Then she turned back
and stooped as if to pick something up. Then the person turned
away again. I hurried out to my lawn and saw the person walking
towards the vacant lot. When she reached it she began to run and
disappeared through the lot."

"Did you know who the figure or person was which you
saw?"

"It was Mrs. George."

As expected, Welty shouted out an objection. He was immediately overruled without comment and Pomerene continued
his examination:

"You say you recognized the figure?"

"I recognized the figure. It was the same as I had before
seen in front of the home. It was Mrs. George. There was an electric light, but it did not shine brightly. There was a light in the
Glick house and in our store. I crossed the street and saw Mr.
Saxton on the sidewalk, lying on his face. The person who did the

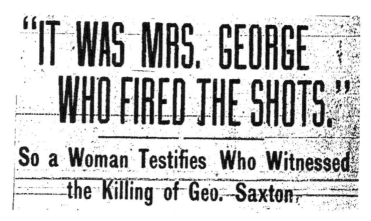

It Was Mrs. George Who Fired the Shots
(Cleveland Daily World, April 15, 1899)

shooting was dressed in dark clothes. As she turned into the vacant lot, it looked as though she threw a wrap across her arm." In response to another question from Pomerene, Christina clarified her memory with respect to the critical moment: "Just as the figure straightened up, after stooping over the body, the electric light flared up and I could tell the figure was Mrs. George."

John Welty took his time getting to the nub in his subsequent cross-examination of Christina Eckroate. He first asked her what the weather and visibility were like when she stared out her window at the Althouse steps. Mrs. Eckroate replied that it had rained that morning but she did not recall any rain later in the day. Welty questioned her closely on the lighting, and she insisted there was ample light shed by the nearest streetlamp (at the corner of West Third Street and Lincoln Avenue), an oil lamp shedding light through a window at the back of Eckroate's grocery store and light streaming from the windows of the Glick house at the corner. Prodded sharply by Welty, she eventually conceded that it was so dark that she didn't recognize Saxton's corpse until someone lit a match. She admitted that there were still leaves on the nearby trees but that enough of them had already fallen to make her rake her lawn. And anyway, it was the flash of the gun, Mrs. Eckroate insisted, that allowed her to see the shape of the shooter, if not her exact facial features.

Welty now turned to Mrs. Eckroate's acquaintance with Mrs. George.

"You never talked to Mrs. George?"

"No, sir."

"You date everything about her from the peace proceedings?"

"Yes, sir."

"You are not sure about the date of that?"

"No, sir."

"You are Mrs. Althouse's friend?"

"No, sir. We are acquainted, but seldom visited together."

"Did you not testify in the peace proceedings before Justice Robertson that you did not know Mrs. George; that you had not seen her before?"

"Yes; I had not seen her to know her."

Welty further elicited from Mrs. Eckroate that the window screen was made of wire netting and that the screen was secured to a nail. He then turned to the suspect chronology of Mrs. Eckroate's testimony:

"When did you first tell anybody that you thought it was Mrs. George?"

"I don't know whether I spoke of it that night or not."

"Isn't it a matter of fact that you didn't say anything about it for months?"

"I didn't tell it fully until they began looking up the case."

"Yes, and that was when the grand jury met?"

"It was sometime before that."

"You saw Mrs. Althouse when she came back?"

"I saw her sometimes."

"You talked with her about that night?"

"No."

"You don't mean to say you talked with her about the Saxton matter and not about that night?"

Mrs. Eckroate shook her head.

"There was no shooting when the figure came back?"

"Yes, sir."

"The figure seemed to stoop and then go away?"

"Yes, sir."

"Did you see the flash north or south of the steps?"

"South."

"Did you see the steps?"

"I did."

"It was a dark night; about the darkest you ever saw?"

"No, it wasn't."

"Was it light?"

"No."

"Well, how dark was it?"

"It was a pretty dark night."

Judge Taylor was irritated. "Oh, pass to something else," he told Welty. Welty was only too happy to oblige. As always, the defense team had done its homework well. Mrs. May Streeter, Annie's Columbus friend, had collected much gossip about likely State witnesses during her months in Canton and she had been especially curious about Mrs. Grable and Mrs. Eckroate. Welty now turned the arsenal of her findings to good account. Moving closer to the trembling Mrs. Eckroate, he asked:

"At the time of Saxton's murder you were then and had been for some time in the habit of eating morphine?"

"Yes sir."

"How long had you been eating it?"

"I have used it for nine or ten years. After treatment from Dr. Leninger, I only used it every other day for the last six months. I probably bought twenty-five or fifty cents, which lasts me a month."

"In what form do you eat it?"

"I have taken it in the form of a powder."

"You counseled with Dr. Leninger about taking you away to an institution to be cured, but before this was done the doctor died?"

"Yes, sir. The doctor died and my husband was not able to bear the expense."

"And you have been taking morphine out here in the witness room?"

"Yes, sir."

Mrs. Eckroate was in bad shape by the time Welty finished his cross-examination. Stammering out her answers, she seemed the very portrait of addled drug dependency he wanted the jury to see. Pomerene moved quickly to repair the damage to her credibility as he opened his redirect examination:

"Who has been doing your housework for the past four or five years?"

"I have."

"Has the morphine habit affected your mind?"

"Not in the least."

Welty objected. "The witness is not competent to answer the question." Judge Taylor turned to Pomerene. "Her condition of mind is a scientific question." Pomerene couldn't conceal his anger, sputtering, "Note an exception [i. e., grounds for appeal]! "Yes, note *two*," dryly retorted Judge Taylor.

Abandoning the question of her mental competence for the moment, Pomerene tried to firm up Mrs. Eckroate's identification of Annie as Saxton's shooter. Admirers of Mrs. George had often commented on her shapeliness and graceful motion, and Pomerene tried to capitalize on these perceptions:

"You said to the defense that you had recognized the figure by its form. Did you also notice her movements?"

"No, sir."

"You say you saw her turn."

Welty interjected sarcastically, "I object; we do not want to be called to answer for every graceful turn." Judge Taylor sustained the objection.

"Was she erect?"

"Yes, sir."

"Was she graceful in her movements?"

"Objection!" shouted Welty. He was again sustained and Pomerene relinquished his witness. During re-cross-examination Welty tried to shake Mrs. Eckroate on her identification of Mrs. George as the shooter. She wouldn't budge, insisting that she probably could have recognized the shape and form of Mrs. George even without the light of the revolver flashes. But Welty could take some consolation in the fact that his cross-examination had committed Mrs. Eckroate to a seeming inconsistency which would loom ever larger as the trial progressed: although she said she could only perceive the outline of the Althouse steps, she nonetheless insisted she could distinctly identify the form of Mrs. George at the same site.

Laura Huwig (*a.k.a.* Louisa or Loretta), Mrs. Eckroate's step-daughter, followed her on the stand. She explained to Pomerene that she had been visiting her family at their Lincoln Avenue home on the night of October 7. While in Mary Boron's kitchen about 6 p.m., she had heard two shots. They seemed to be coming from the west and she ran out of the house and stood by the front gate, peering west towards the Althouse residence:

> I saw a form facing north and some shots were fired north [indicating with her hand that the shots had been fired downward]. I saw a form walk down to the corner of the first vacant lot. Then the form returned to where I first saw it. This was at the Althouse steps. The form stooped down and then turned away and ran through the vacant lot south of the place. As she turned around she faced the grocery store. The form carried itself well and seemed not to be excited. The form was erect and tall and slender.

"Have you at any time since that night seen that person?" asked Pomerene.

"I cannot swear to that; I have seen the form—"

Welty objected that "form" was too vague a word. Judge Taylor sustained him and Pomerene continued:

"Have you seen Mrs. George since?"

"I saw her in the court room; I saw her again in the back room of the court house."

Pomerene here tried several more questions about the form Huwig had seen. All of them were objected to and ruled out by Judge Taylor until:

"Have you since seen the form of a person who resembled that person out there?"

"I have."

"Have you seen a person of about the height of the person you saw out there?"

"I have."

"Have you seen a person who resembles in figure and carriage the one you saw out there; and where?"

"Yes, sir; once in the court room and once in the back room of the court house?

"And who is the person thus resembling the one you saw?"

"Mrs. George, the defendant."

Welty objected but was overruled. Pomerene turned the witness over to him just before the lunch recess. Although Huwig had used the abstract word "form" to describe the figure she saw by the Althouse steps, Welty was only too aware that she had also used the pronoun "she" several times in describing the figure by the body who ran from the scene. Querying her carefully, he finally got her to hedge on the gender of the shooter:

I would not swear that the person who did the shooting was a woman. It might have been a man, wearing a long mackintosh coat. When the person who did the shooting ran away I could not swear whether it was a man or a woman. I saw only one form.

Sterling picked up Huwig's cross-examination when court resumed at 1 p.m. Saturday. In response to his questions about the lighting at the murder scene, Huwig stated it was rather dark; she thought it was cloudy. She could not swear that it was a woman. Indeed, even without Sterling prompting her, she eventually conceded that it might even have been a man in woman's clothing. Huwig also remembered that she—Sterling interrupted her, insisting she call it "the form," not "she"—the form had not walked rapidly as it left the scene. She did not know what kind of lamp was burning in the grocery store but she recalled that it threw a dim light across the street.

Welty now took over from Sterling and brought up a subject that, oddly, had not been raised with Christina Eckroate. Referring to the window through which Christina had peered at the murder scene, he asked Mrs. Huwig, "When you look through that window, don't you look through a peach tree?" Laura brushed off the question, stating that she had looked through it just that morning and clearly seen the Althouse steps. The tree in question was, in fact, a one-foot wide cherry tree, not a peach tree. Welty dropped the matter for the moment but it would loom large before he was finally done with it.

Eva Althouse's brother J. G. Best testified next. Examined by Grant, he stated that his sister Eva was at his home at 1021 North Walnut Street from 5 to 7 p.m. on the night of October 7. Welty objected to the testimony as irrelevant and was overruled. Mrs. J. G. Best then testified, corroborating her husband's testimony. Welty again objected and was overruled. The State then recalled Post Office money order clerk Michael Barr to the stand. In response to Pomerene's questions, Barr satisfied Judge Taylor that he was actually qualified to identify Mrs. George's handwriting. He was ready to do so but his testimony was reserved for later and he stepped down. police officer Henry Piero was then recalled for additional testimony. The only interesting point revealed by him came during cross-examination, when he admitted that since his previous appearance Pomerene had sent him to interrogate some of the witnesses subpoenaed for the defense. Frank O'Wesney was briefly examined by Grant. O'Wesney, a fireman at the pumping station of the Canton city water works, had been on duty and sitting outside it between 6:00 and 6:45 p.m. on October 7. From his vantage point he had had a clear view of the vicinity of the West Third Street-Lincoln Avenue intersection. He now testified that he had seen no one pass through the area during the interval he was watching it. O'Wesney said that it had rained that day and the ground was wet.

At this juncture Grant requested that the legal record of Saxton's injunction barring Anna from the Saxton block be entered into evidence. The presumable motive of the prosecution was to further document Anna's hostile behavior to Saxton. But the defense objected and Judge Taylor ruled it out, probably because of its remoteness in time from Saxton's murder.

Prosecutor Pomerene now called William J. Hasler to the stand. His appearance was eagerly anticipated by the courtroom audience. Although it was not as crucial to Mrs. George's fate as Christina Eckroate's eyewitness identification, it promised lurid hints of scandal at the highest level of Canton officialdom. Pomerene and Grant had been claiming for months that the civil and police authorities of the city had been dragging their feet in the Saxton murder investigation. Now they put the ex-police sergeant on the stand to offer testimony that ex-Mayor Rice had suppressed evidence and obstructed justice in the case. Hasler's story lived up to Arthur Sperry's characterization of it as "about as weird as a man ever told in a murder case."

Pomerene began his examination by having Hasler tell the jury about his acquaintance with Mrs. George. He related that the previous summer he had responded to a call from Mrs. George for police aid. She was living in a room on Walnut Street and when Hasler arrived, Annie had asked him to arrest Saxton and Althouse at the latter's home, where they were involved in illicit relations. Annie had told Sergeant Hasler that he could gain unobserved entrance to Eva's house through a coal chute; she said she had done it herself. Understandably, Hasler had declined to arrest Saxton and Eva and left Annie's room.

At this point Pomerene encountered some difficulty. He wanted to explain just *why* Hasler had gone to search for the alleged murder weapon in an obscure place on the night of October 10. Everyone knew that it was Hasler's contention that it was his titular boss (and also Annie George's lawyer), Mayor James Rice, who had privately commanded him to do so. But every time Pomerene mentioned Rice's name Welty objected and Judge Taylor sustained him, saying, "The testimony is excluded on the grounds that the accused cannot be bound by the statements of another, no matter who, when she is not present." Judge Taylor consistently and frequently renewed his ruling excluding any mention of Mayor Rice during the rest of the trial, which put Pomerene on the horns of a unpleasant dilemma: he could not have the State witnesses talk about Rice — yet he knew that if he tried to subpoena Rice as a witness the ex-Mayor could successfully evade testifying by invoking his privilege as counsel to Mrs. George. Hoping that the jury might apprehend Rice's involvement by context, Pomerene led Hasler to the corner of High and South Streets on the night of October 10:

"What did you do?"

"I went to the walk at the northeast corner."

"What, if any, search did you make there?"

"I felt under the walk for what I was sent after."

Welty here objected to the last four words of Hasler's answer and was sustained.

"What did you find?"

"A revolver."

"What did you do with the revolver afterwards?"

"Brought it to the city hall."

"What did you do with it afterwards?"

THE REVOLVER.

Sergeant Hasler's Famous Revolver
(Cleveland Daily World, April 19, 1899)

"I took it home, put it in a stocking and concealed it between the plastering and the floor in the garret."

"How long did you have the revolver?"

"From October 10 to January 10."

"Then what did you do with it?"

"Gave it to Prosecutor Pomerene."

Pomerene's interrogation here entered the phase of his own involvement, putting him on more perilous ground:

"After this did you at any time see Mrs. George?"

"Once, in the prison."

"When?"

"March 24."

Welty jumped to his feet, interrupting Pomerene and putting every ounce of incredulity he could muster into his voice. "You were sent to the jail by the prosecutor?!"

"Yes, sir."

"To try and entrap Mrs. George?"

"I went there to talk with her."

"You were sent there to secure if possible some evidence against Mrs. George?"

"I was sent there for that purpose."

Pomerene reclaimed his witness:

"What happened when you visited Mrs. George?"

"I asked her, 'What shall I do with that revolver you hid under the culvert and which Rice sent me after?'"

Welty again objected and the last five words of Hasler's answer were stricken from the record.

"And what did Mrs. George say?"

"She said, 'See Welty, and then I will see you again.'"

Would you recognize that revolver if you saw it again?"

"Yes."

"Were there any cartridges in the revolver when you found it?" asked Pomerene.

"No, it was empty."

Not surprisingly, Welty's cross-examination was savage. The defense attorney had hardly been gentle with several of the State's timorous female witnesses and he took the gloves off entirely with the burly Hasler. He focused his attack on Hasler's motive in concealing his knowledge of the alleged murder weapon for three months.

"You did deny that you had the gun?" barked Welty.

"I did deny it to Mayor Rice."

Welty turned to Judge Taylor. "Objection." Judge Taylor again ordered Rice's name expunged from the record.

"You never told a living soul about it?"

"I told my brother-in-law Mont but no one else."

Hasler went on to explain that he had concealed the finding of the revolver until his unsuccessful race for the Democratic nomination for Canton marshal was over. He said he was afraid that it would hurt him politically and that Mayor Rice would fire him from the police force if the gun story got out. He said he had intended to keep the revolver story a secret even longer but it had leaked out before the trial. Hasler lost his cool when Welty accused him of not telling the truth about his real motive, finally provoking Hasler to shout, "You said I lied!" "I did not," said

Welty cuttingly, "but I might have." But Welty saved his final blow for last:

"You are in the pay of the State, are you not? You resigned from the police force because you were told you would be paid right along? Is that not true?"

It took some time but Welty eventually made Hasler admit that Pomerene had assured him that he would be paid for his trial time by the county commissioners if he so wished. Hasler's cross-examination was still underway when Court adjourned for the day at 3 p.m. Judge Taylor's last act was to command that any previous testimony indicating that Mayor Rice was Mrs. George's counsel be stricken from the record.

It had been another great day for the defense. Welty and Sterling had once again turned the State's own witnesses against them. Two alleged eyewitnesses had identified the killer not so much as Mrs. George, but rather as a silhouette or figure resembling her. And one of the eyewitnesses had possibly been discredited as an unreliable drug addict. Ex-Sergeant Hasler, moreover, was a witness of murky motives and dubious plausibility and the State had failed—it had not really even attempted—to connect Hasler's revolver with Mrs. George. Indeed, the State had not even presented evidence that Anna possessed a revolver at the time of Saxton's killing, much less the one discovered by Hasler. And while the State had been unsuccessful at dragging ex-Mayor Rice into the fray, Pomerene had once again been pilloried as less than honorable in his attempts to entrap Mrs. George.

If it was a bad day for the State, it remained another salad day for the media. That evening's edition of the *Canton Evening Repository* crowed that that the twelve correspondents covering the trial were sending out at least 10,000 words of coverage a day over the telegraph wires—and the local Western Union office had been forced to hire extra telegraph operators and messengers. It was the greatest volume of media attention focused on Canton since McKinley's 1896 front-porch presidential campaign. Rising public interest in the trial was also taxing the space of the courtroom and the endurance of its avid spectators. The *Repository* reported that only those who arrived early in the morning could now gain access to Canton's most entertaining spectacle. It was also noted that the lengthy trial had already consumed 700 pages and 18,000 words of stenographic testimony.

Annie George passed an uneventful Sunday in the Stark County jail. Arising at a leisurely hour, she dressed late and then attended the biweekly religious services in the lower jail corridor, the sole female among the ten prisoners. Afterwards she received reporters graciously in her cell. She made her usual good impression and was careful to reiterate her abhorrence to profaning the Sabbath by discussing her case with her attorneys.

Chapter 15   The State Rests

The expectation that the State would finish presenting its case on Monday produced a packed courtroom when Judge Taylor opened the proceedings on April 17 at 10:00 a.m. Courtroom seats were particularly competitive thanks to rumors that Cleveland detective Jake Mintz might testify that day. It was supposed that his testimony would be particularly lurid, exposing the sordid details of Saxton's alleged plots to incriminate, discredit, kidnap or even do away with Annie George.

Welty resumed his cross-examination of ex-Sergeant Hasler, energetically chipping away at his diminishing credibility. He began by insinuating that Hasler and the prosecution were joined at the hip:

"Since the adjournment, Saturday, did you talk to any one about this case?"

"Only with the lawyers," Hasler hesitatingly replied.

"What lawyers?"

"Mr. Pomerene and Mr. Grant, in Mr. Grant's office; Policeman Rohn came after me Sunday night."

Welty then revisited Hasler's motives in the case.

"When did you tell your brother-in-law Mont about the gun?"

"The morning of January 10."

"You and he had been unfriendly?"

"Not for the last three or four years."

"You know he used his influence with the commissioners and wanted them to have a reward offered for the finding of the gun?"

"No sir. I know he is agent for the Wrought Iron Bridge Co. and had business with the commissioners."

"You know that Mont went to the commissioners and tried to have a reward offered?"

"No I didn't."

Welty here sought to have Hasler contradict some of his Saturday statements. He eventually rattled Hasler to the point where the ex-policeman asked plaintively, "Mr. Welty, what do you want me to say?"

"The truth, if I can get it."

After another such exchange, Hasler blurted out:

"I don't know what you are talking about half of the time."

Welty again roasted Hasler for acting as Pomerene's tool in attempting to entrap Mrs. George on March 24:

"When you told Mrs. George you had the revolver and asked what to do with it you lied to her didn't you; you knew you didn't have it?"

"I didn't tell her I had; I told I had found it."

"Didn't she tell you that she didn't talk to anyone about her case; to go to her attorneys?"

"No, she didn't use those words. She did tell me to see Mr. Welty."

"Why didn't you take the gun with you?"

"She might have shot me."

Welty couldn't resist mocking Hasler. "What — shoot a big policeman like you, and with a gun that wasn't loaded; didn't even have the blank cartridges?" As the courtroom spectators laughed, Welty turned Hasler over to Pomerene for redirect testimony. The chief prosecutor was weary of Hasler's hapless foundering, so most of his brief interrogation was confined to clearing himself of the imputation that he had bribed Hasler to testify against Mrs. George:

"What was said between you and me about pay?"

Welty objected and the question was stricken.

"Was there any promise of pay made?"

"No sir."

Pomerene now asked that the revolver be introduced as evidence. Welty and Sterling simultaneously shouted out their objection. The revolver was produced in court and Pomerene pulled it out of its stocking. It was then positively identified by

Hasler and entered into evidence. Welty objected and was over-ruled by Judge Taylor, who stated that it was up to the jury to decide what weight as evidence the revolver should be given. It was a .38-caliber, single action weapon. It was noticeably muddy. After examining it carefully, Welty placed the gun on the table next to Mrs. George. She had dropped her eyes to the table when it was taken out of the stocking and kept her eyes averted from it for the rest of the day.

After Hasler left the stand Pomerene made another attempt to introduce Mrs. George's obscene and threatening letter to Eva Althouse. Welty insisted that before the prosecutor did so that the defense be allowed to cross-examine Michael Barr. Barr testified that he had first seen the letter when the grand jury in Cleveland investigated it. He had seen it opened there but he admitted to Welty that he had no certain knowledge that it was in its original envelope. Barr was certain, however, that the letter was in Mrs. George's handwriting. After listening to arguments from both sides, Judge Taylor ruled out the letter as evidence, explaining:

> The objection to the admission of the letter as evidence is for the present sustained, not on the ground that the witness has not proved himself capable of identifying the handwriting, but to have this letter admitted it must be shown it was not only written by the accused but by her placed in the envelope and put into circulation by her. It must also be shown the letter was received by somebody at some time and place. There has been no testimony to show any of these things.

"Well, but wouldn't it show the frame of mind the defendant was in?" pleaded Pomerene. Judge Taylor slammed that door with the withering comment, "It would not show anything, not any more than a dream."

John S. Hoover, the Stark County surveyor, was recalled by Pomerene. He brought with him a revised version of the chart that had been ruled out of evidence during his previous appearance. Telling the jury that the revised chart was based on actual measurements he had subsequently taken at the scene, he explained its features at some length. When Welty cross-examined him, he immediately zeroed in on the 12-inch wide cherry tree shown on

THAT MUCH TALKED OF CHERRY TREE.
The World staff artist took the exact position which Mrs. Eckroate, who says she saw the shooting, occupied that night. The dotted lines indicate leaves.

The Controversial Cherry Tree
(Cleveland Daily World, April 22, 1899)

the front lawn of the Eckroate house. Pointing out that it seemed to be in the direct line of vision between the Althouse steps and the window through which Christina Eckroate had allegedly seen the killer, Welty asked Hoover whether the cherry tree blocked the line of vision from the window to the steps:

"Well," conceded Hoover, "it is very crooked."

"Which way does it lean?" persisted Welty.

"It leans forty ways for Sunday," replied Hoover.

Welty continued boring in on the cherry tree until he got Hoover to admit that while he was measuring the distance between the window and the Althouse steps his tape had actually touched the cherry tree--evidence that the tree blocked a straight line of vision from the window to the steps. After more argument from Welty, Judge Taylor overruled defense objections and Hoover's plat map was at last accepted into evidence.

Canton Police officer Uriah Henry testified next. He was expected to corroborate Hasler's story about finding the revolver on the evening of October 10. But Henry had not actually been with Hasler when he found it and most of his testimony describing where they went that evening was stricken from the record as irrelevant.

Grant next recalled Nettie McAllister to the stand. He had listened for a tiresome week as many of the State's own witnesses were prodded to repeat a damning list of George Saxton's alleged offenses against Mrs. George. His kindred strategy now was to undermine Annie's character with testimony that she had been sexually involved with other men while supposedly carrying her torch for Saxton. He asked McAllister:

"You were asked the other day if Mrs. George didn't tell you that Saxton was paying her board in 1897. What else was said in that conversation?"

Welty objected. Judge Taylor queried Grant, "What do you expect to show by testimony about that conversation?" Grant replied, "We expect to show what was said as to why he didn't pay her board after 1897." Judge Taylor immediately ruled out the conversation, stating explicitly that he would not allow testimony about the relations of either Saxton or Mrs. George with persons other than Eva Althouse. This seemingly impartial policy was a key blow to the State's case and it would reverberate throughout the remaining testimony in the trial.

Augusta Susky's testimony was a welcome respite for the prosecution. A resident of Lawn Avenue (one block west of Lincoln Avenue and parallel to it), she had been walking home from her downtown job in a millinery store at the time of Saxton's murder. She told the jury that she had left work at 5:30 p.m., accompanied by her sister Louisa, and walked west on Tuscarawas Street, turning north on Hazlette Avenue (one block east of Lincoln Avenue). As they walked up Hazlette she heard three shots. A little while later, as they walked by the Bederman house near the corner of West Third Street and Lincoln Avenue, she heard two more shots. Drawn by curiosity, they went over to Lincoln Avenue and saw the crowd standing by Saxton's body across the street. Augusta testified that it was a dark evening but that she had had a very clear view of West Third Street and Lincoln Avenue as far north as the Althouse residence. She insisted that she could have seen anyone on the street but no person had passed from the time she and her sister turned onto Hazlette Avenue until they saw the crowd by the Althouse steps. Welty couldn't shake Augusta during his initial cross-examination. Although she admitted that it was a dark night, she also stuck to her story that she could see objects distinctly at the time. And when Pomerene questioned her in redirect, she named several men by name she had clearly recognized in the crowd by Saxton's body, even from across the street. To the prosecutor's chagrin, however, Welty's re-cross-examination exposed Augusta's misidentification of some of the men at the murder scene.

Louisa Susky followed her sister on the stand and corroborated virtually every detail of her testimony. She said there was light shed on the murder scene, both from the electric street lamp at the corner and from windows in the Glick house, just north of the Althouse residence. She named several persons whom she had recognized in the crowd while standing across the street. She said she could also see Saxton's body lying on the sidewalk.

Sterling cross-examined Louisa Susky. He focused on the lighting at the scene, asking Louisa, "Didn't they light matches to see whose body it was? Why was that necessary if it was light enough to see across the street?" Susky replied that Saxton's face was turned downward, making it difficult to identify him even if you were close. But before she left the stand, Sterling's interrogation revealed that Louisa, like her sister, had misidentified some of the men at the scene of Saxton's killing.

Although the examination of the Susky sisters was conducted with relative civility, it occasioned the usual petty sniping between the attorneys for the State and the defense. While Augusta was being examined by Pomerene, it was noticed that prosecutor Grant was not in the court room. When someone wondered aloud where he was, Sterling quipped, *sotto voce*, "Oh, he is out there drilling witnesses." Sterling, in fact, was telling the bald truth: at that very moment Grant was rehearsing State witness Mary Glick for her upcoming appearance on the stand.

The testimony of the pretty Susky sisters was, on balance, a plus for the State's case. With no apparent ulterior motives or any obvious animus against the accused, their testimony was plain, detailed and convincing, especially after the nervous implausibility of William Hasler and the conflicting opinions of other State witnesses about the visibility at the murder scene. Their failure to see anyone while walking south of the murder scene seemed to preclude the possibility that Saxton's assassin had fled far in that direction. The only problematic elements of their testimony were their misidentification of several witnesses and their insistence that they had heard three shots, followed, after an interval, by two more. Every other witness who had thus far testified had sworn that there were two initial shots, followed by two more. More puzzling still was the novel chronology offered by the Susky sisters. Previous witnesses had estimated the time between the first shots and the last two as no more than thirty seconds. But if Augusta and Louisa had walked the distance up Hazlette Avenue to West Third Street to which they had testified, the interval between shots must have been considerably longer.

After recess for lunch, the State called Mary Glick to the stand. A housewife who lived in the house just north and next door to Eva Althouse, Glick had been home on the murder night and had run to her parlor window after hearing two shots outside. She couldn't see anything significant, but testified there had been an electric lamp burning in the front room of her house and that its rays had extended out onto the Althouse lawn. Glick could not say whether the light reached as far as the Althouse front steps on the night of Saxton's murder.

Welty tangled sharply with Glick during her cross-examination. Contrary to his previous practice, he wanted her to say that there was ample light shed through her parlor window, which would imply that she would have seen any killer fleeing past her house. Welty didn't succeed, but he certainly demonstrated that Pomerene and Grant were not the only lawyers coaching their witnesses:

MRS. MARY GLICK.

Mrs. Mary Glick
(Cleveland Daily World, April 18, 1899)

"One night last week I was at your house and Brother Sterling was with me?"

"Yes, sir," replied Glick.

"You put the lamp where it was the night of the death?"

"Yes sir."

"We tested what could be seen from across the street and you said you could recognize anyone?"

"No sir; you are trying to make me say what I didn't say."

"Didn't Brother Sterling put a handkerchief on his head so we could see him?"

"You didn't ask me to recognize him; you asked me if I could see the handkerchief, and I could."

Having Eva Althouse's next-door neighbor on the stand, Welty tried to question her about Saxton's alleged illicit relations with Eva Althouse:

"Did you ever hear rackets over at the Althouse residence?"

"Yes."

"Did you see washing on the line over there?"

"Yes sir."

"There was men's clothing on the line, wasn't there?"

Pomerene roared out his objection and Welty's question was stricken from the record.

Returning to the subject of the parlor window lamp, Welty got Glick to admit that she had noticed since the murder that the light from her front window did not extend *quite* as far as the Althouse steps. During Pomerene's redirect examination, however, Glick volunteered the interesting observation that just the previous morning she had stood at Christina Eckroate's window and had been able to obtain a clear view of the Althouse steps. Welty understandably made a vigorous objection to her statement, arguing that the conditions of the previous morning were not the same as on the night of October 7. Judge Taylor sustained the objection, noting that the witness's line of vision would have passed close by the controversial cherry tree, whose now bare boughs would likely have been covered with rain-laden leaves on the night of Saxton's death.

Mary Boron testified after Mary Glick. Her brief testimony was elicited by Pomerene to support her mother Christina Eckroate's assertion that she had enjoyed a clear view of the Althouse steps. Mary testified that the back north window opened easily and that its screen was easily detached from its securing nail. She insisted that there were no trees blocking a direct view of the Althouse steps, and that the branches of the cherry tree were too low to obstruct the line of sight. Mary added that just that morning she had made the experiment anew and had seen the steps quite clearly. Her remarks about the current view were stricken from the record and she stepped down, if nothing else a fine exemplar of filial behavior.

The State's attorneys moved quickly now to wrap up their testimony. Quavering Mary Finley was recalled to identify the obscene letter as being written and mailed by Mrs. George. She was no more successful than Michael Barr and her testimony was ultimately eclipsed during Welty's cross-examination by ineffectual but acrid sniping between him and Grant over the admissibility of the letter. After several minutes of such sparring, Judge Taylor noted that he still judged the letter inadmissible but pointedly warned Welty that he might change his mind "by the time this cross-examination is completed." "Perhaps I had better quit," quipped Welty and shrewdly sat down.

Finley was followed by former Justice of the Peace James H. Robertson, who had examined the obscene letter while presiding over Annie's peace proceeding. His testimony did not persuade Judge Taylor to allow the letter into evidence, nor did that of United States Post Office Inspector Alonzo P. Owens during his brief appearance on the stand. Owens testified that he had seen the letter in the hand of George Saxton in 1897. But he could not tie the letter strongly enough to Mrs. George to satisfy Judge Taylor and he sustained the defense objection to admitting the letter in evidence. Its ultimate suppression was surely a disappointment to Pomerene, as it was described by a *Cleveland Plain Dealer* reporter as a "sulphur hued epistle, [which] contained many unprintable expressions and words."

The State now offered into evidence Dr. Pontius' packet of burrs and Spanish needles collected from Mrs. George's dress. Predictably, Judge Taylor sustained defense objections that it had been obtained from the accused under duress. Moreover, the judge opined, in ruling it out, that it was inadmissible because the burrs and needles were now matted together and not in the same condition as when removed from Mrs. George's dress.

When Pomerene announced that the State had no more witnesses to call, Welty requested that W. O. Werntz, Charles Dickerhoff and Charles Frazer be recalled for additional cross-examination. Pomerene objected but the procedural decision was at the discretion of the court and Judge Taylor told defense counsel to proceed. So Sterling once again led Werntz through his recollections of Annie's manner when she ranted about her sufferings at Saxton's hands. Werntz said her face became noticeably flushed and she gesticulated wildly when she talked about Saxton's wrongs. This emphasis on Annie's overwrought behavior renewed suspicions among trial observers that her lawyers were preparing a defense of emotional insanity. Once more, during his redirect examination, Pomerene couldn't resist trying to drag Mayor Rice's name into the record, and once more Judge Taylor excluded any mention of him as Mrs. George's quondam counsel.

After it was announced that Charles Dickerhoff could not be located, the defense finished with a recall appearance by Charles Frazer. Sterling wanted Frazer to testify that it had been very dark at the scene of Saxton's murder. He was quite unsuccessful:

"The night you went after Saxton's body, wasn't it so dark that when you lost your hat you had to light a match?"

"No sir."

"Did you use a lantern to find it?"

"No sir."

The State rested its case at exactly 3:25 p.m. It seemed to observers that the crowd was disappointed by the anti-climatic conclusion of the prosecution's case. "Never," noted seasoned trial scribe Arthur Sperry, "did a murder case close less sensationally."

Immediately after Pomerene's announcement, the defense called the first of its 126 witnesses. (Before the trial was over the defense would subpoena an even 150 witnesses.) The courtroom crowd, already deflated by Pomerene's weak finish, must have been further disappointed by Welty and Sterling's mundane beginning. They had hoped for Jake Mintz; what they got was a reading of Abraham Goldberg's deposition. Pomerene first objected to its being heard or entered into evidence. His stated reason was that the time covered by Goldberg's testimony was too remote from Saxton's murder. Pomerene's real reason, of course, was that he that he knew Goldberg's recollections covered only the period of Annie's seduction. The State's chief prosecutor was in no mood to hear yet another pity-provoking narrative of Annie's ruined innocence. But Judge Taylor ruled otherwise, stating that if the defense wished to show Mrs. George's irrational state at the time of the murder as potential evidence of insanity, it would be proper "to show the relations between parties, that it may be established whether or not there is reason for the insanity or frenzy claimed." Throwing salt on Pomerene's legal wound, Judge Taylor added that "it was proper in this case to show the relations by testimony for the defense, because the State had all along shown the relations claimed between the accused, Mrs. Althouse and Saxton." Interestingly, at least to the lawyers present in the courtroom, Judge Taylor based his ruling in part on a precedent cited initially by the defense, the Barberi case in New York City. Maria Barberi [Barbella] was a girl who had murdered the man who seduced and betrayed her, and a key judicial ruling in the appeal of that case had allowed the ventilation of the sordid facts of their relationship.

Abraham Goldberg and his brother Jacob had run their dry goods store in the Saxton block from its opening in 1881 until their move to Detroit in 1892. Abraham's deposition, taken before notary public George P. Codd and based on questions submitted by Pomerene and Welty, documented his memories about the relations between Saxton and Mrs. George. Actually, if Abraham was telling the truth in his deposition, he didn't remember much. He could not even recall seeing Saxton in the George family flat on the third floor of the Saxton block during the early period of their alleged relations. He did recall Annie's return to the block in the spring of 1890 and her leaving for Dakota in October of the following year. During that latter period Goldberg had had occasion to consult with Annie about cloaks she was altering for his firm and he often saw Saxton in her second-floor rooms. Reflecting most likely his own business habits, Abraham had seen Saxton in Annie's rooms only twice at night. His characterization of their relations did not bespeak a perception of grand passion:

> It appeared to me that he was very friendly to her and was very solicitous as to her having pleasant times and spoke to me frequently about it. I remember especially one occasion when I was going to Cleveland and he heard about it, he came to me and asked me to take her with me and see that she had a pleasant time.

Goldberg stated further that he had never seen Mrs. George sitting on the lap or knee of Saxton. He said he had never seen them going out driving together and he knew nothing of any presents Saxton might have given her.

Many of Pomerene's questions submitted at Abraham's deposition had probed possible bias Abraham might have harbored toward George Saxon, even accusing him of having threatened Saxton with exposure of his private life:

"Are you not one of the defendants in the suit which was formerly brought by George D. Saxton against yourself and others at the firm of Goldberg Brothers?"

"Yes."

"Is it not a fact that after George D. Saxton had sued you and your brothers as the firm of Goldberg Brothers you then pretended or offered to tell the matters which you have stated in your examination herein in chief?"

"No sir."

"While the jury was out considering their verdict in the suit of Saxton vs. Goldberg Brothers, did you not say to Attorney James Grant that you would do George Saxton all the harm you could in this law suit with Sample C. George or words to that effect?"

"Never; no sir."

"Did you not entertain some feeling towards George D. Saxton after he instituted the lawsuit against your firm?"

"None at all; we were the best of friends."

"Do you not now entertain some feeling against him?"

"No, sir."

While Goldberg's deposition was read, Annie stared downward at the table, her face visibly twitching with distress as the ecstasy and shame of her early days with Saxton were recalled.

When court adjourned for the day Pomerene tried to put a brave face on the State's case for inquiring reporters. "The State is very well satisfied with the case it has presented," he exulted confidently. "Yes, it is true that some things we had hoped to introduce were excluded, but we do not view any of these in a serious light. We think we have made a clear case." But Arthur Sperry's evaluation in the following day's *Cleveland Evening World* offered a more accurate judgment of the totality of seven days' testimony by State witnesses. Sperry tried to imagine the current state of the case from Annie's point of view:

[Mrs. George's face reflected] satisfaction, surprise and interest. It seemed as though she were saying to herself, "Well, they have got me within three squares of the killing and within a few minutes of the time it was done. They have found a revolver that they couldn't prove was mine, or had ever been mine, or that I had ever seen. They have not even proved that I had a revolver at the time of the crime. They have not proved the revolver that was found under the sidewalk was the one with which George Saxton was killed. They have not proved that the bullet that inflicted the fatal wound was fired from the same sized revolver that the others were, though the three other wounds were inflicted with a revolver the same caliber as the one found under the sidewalk. They tried to get in as evidence against me a letter, but they were not able to get either the letter or its contents admitted. They have proved that I made threats against Saxton but that is not proving that I carried them out. They have put on the stand a witness who says she saw me shoot Saxton, but that witness must have looked through a cherry tree on a dark night to see it, as my lawyers have proved. They have proved that I was looking for George Saxton that night, but they have proved, too, that I looked for him many other nights. And then, after they have proved that and nothing more, the prosecution rests.

The evening after the State rested, the newspaper correspondents covering the trial took another informal vote on the probable verdict. It showed five for outright acquittal, one first-degree murder with a recommendation of mercy, three for manslaughter and three for a hung jury.

Chapter 16   Mrs. George's Defense

Another large crowd packed Judge Taylor's courtroom to capacity as court opened on Tuesday morning, April 18 at 8:30. Welty was being quoted on the street to the effect that the defense would complete its testimony in three days, and the most faithful trial spectators were anxious not to miss a moment of it. The crowd at the door of courtroom No. 2 was even larger than usual, as the entrance of spectators was barred until most of the witnesses called by the defense had been sworn in. Mrs. George was attired in a crowd-pleasing outfit featuring a white waist with purple stripes and a white sailor hat with a black band and jaunty turkey feather.

Most of Tuesday morning was consumed with John Welty's dry recitation of the depositions taken concerning Annie's early relations with George Saxton. The first deposition the jury heard was that of Jacob Goldberg, the brother of Abraham Goldberg. Jacob's memories of Annie and Saxton's relationship were much the same as his brother's. His most specific recollection was of the day Saxton first spied Annie in the Goldberg's store and stated his intention of getting to know that "deuced pretty woman." As with Abraham, most of Jacob's testimony concerned the period after Sample C. George had left and Annie had moved into rooms across from Saxton's private quarters on the second floor of the Saxton block. Jacob testified that he had often seen Saxton in Annie's rooms. He had never seen her sitting on Saxton's knee and he did not recall Saxton taking her out driving in his rig. Jacob couldn't recall Saxton giving Annie specific presents, although on occasion Annie would flourish a wad of cash and boast that Saxton had given it to her. Most interestingly, Jacob declined to say a negative word about anyone involved in the Saxton-Sample-Annie triangle. He denied under oath that Annie had ever complained to him that her husband was harsh or cruel to her or that he was of a jealous disposition. And he had never heard Sample and Annie quarreling during their residence together in the Saxton block.

The live testimony of United States government weather observer Charles F. Stokey provided a welcome break in the monotonous reading of the depositions. Stokey had held his position since 1886 and the defense badly wanted his testimony to support their contention that it was muddy throughout Canton on the night of October 7. Stokey testified that there had been rainfall amounting to .06 of an inch between 9 a.m. and 2 p.m. on October 7, 1898. There had been another .015 inch of rain between 2 p.m. and 9 p.m. and the sky had been overcast. Welty pressed Stokey hard to make him say that there was a general muddiness resulting from the rain, prompting Pomerene's strenuous protest. Judge Taylor sustained the prosecutor's objection, chiding Welty, "If you intend to go at your proof in this roundabout way you will not get through until the middle of July." He went on to say that proof of muddiness would have to be made by persons familiar with the specific route said to have been taken by Mrs. George on that night.

The defense now turned to documenting its contention that George Saxton had treated Annie as a virtual wife before callously discarding her without cause. The deposition of Robert Hunter was read into the record. Hunter, a lawyer of Sioux City, Iowa had apparently been working as an investigator for N. E. Rudolph, the lawyer handling Sample C. George's interests in Annie's Dakota divorce suit. Hunter testified that he had stopped at the Booge House Hotel in Sioux City several times in 1892 while on the track of Annie and Saxton's movements. On March 10, 1892, he had examined the hotel register, where he found a "George D. Saxton and wife, Canton" enrolled for Room 20 under the date of February 16. Hunter had made a tracing of that registration and he had seen the original again in April, 1892. When he returned in July of that year, however, he found that the page containing Saxton and Annie's registration had been cut out of the register. Hunter's tracing had shortly thereafter been used as evidence in Annie's divorce suit. The tracing was attached to Hunter's deposition and Welty now asked Judge Taylor to enter it into the record as evidence. Pomerene objected, citing the doubtful authenticity and uncertain provenance of the tracing and Judge Taylor ruled it out.

SAXTON CALLED HER HIS WIFE

Evidence to That Effect Brought Out By the Defense.

Was First Degree Murder Proved by the Prosecution?--Her Lawyers Expect to Finish in Three Days--The Prisoner's Side of the Case.

Saxton Called Her His Wife
(Cleveland Daily World, April 18, 1899)

The deposition of Charles Seeley was next read into the record. Annie and Saxton had been guests at his Canton, South Dakota Hotel, the Harland House, during the winter of 1891-2. Annie had lived there to establish residence qualification for her divorce and Saxton had visited her for about a week during that time. Seeley testified that Annie lived in room No. 10 and room No. 14 on the first floor. Although they took their meals together, Seeley never saw them in each other's room or witnessed anything improper between them. Mrs. George, he recalled, always had cash, always paid her bill promptly and was always well dressed.

261

The deposition of N. E. Rudolph, Sample C. George's divorce lawyer, was read into the record. His sole, barely relevant memory of Annie and Saxton was of seeing them briefly after her divorce degree was granted. They were standing on the upper porch of the Harland House Hotel and Saxton was apparently pointing out places of interest to her.

Welty and Sterling now brought forward witnesses to verify Annie's financial dependence on Saxton. Their testimony was of varying quality and relevance. T. H. Heigerson, the cashier of the Lincoln County National Bank in Canton, South Dakota, testified that he knew nothing about the case and had not cashed any checks for Annie George. Oscar K. Brown, a cashier of the same bank, testified in his deposition that he had known Annie George when she lived at the Harland House in 1891 and 1892. Brown stated that during that period she had no occupation that he knew of. He had cashed nine drafts for her for a total of $450.00 during her South Dakota residency. All of them bore the signed endorsement of George D. Saxton.

The deposition of hardware man Claude Treet was next read into the record. A resident of Canton, South Dakota, he had become acquainted with Mrs. George while she waited out her divorce residency there at the Harland Hotel. He knew of no particular occupation she practiced but had seen her doing needlework, including making neckties and the embroidery on two gentleman's silk nightshirts. Treet had also seen Saxton and Mrs. George together at various times and testified they seemed very affectionate towards each other.

Charles B. Judd's deposition was read into the record. A distinguished citizen of Canton, South Dakota, Judd was the President of the First National Bank of Canton, and had held virtually every civic office in his city's gift. Although he didn't know Mrs. George personally, he had seen her frequently at the Harland House and on the streets of Canton during her residency there. He had later encountered Annie one afternoon while passing out of the dining room at the Booge House hotel in Sioux City.

She was accompanied by a man, whom Judd later learned was George D. Saxton. Judd, apparently a curious fellow, kept his eye on the couple as they walked through the parlor and into room No. 201 and closed the door. Aware that Mrs. George had been residing in South Dakota in pursuance of a divorce, Judd was moved to consult the hotel register. Sure enough, there under the registry for Room No. 201 was the entry, "George D. Saxton and wife." Judd added that it was between 1 and 3 p.m. in the afternoon when he saw Annie and Saxton enter Room No. 201.

The relentlessly mundane detail of the defense's depositions continued on through that Tuesday morning. Lesley M. Foote stated that he had been a clerk at the Harland House during Annie's residency. During Saxton's visits there, he had often seen Annie in his room, sometimes with the door closed. More luridly, he recalled evidences of alcoholic refreshment:

> I know there were bottles left there in that room that were emptied when I saw them. I know they were taken there by him because no one else could have taken them there if he did not.

Less scandalously, Foote recalled Saxton driving out in a rig with Mrs. George and his giving her a box of Gunther's candy. He was vaguer on the subject of Annie's apparently invisible means of support; he had a faint recollection of some money drafts and had seen at times considerable cash in Annie's possession. The deposition of Foote's wife Mary was read aloud next. It largely supported the more irrelevant details of his testimony but added a recollection of seeing Annie doing needlework on garments apparently intended for Saxton.

As agreed at the outset of the trial, Russell Hogan's inquest testimony was now read into the trial record. Hogan had told Coroner McQuate that he had been standing across the street from the Althouse steps when he saw a figure in black run south from the murder scene and pass west through a vacant lot by the Quinn house. He stated he could not tell whether it was a man or woman or whether it was Mrs. George or Mrs. Althouse. He had then run to the side of the body and had recognized it as George Saxton when someone lit a match.

The defense managed to squeeze in one live witness before the Tuesday noon recess. Mrs. Cora Cripe. Her testimony was not very useful to either the defense or prosecution. A resident of Meyers Court, the young housewife had heard four shots while she was making dinner on the evening of October 7. She described it as a dark and cloudy night. Unfortunately, Cripe fixed the time she heard the shots at 5:40 p.m., a chronology widely at odds with every other auditor of the shots. Before she stepped down, Pomerene objected to her statement about the time and it was stricken from the record.

Court now recessed for lunch. While talking to reporters during the break, Welty ended months of intense speculation by declaring that the defense plea and strategy would be an uncompromising "not guilty." Welty's unequivocal statement puzzled and probably irritated many of the newspaper correspondents covering the trial. Like most Cantonians, they had assumed that Mrs. George's defense would be either justifiable homicide or temporary emotional insanity. The defense team's cross-examinations of the State's witnesses had seemed to support either of the two pleas: the revelations about Saxton's vile conduct bolstering the first and the testimony about Ann's frequently agitated manner buttressing the second.

Welty and Sterling wasted no time in demonstrating that their now declared plea was in earnest. The first witness after lunch was Joseph Eckroate, the husband of Christina Eckroate. His testimony did everything the defense desired, baldly contradicting his wife's key assertions. Joseph said he had been in his grocery on the night of October 7 when he heard somebody shout, "Somebody's shot!" He ran out to the sidewalk in front of his house and looked across the street towards the Althouse residence. He testified that he could see a crowd gathered around Saxton's body but he could not recognize any one, despite the fact that he later learned that he knew some of the persons standing there. He said it was a dark night and that the only available light was a lamp in his grocery store window; visibility was further obscured by the dense foliage on nearby trees. He also stated that he and Coroner T. T. McQuate had made an experiment on the night after the shooting. They had placed the lamp in the grocery window again and Joseph Eckroate had stood where he had the night before. They then had a boy stand by the Althouse steps but Eckroate was unable to recognize his features by the available light. This directly contradicted his wife, who insisted that she had recognized Mrs. George from a vantage point at least thirty feet farther from the steps. Joseph had also tested his wife's claimed visual acuity the previous day (April 17) by leaning out of the window on the north side of his house. He now testified that he could not see the steps because the cherry tree blocked the direct line of sight to them.

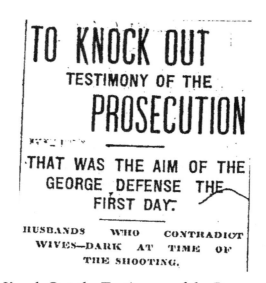

To Knock Out the Testimony of the Prosecution
(Cleveland Daily World, April 19, 1899)

Prosecutor Grant was loaded for bear as he confronted Eckroate in cross-examination. He immediately attacked the quality of his vision:

"Are you a man of good eyesight?"

"Tolerably good."

"See out of both eyes?"

"No sir."

"Blind in one eye?"

"Yes sir."

"Don't see very well out of the other?"

Eckroate grinned at Grant. "I see well enough to do business."

"Don't get comical with me!" screamed the irate prosecutor.

Grant harped on the issue of Eckroate's eyesight, getting him to admit that besides being partially blind, he was 66 years old and had not been wearing his eyeglasses on the night of October 7. When Eckroate repeated that he could not say whether there had been men or women standing by the Althouse steps, Grant snapped angrily, "Could there have been anything else over there but men and women?" "There might have been," was Eckroate's amused reply.

Grant tried hard without success to intimidate the grocer. A little, loquacious old man with Uncle Sam-style whiskers, Eckroate seemed, as Arthur Sperry remarked, a diminutive Jack Sprat to his stout wife and was positively dwarfed by the imposing Grant. The prosecutor confronted Eckroate with his grand jury testimony in January, demanding to know why he now seemed more positive in his statements. Eckroate replied that it was because he had been questioned differently. When asked if he had discussed his testimony with anyone, he said he had conferred with Welty, Sterling, Pomerene and Grant himself. He added, bitterly, "When you found out what I was going to testify to, you would not speak to me." "Never mind that!" shouted Grant, realizing he had been made to look like a spiteful hypocrite. Before he could stop Eckroate, the chatty grocer went on, reprovingly, "I've known you from a little boy up," (Grant turned visibly red to the amusement of his courtroom audience) "and the other day I nodded my head to you and you never noticed me." Before leaving the stand, Eckroate explicitly denied trying to prevent his wife from testifying, as implied by Pomerene

Thirteen-year-old Joseph Schmidt was next on the stand. He told how he had heard the shots from inside his home at Lincoln Avenue and Third Street. He had then run to the murder scene and after that to Weiss' saloon to telephone the police. His relevant testimony was limited to his statements that it was dark by Saxton's body and that men were lighting matches to see who it was laying by the steps. The only anomaly in his testimony was his insistence that he had heard *five* shots fired. It is interesting to note that Schmidt, like the Susky sisters, who also heard five — not four — shots, was south of the scene when he heard the shots that killed Saxton.

John Berger testified next. A boarder at the Schmidt family's house at West Third Street and Lincoln Avenue, he had been a member of the crowd that quickly gathered around Saxton's body. He testified that the night was dark and cloudy and that he had not recognized Saxton's face until matches were lit above it. He said it was not very muddy at the murder scene, nor had he gotten his shoes muddy while searching the side lots and backyards off Lincoln Avenue. He had, however, picked up a few burrs on his clothing while combing the neighborhood for the supposed killer.

As Berger stepped down, a still-seething Grant decided to recall Joseph Eckroate to the stand for another tussle. It was a mistake. Grant was unable to discredit his eyesight further; the scrappy grocer insisted that he could see just about as well without his glasses as with them. Grant then returned to the cherry tree, insisting that it was not in the line of vision from the north window to the Althouse steps. He only succeeded in provoking another losing exchange with the imperturbable grocer:

"Don't you know that you can see 75 feet south of the steps from the window?" roared Grant.

"Not without moving my house!" riposted Eckroate. As the courtroom erupted in laughter, the frustrated Grant again shouted, "Don't get comical with me, Mr. Eckroate!"

Jacob Deppish testified that he had heard the shots from inside his Lincoln Avenue home. He was one of the men who had gathered by Saxton's body. He said it was an "ordinary, dark night" and that Saxton's face could not be recognized without the aid of matches.

Joseph Eckroate's son-in-law August Boron was called to the stand. He had originally been subpoenaed by the State but not called; his testimony for the defense soon made clear why. He was clerking in the grocery store the night of Saxton's murder. He shocked the prosecutors by stating that there was a lamp burning in the Eckroate grocery store that evening — but that it was a small lamp that shed no light near the Althouse steps. There was a larger lamp in the store, he said, but it had not been lit on October 7. He had joined the crowd around Saxton's body and said it was too dark to see anything without lit matches. He further stated that since the murder he had tried to see the Althouse steps from the north window but could not, as the line of sight was blocked by the cherry tree. He had also been present when Joseph Eckroate and Coroner McQuate tested the visibility of the Althouse steps on the night after the murder. He now swore that he could not recognize anyone from that distance.

Grant's cross-examination was predictably fierce, implying that Boron had altered his previous testimony and was now hostile to the State's case:

"Did you ever tell me that [large] lamp was not lit?"

"No sir."

"When did you tell Mr. Pomerene that lamp was not lit?"

"Before the grand jury."

"When did you tell the coroner?"

"The next night."

"You have not been friendly to the prosecution, have you?"

"Yes, sir."

"Haven't you and your father-in-law [Joseph Eckroate] spoken against the prosecution?"

"No, sir."

The only point helpful to the State that Grant could wring from Boron was that one *might* be able to see around the cherry tree to the steps if one leaned far out the north window. He also said that Welty and Sterling had been out to the Eckroate place the night before (April 17) to look around and talk to Boron. On redirect examination Welty gleefully highlighted the fact that Boron had originally been called as a State witness but was dropped when the prosecutors learned the character of his likely testimony. Welty also elicited Boron's recollection that the cherry tree still retained most of its leaves on October 7

Henry Bederman's wife Frances testified next. She had been in her West Third Street home when she heard shooting on October 7. She said it was a very dark night and the ground was muddy. She had first stood across the street from the Althouse steps but it was too dark to recognize anyone in the crowd over Saxton's body. And when she crossed the street, she didn't recognize Saxton until matches were lit over his face. Like the Susky sisters and Jacob Schmidt, Frances had heard five shots from her home south of the Althouse steps.

Welty now turned the conversation back to Saxton's sordid sex life:

"Did you see Saxton going to Mrs. Althouse's house often?"

"Yes."

"How did he get in?"

"He seemed to have his own key. He unlocked the door and let himself in."

The last two witnesses of that eventful Tuesday were Charles and Helen Huth. Charles, an express wagon driver, had gone to the Valley Railroad depot at Tuscarawas Street on October 7 to pick up packages from the Valley Railroad freight train due at

5:44 p.m. The train had been late, and it was still blocking the westbound progress of streetcar No. 21 when Helen arrived at the depot with her husband's dinner. Charles testified that he was certain that the Valley train had not moved off the streetcar crossing until 6:04 p.m. He had also seen Mrs. George later in the evening, as she was being marched down Tuscarawas Street by her police escort. He recalled that she was wearing a white skirt and that she was holding its hem as she walked. Huth said that he could see the skirt clearly and that there was no mud on it, despite the rain that day. Pomerene could not shake his testimony in cross-examination and Helen Huth's brief testimony corroborated her husband's recollection about the time the track for streetcar No. 21 was cleared at the depot. Most court observers agreed that the impact of the Huths' testimony was increased by their homely, matter-of-fact demeanor.

When Tuesday's court adjourned, Sterling could not resist gloating to the assembled reporters over the day's testimony. "We are greatly indebted," he chortled ironically, "to our brothers on the other side of the case. Questions we could not ask, they asked on cross-examination, and then we were able to bring out what we wanted." Sterling was particularly delighted with Joseph Eckroate's dramatic contradiction of his wife's testimony. Anticipating her recall, he promised, "Wait until we get through with her. Her testimony will be smashed to smithereens."

If lacking the crowd-pleasing fireworks of Joseph Eckroate and August Boron's appearances, the testimony of Charles and Helen Huth had been, perhaps, even more helpful to Annie's defense. If their recollection that streetcar No. 21 had not left the Valley Railroad crossing until 6:04 was correct, it would have been difficult, if not impossible for Annie to have later exited the streetcar at Hazlette Avenue and walked 1,000 feet to 319 Lincoln Avenue in time for a fatal rendezvous at 6:10 p.m. As *Cleveland Press* correspondent Jacob Waldeck put it the next day: "If Huth's statement is not contradicted, the State will be obliged to say that Mrs. George rushed to the Althouse home like a courier from the front and that by a remarkable coincidence Saxton arrived there at the same moment."

THURSDAY, APRIL 20, 1899.

THE GEORGE TRIAL.

GRANT GLOATS.

MRS. UNDERMAN MOST IMPORTANT WITNESS FOR THE DEFENSE

MRS. K. GOETZINGER

POMERENE GETS EXCITED

MRS. GEORGE LAUGHS

WELTY APPEALS TO THE JUDGE

MISS ADA CASSELMAN

Center Scene—When Howard, Mrs. George's younger son, was brought into court Wednesday afternoon, his mother showered kisses on his face.

Scenes and Characters from the George Trial, Wednesday, April 19
(Cleveland Daily World, April 20, 1899)

When court opened Wednesday morning Annie was dressed as on the previous day, except that she had exchanged her feather-decked sailor hat for a jaunty straw model. Surprise witness Jacob Adams immediately riveted the attention of everyone present with his startling testimony. A carpenter by trade, Adams testified that he had been walking south on Lincoln Avenue about 6 p.m. on October 7. About halfway between West Third Street and Tuscarawas Street, he had passed a man walking north in the direction of the Althouse residence. Adams said the man was a stranger to him and about 5 feet, 8 inches tall. Adams couldn't recall anything else about the stranger and he had given him no more thought at the time. When he reached Tuscarawas Street, Adams turned east. Several minutes later he passed George Saxton, riding toward Lincoln Avenue on his bicycle. He asked Saxton whether he had attended the Minerva fair; Saxton said, "Yes," and cycled on. Adams had walked about three blocks farther when he heard three shots, followed by two more. Adams had also encountered Annie George as she walked westward on Tuscarawas Street about 8 p.m. that same evening. Adams said she was not agitated, flushed or otherwise "unusual" in her appearance. He also recalled that it was dark and the ground was wet and muddy that night.

Grant realized immediately that Adams' testimony was a serious obstacle for the State. It raised for the first time in the Annie George trial what Welty and Sterling had hoped for: a credible alternative candidate for Saxton's killer. The most Grant could do, however, was to quibble with Adams about the exact time he saw the stranger and to try to suggest to the jury that the witness was in bed with the defense. He first fired many questions at Adams about the precise time he saw the mysterious stranger. It developed that Adams, like many Ohioans of the era, did not operate on standardized or "clock" time. His memories were arranged by "sun time," a less rigorous calculation based on the amount of daylight and the schedule of his work day. The fact that Adams's sighting of the stranger occurred just before he saw Saxton nearing Lincoln Avenue, however, established it close enough to the time of the murder. Grant next turned to Adams' relations with Andy Wielandt, a Canton private detective employed by Annie's defense:

"You have talked a good deal about this matter. Who with — Mr. Welty?"

"Yes sir."

"And Andy Wielandt?"

"Yes, I talked to Andy."

"How often did you talk to Andy?"

"Andy and I hunted for the [Saxton murder] revolver."

"Never mind that," snapped Grant. "How often did you talk to Wielandt?"

"About a dozen times. I have talked to hundreds of people about passing the man."

"Mr. Pomerene talked to you about this case?"

"Yes sir."

"Did you tell him about the man you met?"

"No, he didn't ask me?"

"Did you tell him about meeting Saxton?"

"No, he didn't ask me. He asked me about a man named Numan."

"And yet you pretended to talk freely to him!" ended Grant sarcastically.

George Rex, a former mayor of Canton, was examined next by Sterling. Although originally subpoenaed by the State, he now testified for the defense. He stated that two days before he had accompanied Edward C. Baumberger and George Fox to examine the view from Mrs. Eckroate's north window. Rex said the cherry tree interfered with the line to sight to the Althouse steps when the window was closed. Pomerene pushed Rex hard in cross-examination to modify this judgment. He succeeded in getting Rex to say that it was possible to see the steps if one leaned out far enough from the window. During redirect examination Welty elicited the fact that it was at the solicitation of Pomerene that Baumberger, Fox and Rex had made their investigation of the view from Mrs. Eckroate's window. Baumberger and Fox followed Rex on the stand and perfectly corroborated his testimony.

Welty next examined Frank Hildenbrad. Possibly the first witness who actually saw Saxton's body, Hildenbrad had heard four shots while in his room on Meyers Court, just behind the back of the Eckroate grocery. Running west toward the direction of the shots he had passed by a woman who screamed, "My God, some one has been shot. He is lying there dead!" He testified that it was an unusually dark night and when he first arrived at the Althouse steps he could not see the body. Hearing groans, he struck a match and saw Saxton's body on the sidewalk. He said the ground in the area was muddy from the rain and that no light from the street lamp at Third Avenue, the Glick's parlor window or the small lamp in the Eckroate grocery reached the Althouse steps.

During Grant's cross-examination Hildenbrad was unable to remember anything about the woman who screamed, except that he didn't recognize her and that she was wearing a light-colored skirt. He thought he had heard Saxton groan just as he reached him.

Upton Shultz was asked by Welty to describe the weather and ground conditions on October 7. Shultz had been hunting for much of that day, and he stated it was wet and muddy in the northwest part of Canton. He testified further that the leaves on the trees in the Lincoln Avenue area were still very dense and that there were a lot of burrs and Spanish needles growing in the lots along Tuscarawas Street. Shultz was followed by George Sweatt, who likewise testified that burrs and Spanish needles grew in profusion along Tuscarawas Street. Welty did not have to tell the jury that the import of such testimony was that Mrs. George's skirt had picked up its burrs and needles there, rather than in the vacant lot near the Althouse residence.

The defense next put Adam Jackman on the stand. He had known Mrs. George for some years and as a Canton constable had been involved in some of the police actions sparked by her own lawsuits and the ones filed against her. His testimony now was largely a tedious recital of the prolonged bickering involved in Annie's replevin suits against Saxton to recover her belongings in the Saxton block. Jackman testified he was present on one occasion when he accompanied Annie on an expedition to reclaim her goods and Saxton had demanded Jackman remove her or he would summon another policeman to eject her. Jackman said he had seen letters presented as evidence at one of the replevin trials in which Saxton addressed Annie as "My dear wife" and used other terms of strong affection. Saxton had legally admitted authorship of these letters and Annie had later submitted them, Jackman testified, as evidence in her suit for breach-of-promise. More importantly, Jackson recalled the conversation in Mrs. George's room in mid-1897 during which, as State witness Charles Lloyd had testified, she had threatened Saxon's life. Jackson now swore under oath that he had been there with Lloyd but that he didn't hear Annie make any such threat.

Grant attacked Jackman's credibility directly in his caustic cross-examination. He accused him of talking to Welty, Sterling and Wielandt in the preparation of his testimony. He also challenged him on his veracity in recounting Mrs. George's conversation with him and Charles Lloyd. Much of Grant's angry interrogation was devoted to rehashing his own participation in Annie's replevin suits, in which, as Saxton's personal attorney, Grant had played a leading role. After many questions about the replevin actions, Grant exposed his purpose, which was to suggest that Annie's real motive had not been to reclaim her goods but to embarrass Saxton through his family:

"Didn't these proceedings begin the very day Mr. McKinley came home?" Grant bellowed. His reference was to the day McKinley returned to Canton in 1896 to announce his campaign for president. Welty shouted out his objection, telling Judge Taylor that such evidence was not competent. Grant shot back, "We claim it is competent." Judge Taylor asked, "How is it competent?" Grant responded, "Because it shows that the whole proceeding was brought to annoy and harass." Welty, who was hardly loath to bringing McKinley's name into the case, riposted with sardonic piety: "We don't want to bring the relatives of Mr. Saxton into this suit, but since you desire it, we will open the door if you want it open." Judge Taylor intervened, ruling the reference to McKinley out of the record. Grant turned back to Jackman, sneering, "You don't like Mr. Saxton because he didn't pay your costs in the replevin suit." Jackman replied, "I have nothing against him."

Welty and Grant clashed again when Grant returned to the subject of Annie's replevin suits. Grant suggested that Anna's expedition to the Saxton block with Jackman was merely a fishing expedition to inventory the entire contents of Saxton's room, all of which she subsequently attempted to replevin. Grant once again brought up his own role in the episode, recalling that no one had seemed to take it amiss when he sarcastically accused Anna of trying to replevin the wallpaper on Saxton's walls. This was too much for John C. Welty, who angrily interjected:

"If *you* want to testify, take the stand and *I'll* cross-examine *you!*"

"I'll take the stand at the proper time, Mr. Welty," retorted Grant, mimicking Ann's mantra on the night of October 7.

"And I'll be here," promised Welty.

After Jackson finished his testimony, Kate Gretzinger gave the courtroom audience some moments of needed comic relief. Her testimony on direct examination was merely that Saxton and Annie had twice stayed overnight at the Zoar Hotel, about twelve miles from Canton, where Gretzinger had worked during the early 1890s. This information was inconsequential, particularly after Judge Taylor sustained Pomerene's objection to her stating how the couple had registered at the hotel. The humor came during Pomerene's cross-examination of Gretzinger:

"Where do you live now?"

"At Canal Dover."

"What are you doing there?"

"I live there." The courtroom audience tittered.

"Oh, you are married then?"

"Yes."

"I didn't understand that. What is your husband's name?

"John Gretzinger."

"What is his business?"

"I don't know — he's dead."

The entire courtroom audience erupted in laughter, including, for the first time, Annie George. Her merriment moved wordsmith Arthur Sperry to muse: "Mrs. George looked 20 years younger as she laughed. She looked the woman Saxton loved, loved till he got tired of her and got killed."

The ubiquitous Charles Frazer was recalled to talk more about the visibility at the murder scene. Sterling led him back to the memory of how he lost his hat as the police wagon sped to the murder scene. Sterling finally got what he wanted when Frazer testified that it was so dark that he had had to fumble on his hands and knees while searching the ground for his hat. He also disclosed that eyewitness Christina Eckroate had consulted him about two years before about going to a medical institution to cure herself of her morphine addiction. Frazer testified that she had not taken the cure but she had confessed to him that she had been a slave to the drug for ten years and that she knew she would not recover her health until she kicked the habit. But during Pomerene's cross-examination, Frazer admitted that he had not noticed anything unusual in Mrs. Eckroate's manner during that conversation. She had talked "clearly and plainly."

Thomas Shepard was called to the witness stand. Now a miner in Coshocton, Shepard had been a janitor at the Saxton block during the mid-1890s. He well remembered Annie's personal siege against Saxton at the Saxton block and remembered Saxton telling him, "If Mrs. George comes here again, you order her away. If she doesn't go, come up and tell me, and I will kick her away." Sheppard said until the injunction against her was granted, Annie stood sentinel for weeks before Saxton's second-floor door, sometimes morning, noon and night. He went on to recall an incident during the summer of 1896, when Saxton was away at the St. Louis Republican convention that nominated McKinley for president. One night he had found Annie and her friend Florence Klingler in Saxton's office. They went through Saxton's wastebasket and took away some letters he had torn up and discarded. Welty did not pursue the content of those letters. Instead he tried to reopen the subject of Saxton's sex life:

"During the time you were janitor of the Saxton block did not a great many women visit Mr. Saxton's rooms?"

Pomerene was on his feet, objecting. Judge Taylor asked Welty, "What are you trying to show by this testimony?" Welty replied that he hoped to show that William F. Cook, the deaf Saxton block janitor, might have mistaken some other woman for Mrs. George when he saw a female standing by Saxton's door with a pistol. Judge Taylor then asked Sheppard whether he knew Mrs. Althouse. When Sheppard said he didn't, Judge Taylor asked Welty, "Are you seeking to show that other women visited Saxton for licentious purposes?" Welty replied, "We don't care for what purposes." Judge Taylor then sustained Pomerene's objection, explaining that, consistent with his rulings on the State's witnesses, only evidence about Eva Althouse would be allowed. "You cannot at this time," he told Welty, "attempt to drag in a hundred other women or any women for that matter."

Judge Taylor's decision to slam the door once and forever to any testimony about Saxton's other women proved to be one of the most important of the trial. First of all, it considerably shortened it, as it enabled the defense to drop dozens of witnesses they had subpoenaed to embroider their portrait of Saxton as a ruthless and relentless Lothario. More importantly, it paved the way for Taylor's kindred decision to exclude any testimony about Annie's alleged relations with other men. While these two decisions, on the surface, seemed impartially fair, they were disproportionately helpful to the defense. Welty and Sterling had already succeeded in painting a squalid portrait of Saxton for the jury as the heartless seducer of a married woman and the playmate of a dubious widow. Exclusion of any testimony about Annie's alleged sexual irregularities, other than with Saxton, allowed her lawyers to maintain their portrait of her as a once innocent spouse ruined by her one fatal lapse. Not incidentally, too, as the *Canton Evening Repository* reporter noted, Taylor's decision not to allow the ventilation of the full catalogue of Saxton's affairs "brought relief to many homes" in Canton.

Grant achieved little with his cross-examination of Shepard. After his interrogation chronicling Annie's harassment of Saxton in his block continued for some minutes, Welty finally objected, pleading that the testimony was hardly competent as evidence to the charge of murder. "What does the State claim for his conversation?" inquired Judge Taylor of Grant. "That it shows her menacing and annoying manner." "It is not competent on these grounds," Judge Taylor ruled briskly. "It may all be stricken from the records."

Charles Summers now took the stand. Another janitor, the Columbus, Ohio resident had been employed by Saxton at the Saxton block during the mid-1890s. Most of Sterling's examination was devoted to chronicling Eva Althouse's supposed assignations with Saxton after he had discarded Annie. Summers stated that he had seen Eva in the block at least a "hundred times" at all hours of the day and night. He told of how she would often come to Saxton's rooms on Saturday evening and stay right through until Monday morning. Summers could often smell coffee brewing in Saxton's rooms on Sunday mornings and he recalled that Saxton and Eva sometimes spent the whole Sabbath there. On Monday afternoons he would often find "many" empty beer bottles and dirty dishes while cleaning up after them. He said he had never seen Mrs. George in the Saxton block but had often seen many other women there. His first memory of Eva Althouse probably dated from 1896 and contained details illustrative of Saxton's furtive love life:

> One night when it was raining and the roof was leaking, Mr. Saxton took a light to go upstairs with

me and put a bucket under it. That was the first time
I saw Mrs. Althouse. She came up the side stairs
while we was in the hall. Mr. Saxton seemed kinder
mad at seeing her then. He grabbed her and rushed
her into his private room and slammed the door. It
had a spring lock on it.

Pomerene didn't like what he was hearing from Charles
Summers. His cross-examination was bluntly contrived to suggest
to the jury that the janitor had a number of unseemly motives in
testifying:

"You had some difficulty with Saxton?"

"Yes, he talked cross to me and I quit him. But I worked for
him three times after that."

"What do you do in Columbus?"

"I am a janitor."

"Did you formerly run a gambling room in Columbus?"

"No sir."

"You paid especial attention to Mrs. Althouse, didn't you?"

"No."

"She was the apple of your eye, wasn't she?"

"No."

"You have talked about your testimony with Mr. Welty and
Mr. Sterling, have you not?

"Yes sir."

A star defense witness now appeared in the person of Lena
Lindeman. Lindeman lived at 1525 South Market Street, about two
miles from the murder scene. She had once been employed to
clean Saxton's rooms at the Saxton block and she still did his
weekly ironing at the time he was murdered. In a calm and clear
voice, Lindeman testified that Annie George had been visiting
with her at her home from 12 noon until 5:30 p.m. on October 7.
Her memories of Annie's behavior that day offered a strong
contrast to the stories told by John J. Jackson and Judge Thomas
McCarty. Lindeman testified that Annie was blissful that after-

noon, almost giddy with the possibility of marrying her dear lover at last, now that the Sample C. George lawsuit was settled. She recalled how Annie had talked, with happy tears in her eyes, of how Saxton loved her and how certain she was that he would now honor his promise to marry her. She particularly remembered how Annie had gushed upon seeing a pile of tidies in Lindeman's ironing pile; how she had reminisced about sewing them for Saxton during her long Dakota divorce winter; how she had repaired one of them with her needle and asked Lena to let her know if "Toby" (her affectionate nickname for Saxton) recognized her loving handiwork. Many in the courtroom noticed that Annie, apparently deeply moved by the recitation of her conversation with Lindeman, becomingly put a handkerchief to her eye at this juncture of the testimony.

Moving on to less sentimental matters, Welty called for the revolver that had been introduced into evidence. Showing it to Lindeman, he asked her if she had seen it before:

"No."

"Was it possible for Mrs. George to have had a revolver concealed about her that day?"

"No."

Lindeman went on to explain why it was impossible. It seemed, by happy coincidence, that she had much admired the dress Annie was wearing that Friday afternoon. Generous spirit that she was, Annie had immediately promised to give it to Lindeman after she married Saxton. Lena stood up and Mrs. George pointed out the various components of the garment as Lindeman felt the material. The point, Welty now led Lindeman to explain, was that if Mrs. George had been carrying a revolver on her person, Lindeman would have felt its shape as she ran her fingers all around Annie's garments. Lindeman added that she had taken Annie's hat and coat when she arrived and there was no gun concealed in them. She also remembered that Annie had wandered into her back yard, which was filled with Spanish needles and burrs, several times that Friday afternoon. Lindeman's last memory of Annie was when she said goodbye to her at 5:30 p.m. Still happy, Annie had told her that she was going to supper and would then see Judge McCarty to see if she could get the injunction against her lifted. She promised she would talk to Lindeman after she had seen Saxton again.

Welty provoked a burst of laughter during his amicable interrogation of Lindeman. Querying her about what she saw during the period when she cleaned Saxton's rooms, he asked:

"Did you see revolvers about this room?"

Pomerene objected and Judge Taylor asked Welty, "What do you claim for this?"

"We expect to show that he had revolvers and carried them, and that it may have had something to do with the occurrence on Lincoln Avenue."

"Do you expect to connect it in that way?" pressed Judge Taylor.

"We cannot say that."

"Unless there is some claim of accidental shooting," replied Judge Taylor, "this is not competent testimony — unless you have a theory of self-defense or accidental shooting." As the courtroom erupted in laughter, Judge Taylor commanded, "Pass on to something else." Noting an exception to his ruling for possible appeal, Welty said he could prove that Saxton kept revolvers in his room and that once Lindeman had picked up a pair of his trousers and a .38-caliber revolver had tumbled out of a hip pocket. As Judge Taylor repeated his injunction to drop the matter, Pomerene remarked, *sotto voce*, that Mrs. Lindeman would not have known a revolver from a cannon.

Lindeman stood up well under Grant's testy cross-examination. He tried to provoke her into admitting that she was angry at the prosecutors. She allowed that she was a "little annoyed at what you told one of the witnesses about me. I told the officers I would talk if you came to me." He accused her of refusing to talk to the State's lawyers. Lindeman blandly denied any animus, insisting that she had only refused to talk to Patrolman

Henry Piero when he tried to interrogate her at Grant's request. Grant pressed her hard on her claim that Mrs. George had no revolver concealed on her person:

"You didn't open Mrs. George's dress to see if she had a revolver?"

"No, but I felt her waist and know she had no revolver."

Grant was now entering delicate terrain. This was an era when even full-figured women used corsets and various types of cloth pads and other supplements to enhance the shape of their bosoms and hips. It was not genteel, however, to talk about it:

"Did Mrs. George wear anything to improve her form?"

"I didn't see anything."

"But you admit that you can't tell as to this and yet say she had no revolver?"

Lindeman was adamant in her denial. "I know if she had a revolver I would have found it." Nor could the dogged prosecutor shake her insistence that her back yard was simply overflowing with Spanish needles and burrs. But before leaving the stand, Lindeman frankly admitted to Grant, "I like Mrs. George and can't say anything against her."

The defense next brought two witnesses forward to corroborate Lena Lindeman's testimony. Jacob Lindeman, Lena's brother-in-law, testified that her back yard was infested with burrs, although he couldn't recall whether it had Spanish needles. Insurance investigator J. C. Moore testified that he had stopped by Lindeman's house between 4 and 5 p.m. on October 7. He said he had been there for several minutes and had seen both Lindeman and Mrs. George.

Dr. Douglas Schwartz was the last defense witness of the day. He had been near Lincoln Avenue on the early evening of October 7 on his bicycle. He testified that he had been looking for the home of a patient on Smith Street and had great difficulty in finding it because of the extreme darkness. He also testified that it was quite muddy in the area, with many mud holes full of water. Pomerene's cross-examination was brief and focused on the available lighting in the neighborhood. Before Schwartz finished, Pomerene got him to admit that the electric street lamps on Tuscarawas Street might have made the unlighted portion of Smith Street seem darker when Schwartz turned on to it.

Wednesday had been another encouraging day for Annie George's defense. Pomerene demonstrated his mounting frustration with the trend of the trial while talking to reporters afterwards. "If that she-devil goes free," he barked bitterly, "I will leave the county!" "Well, good-bye!" chortled Sterling as he walked past him. "You had better pack your clothes and go." Meanwhile, outside the courtroom, Grant confessed to reporters, "I'm afraid they have got us up in the air." The tally of defense victories was the most impressive yet: they had raised the tantalizing possibility of an alternative shooter with Adams' testimony about the mysterious person on Lincoln Avenue; they had significantly impeached Christina Eckroate's eyesight with the testimony of George Rex, Edward Baumberger and George Fox about the intervening cherry tree; Lena Lindeman had painted a sunny portrait of Annie's disposition on the brink of Saxton's murder; and almost all the witnesses had sworn that it was a dark night with poor visibility. The only seeming setback for the defense was Judge Taylor's ruling slamming the door for good on testimony about Saxton's other women. Thrifty Cantonians were quick to acclaim his decision, as it promised to abbreviate the already lengthy trial by a considerable amount. Many of the defense witnesses who had been subpoenaed to talk about Saxton's love life would now be dismissed. It was said, too, that Judge Taylor's decision brought relief to many a Canton female who had been involved with the hyperactive bachelor.

Wednesday's sessions had even provided some laughs. The first came during Grant's interchange with Kate Gretzinger. The second was provoked by Welty's injection of the notion that Saxton might have committed suicide. The third came courtesy of the unfortunate Mr. J. A. Giffin. A photographer who had once had his shop in the Saxton block, Giffin was a regular spectator at the trial. He was a large, handsome, extremely dignified old gentleman and the only person in the courtroom who wore a silk hat. Every morning he placed it carefully beside his chair as he listened raptly to the testimony. Like many men of the era, he also chewed tobacco. That afternoon, as he listened intently to one of the witnesses, he had absent-mindedly leaned over and expectorated carefully into his beautiful silk hat. The expression on his face as he realized what he had done convulsed even Judge Taylor and it was some time before courtroom decorum was restored.

Many of the trial observers remained entranced by the attractive defendant. As usual, Mrs. George had pleased the courtroom crowd with her handsome appearance and unruffled calm. The spectators were particularly gratified by a touching family tableau which occurred as Judge Taylor gaveled the afternoon session to a close at 4:20. Mrs. George's younger son Charles Howard, just arrived on the train from Hanoverton, had waited patiently to see his mother through the long afternoon. When the doors were opened, he came running to his mother's side and buried himself in her arms and Annie covered his face with kisses. Meanwhile, Welty gave reporters a preview of coming attractions. Sample C. George, he told reporters, had just arrived in Canton to testify at his wife's trial. And, Welty now promised, he expected to put a surprise alibi witness on the stand tomorrow.

As usual, correspondent Arthur Sperry put his finger on the dramatic resonance of the day's testimony. After noting Lena Lindeman's touching evocation of her friend Annie as a woman deliriously in love, he found the common chord that had motivated many of the witnesses in their supportive testimony for the defense:

> Most of . . . those who gave their testimony yesterday to save the neck of the woman charged with killing George Saxton were those who had been Saxton's dependents, his employees. They were the jani-

tors of buildings and the woman who took care of his rooms.

Sperry didn't have to draw the obvious homily for his readers: that George Saxton had been no hero to the more humble folk who smoothed his path in life.

*Charles Howard George
(Cleveland Daily World, April 9, 1899)*

Chapter 17   Another Mysterious Stranger

Trial correspondents reported that Annie looked exceptionally calm and confident as Judge Taylor opened court on Thursday morning, April 20. She was wearing a white-striped shirtwaist, a dark skirt, a white collarette and sported her sailor hat. As she marched to her seat, her friend May Streeter presented her with a gorgeous bunch of red roses in a dark green vase.

HARD BLOW AT THE PROSECUTION IN THE GEORGE CASE

A Morphine Fiend Absolutely Unreliable, Swears Dr. Eyman.

Mrs. Eckroate's Testimony Knocked Out—Now Said That the Prisoner's Lawyers Will Prove an Alibi—Mrs. George May Go on the Witness Stand.

Hard Blow at the Prosecution in the George Case
(Cleveland Daily World, April 20, 1899)

Welty had publicly vowed to reduce Christina Eckroate's testimony to "smithereens." He now set to work fulfilling that promise by putting Dr. H. C. Eyman on the witness stand. Eyman began by stating his credentials. Superintendent of the Newburg Insane Asylum in Cleveland for eight years, Eyman said he had treated many persons addicted to morphine, laudanum or opium throughout his medical career. He now told the jury that the effect of all such addictions was the same:

The first effect is loss of moral tone. The victim has a total disregard for honor and truth and is devoid of principle. The mind is in a diseased state. A physician is not justified in prescribing morphine for a longer period than 30 days, owing to the danger that the habit may become fixed.

Buttressing his statements with a plethora of citations from medical authorities, Dr. Eyman testified that the effects of the morphine habit were predictable and consistent in the many patients he had treated. "What artifices do those having formed the habit use to get the drug?" asked Welty. "They will resort to any means or device to secure it," replied Eyman. The net effect of Welty's examination was to force the chief prosecutor into the unenviable position of defending the credibility of a drug addict. But Pomerene was determined to salvage some of this key witness's credibility and he grilled Eyman vigorously, trying to get the physician to concede a positive exception to his experience with drug addicts' veracity:

"Is not untruthfulness in those addicted to the habit largely confined to efforts to get the drugs?"

"Yes, it is more especially noticeable in this respect, but is not limited to it. Hallucinations would probably come before the loss or material impairment of the faculties. Unreliability, however, is one of the very first stages of the disease."

"Does the habitual use of morphine render a person totally unreliable?"

"I have never known of an exception."

"Is it not true that men addicted, say, to the intemperate use of alcohol, have been successful in business and eminent in professions?"

"Yes."

"Is this not true, also, of morphine eaters?"

"No, it is not."

Struggle as he might, Pomerene could not get Eyman to qualify his opinion that morphine addicts were habitually untruthful.

Alva Whipple testified after Eyman. Whipple had heard the shots that killed Saxton from his house at the northeast corner of Third Street and Lincoln Avenue. He had joined the crowd milling around Saxton's body and he testified that it was a very dark night, necessitating lit matches to see Saxton's body clearly. Whipple added that he had since examined the view of the Althouse steps from Christina Eckroate's north window and found it obstructed by the cherry tree.

W. B. Deweese, a neighbor of Mrs. Oberlin's, told the jury that there were burrs and Spanish needles growing along much of Tuscarawas Street on October 7. They were liable to cling to the skirts of women walking along the street. Maud Randall followed Deweese, stating that she had met Mrs. George on Tuscarawas Street shortly after 8 p.m. on October 7. She testified that that burrs and Spanish needles had adhered to her own skirt as she walked there. She said there was nothing unusual about Annie's appearance as they passed. Grant tried to nullify part of her testimony in cross-examination:

"You often passed that sidewalk without getting burrs on you?"

"Yes sir."

Welty was quick to retrieve the lost ground:

"And you often got them [there], too?"

"Yes."

A Mr. and Mrs. B. C. Moock next testified that it was very dark on the night of October 7 in the Lincoln Avenue neighborhood. Mrs. Moock said that it had rained there about 7 p.m.

Grocer Joseph A. Lippert, who had already testified for the State, now took the stand for the defense. Most of his testimony dealt with the weather on October 7 and the flora along Tuscarawas Street. He stated that there were a lot of Spanish needles and burrs growing along the sidewalk near his grocery. He then told of seeing Mrs. George pass by it on the evening of October 7 and how he had noticed her stepping around a large puddle, a detour which brought her skirt near a large growth of burrs and Spanish needles.

H. S. Kaufman finished out the morning's testimony with some details of Saxton's financial support of Mrs. George during her Dakota divorce sojourn. Kaufman, who had worked as a cashier at the family Saxton Bank in Canton, identified nine bank drafts to the amount of $525 that Saxton sent to Annie.

An incident just before the lunch recess dramatized the increasing rancor between the opposing attorneys at the Annie George trial. First, James Grant complained to Judge Taylor that the defense had refused to furnish the State copies of depositions taken in evidence as part of Sample C. George's original 1892 alienation-of-affection suit. These documents included testimony from both Annie and her Hanoverton relatives concerning Annie's marriage. After listening to both sides bicker for some minutes, Judge Taylor told Grant he would have to go through the normal legal protocol to get the depositions. Welty then countered Grant's charge with the complaint that the State's lawyers were withholding copies of some of Saxton's letters to Mrs. George that the defense had subpoenaed from Mary Barber. The letters sought had originally been used as evidence in Annie's replevin suits against Saxton. Welty said he had tried to get the papers from Mrs. Barber but he was told she was too ill to appear in court. After Pomerene and Grant denied any knowledge of the letters, Welty demanded that Judge Taylor order Mrs. Barber to appear in court after the noon recess. After listening to both sides, Judge Taylor deferred the matter for further argument later.

The rising tensions in the courtroom finally exploded early that Thursday afternoon. Stalled in his efforts to obtain from Mary Barber the letters Saxton had written to Annie, Welty put ex-Justice of the Peace Frank H. Darr on the stand. Darr had heard the replevin suits filed against Saxton in November, 1895. Although the relevant letters were not available, Darr recalled them vividly and he now testified that Saxton had admitted authorship of the letters. Darr was droning on about the various items inventoried in the replevin suits when Pomerene jumped to his feet and angrily addressed Judge Taylor:

"If your honor, please, while this witness is testifying he is looking toward the defendant, who is shaking her head!"

"*I object!*" hollered Welty at the top of his lungs.

SKETCHED IN COURT THURSDAY.

Scenes and Characters from the George Trial, Thursday, April 20
(Cleveland Daily World, April 21, 1899)

A fulminating Pomerene now informed Judge Taylor that he had observed Mrs. George repeatedly coaching defense witnesses, nodding her head to signal to them whether they should give an affirmative or negative answer to questions concerning her. The prosecutor said he had first noticed it the previous day during Thomas Shepard's and Lena Lindeman's testimony and he demanded that Judge Taylor stop such behavior. After listening calmly to Welty's impassioned denial, Judge Taylor ordered Pomerene's accusation stricken from the record and directed

Grant to proceed with his cross-examination. "All right!" remarked Welty exultantly. Annie kept still as a mouse with her eyes downcast during this episode but smiled slightly as Judge Taylor quashed the accusation.

After the excitement died down James Huddell came forward to testify for the defense. Huddell was the night clerk at the Hotel Federal in Allegheny, Pennsylvania, the scene of Saxton's temporary reconciliation with Annie in 1896. Huddell stated that he had been on duty when Saxton and Mrs. George arrived at the hotel on March 24, 1896. Saxton had demanded the best room and the couple had been given room No. 8 on the second floor. Huddell recalled that the George and Annie had registered as "G. B. Smith and wife, Toledo," and that he had escorted them to their room and showed them how to operate the gas fire. Sterling then produced the hotel register and asked Huddell whether he could show him the registration. Huddell stated that it was missing; it had been removed at a previous time for use in one of Annie's lawsuits. Huddell was able to identify Saxton from a newspaper photograph and he could identify Annie by sight in the courtroom. He did not know, he insisted to Pomerene on cross-examination, what had happened to the missing leaf from the hotel register.

Freeman A. Leeser of Canal Fulton, Ohio testified after Huddell. The schoolteacher-farmer said that he had taken the train to Allegheny, Pennsylvania on March 24, 1896. The next morning, while in the dining room at the Hotel Federal, he had observed Saxton breakfasting there with Annie. He was told at the time that Saxton's name was "Smith." Although Grant was particularly irascible in his cross-examination of Leeser, their dialogue nonetheless provoked laughter in the courtroom audience:

"There was nothing remarkable in this couple. Why did you notice them so particularly?"

"Why, Mrs. George was a pretty woman!"

"You are a single man?"

"Yes."

"You took at good look at Mrs. George, I suppose?"

"Yes, sir. She was a very attractive woman."

"Yes, sir."

"Then you notice such things?"

"Yes sir."

"And you are very attentive to attractive women?"

"Y-E-S," replied Leeser in a slow drawl. "It's human nature. Don't you look at pretty women?"

The courtroom audience exploded in laughter. Grant then tried to shake Leeser on his identification of Saxton:

"When did you first remember seeing this couple?"

"Why, when he was shot."

"Why? You knew him as Saxton, you say?"

"I don't care. I knew it was Saxton. I saw his picture in the paper."

"Did you notice the collar he was wearing?"

"Yes sir. It was a standing collar."

"He never wore a standing collar in his life!" spluttered Grant contemptuously, and he dismissed Leeser from the witness box.

John Treeman, the gatekeeper at the Valley Railroad crossing on Tuscarawas Street, testified. He told the jury he had been working the gates at the streetcar crossing there on the evening of October 7. He recalled that the Valley Railroad freight train was late that night, arriving at 5:57 p.m. and not leave and clear the streetcar track until at least five minutes later. Treeman's testimony was helpful to the defense, corroborating Charles Huth's testimony that streetcar No. 21 could not have left the depot until after 6 p.m. Pomerene tried hard to rattle him on cross-examination, mocking what he insinuated was a suspiciously selective memory:

"How [late] was the train the next night [October 8]?"

"A couple of minutes late."

"What time did it arrive?"

"I don't know."

"What time did it whistle?"

"I don't know."

"What time did it arrive Sunday [October 9] night?"

"On time, I think."

"What time did it whistle?"

"I don't know."

"How about the other nights?"

"I don't know exactly. I think it was just about on time."

"Can you name another *day* on which you looked at your watch and can remember *just* what time it arrived?"

"I can just name the one day," conceded Treeman.

Lizzie Miller was a surprise but stellar defense witness. A Canton resident for twelve years, she lived on Linden Avenue, one block north of West Third Street and west of Lincoln Avenue, three-eighths of a mile and 15 minutes from the murder scene. She told the jury that sometime between 6 and 6:30 p.m. on October 7, she had been out on her front porch. She had gone there to call her ten-year-old daughter Lizzie home to dinner. As she turned around to go back into the house, she heard a noise and spun around. It was caused by someone stumbling over a loose board on the wooden plank sidewalk. (The wooden sidewalk had been used by pedestrians since the street had been excavated that summer for the laying of water mains.) Mrs. Miller peered into the hazy darkness. She saw a dark object approaching as it walked eastward on the sidewalk. At first she thought it was a woman. As it got closer she realized it was a man. He was tall, wearing a white sailor hat with a dark band, a black mackintosh with a white lining and wearing a cape over his shoulders. The man turned his head away from Mrs. Miller as he passed by an electric vapor street lamp and soon disappeared, walking rapidly into the darkness. She watched with curiosity until he vanished beyond the next street light. She said she had not thought any more about the man until she read about Saxton's murder in the next morning's newspaper. She said the press account had produced a "strange impression" upon her, ultimately persuading her to make her story public.

James Grant's cross-examination of the trembling, wan Miller was his harshest yet. But he could not successfully impeach Miller's memory of a single detail about the mysterious man. He realized, as did other astute courtroom observers, that her story represented a serious threat to the prosecution's narrative of Saxton's killing. Adam Jackman had already introduced an unwelcome alternative gunman in the form of the pedestrian walking on Lincoln Avenue around the time of the murder. Now here was another mysterious man lurking in the neighborhood, well within striking distance of 319 Lincoln Avenue at just the right time. Worse yet, the decidedly male figure seen by Lizzie Miller had an uncanny—not to say suspicious—resemblance to Annie George. Both the hat and cape described by Miller could have come right off Annie's person, and the man's presence on Linden Avenue was not incompatible with the shooter's supposed flight westward through the vacant lot to Lawn Avenue. True, the State's scenario assumed that the shooter had then wheeled south and east to hightail it to South and High Streets (where she ditched the gun under the wooden sidewalk). But if Mrs. George—or her mysterious double—had had an accomplice, she or he could have handed off the revolver and then fled north up to Linden Avenue, where she/he was seen by Lizzie Miller.

Between witnesses, Welty and Sterling offered into evidence the legal records of Mrs. George's breach-of-promise and replevin suits. The journal entries verified that all her suits had been settled out of court after Saxton reconciled with her at the Hotel Federal in 1896. Also entered into evidence was a copy of the injunction preventing Annie from entering the Saxton block and a later ruling that had made it perpetual. Pomerene then triumphantly produced an affidavit from Mary Barber's physician affirming that she was too ill to testify in court.

Being a witness for the defense, Newton, the 17-year-old son of Mrs. George, is excluded from the court room. But he is anxious and strung up to the highest degree and perches all day on a box outside of a court room window watching every movement within.

Newton George
(Cleveland Daily World, April 20, 1899)

The courtroom was unusually hushed as the next witness was called. Everyone present fully realized the anguish and shame felt by seventeen-year-old Newton Robert George as he took the stand to testify at his mother's murder trial. Wearing a gray suit, with a high, gaily-striped collar and shirt, the gangly teenager testified in a low, nervous voice while James Sterling and James Grant successively led him through his memories of his mother's early years with George Saxton. He recounted his childhood days in the Saxton block and how George Saxton had frequently visited his parents' rooms when his father was absent. He recalled their move to a flat on Ninth Street, then to Hanoverton and how his mother had moved into the Saxton block after his father left.

Newton remembered Annie's sojourn on the second-floor of the Saxton block in vivid detail. She and her sons lived in two rooms across from Saxton's quarters and he recalled Saxton being in their rooms almost every evening. Sterling led him gently through his reminiscences of Saxton's presence in the lives of himself and his brother Charles Howard:

"Did Saxton ever make you boys presents?"

Pomerene objected to the question but was overruled by Judge Taylor.

"Yes. He gave me a bank and gave us both candy and such things."

"Did he make presents to your mother?"

"Yes, candy and fruit and such things."

Newton further recalled the exact arrangement of his mother's Saxton block rooms and how Saxton would order him and his brother to go to bed or to be quiet. He said his mother seemed friendly with Saxton and sometimes would sit on his lap in the presence of her sons. Once, Saxton had taken them all to the circus and then splurged on a cab ride home. Arthur Sperry noted that the courtroom audience stared as much at Annie as at her son during his testimony. Although deathly pale, Annie did not otherwise reveal what must have been her violent emotions as she listened to her son's chronicle of her downfall. "Whatever her manner," wrote Arthur Sperry, "she would have been criticized," although he also suggested that Newton's testimony "brought to the minds of some of those who heard it more strongly than ever, the idea that, perhaps. Mrs. George was rather proud than otherwise of her relations with the brother-in-law of the president of the United States." Spectators used to James Grant's increasingly savage manner with witnesses were surprised by his almost tender manner while cross-examining Newton George.

Thomas Shepard, the janitor, was recalled for more testimony. Sterling had decided he wanted some more of Saxton's beastly behavior on the record and he led Shepard again through the catalog of his cruelties to Annie. Shepard now also recalled that Saxton had threatened to use violence to keep her out of the Saxton block. Grant began his cross-examination by asking Shepard if he had told Saxton that he had allowed Annie and Florence Klingler to ransack his wastebasket and take away the torn letters. "No sir, he didn't ask me," replied the janitor, uncomfortably. Grant pushed hard and eventually forced Shepard admit that he had "remembered" these additional details only after having his memory refreshed by Sterling the previous night.

W. O. Werntz had already unwillingly testified against Mrs. George for the State. He was now summoned by the defense to testify about details of some of the divers lawsuits he had handled in his capacity as her lawyer.

Werntz had been present at Justice Robertson's peace proceeding and had heard Mary Finley's testimony there. He now told Annie's jury that, contrary to Finley's recent court testimony, she had sworn to Robertson that Annie was entirely harmless, a "perfect lady" who "wouldn't hurt a cat." Mary had also testified at the peace proceeding, Werntz swore, that Annie had never had a revolver and that she (Finley) would have known if she had one.

Werntz was also queried about the Saxton's letters to Annie which had been used as evidence in the replevin cases. Although the originals were not available, it was now disclosed that they had at one time been printed in the *Canton News-Democrat*. Copies of the relevant newspaper clippings were handed to Werntz and he identified them as accurate specimens of the original letters. Fannie McLean, the daughter of deceased attorney Nat McLean, who had once possessed the letters, now corroborated Werntz's authentication of the text of the letters.

The last witness of the day was Justice Jacob Regnier, who had presided at Annie's murder arraignment in lieu of Mayor Rice. He had been a reporter with the *Canton News-Democrat* at the time Saxton's letters were printed there. After he also authenticated the text of the letters, they were offered into evidence by Welty.

Pomerene objected on the grounds that they were improperly identified but Judge Taylor overruled him. All three letters were then read aloud to the jury. In retrospect, however, it would become clear that the extended bickering over Saxton's letters was only a tedious and irrelevant diversion. Other than offering evidence that he treated Annie as a quasi-wife — a status proved by an abundance of other evidence — the letters would have virtually no impact on the decision of Annie's jury.

Both sides plunged into spin control as soon as court adjourned on Thursday afternoon. Pomerene bragged to reporters that the defense had not shaken the State's airtight case against Mrs. George. More specifically, he reiterated his accusation that Annie had been coaching witnesses with head motions during the past two days of testimony. He claimed that a number of persons had called it to his attention the previous day but that he had patiently waited until his own observation armed him with irrefutable evidence. There may have been something more than angry paranoia or calculated outrage behind Pomerene's charge. The anonymous correspondent for the *Cleveland Plain Dealer* mentioned Pomerene's accusation and conceded:

> As a matter of fact while witnesses were on the stand the accused did incline her head so much as to be plainly noticeable, sometimes affirmatively, other times negatively. Whether she did this consciously or not, the state was not allowed to show, nor will the record contain the state's accusation.

Pomerene also accused Annie's defense team of packing the courtroom, charging that Welty and Sterling cynically subpoenaed dozens of Annie's known partisans, persons they had no intention of actually calling as witnesses. Their strategy, Pomerene maintained, was to attract a sympathetic audience using as bait the extra enticement of the $1 witness fee due all subpoenaed witnesses. The prosecutor also vowed to put Lizzie Miller back on the stand. Pomerene said he wanted to question her about that that "strange impression" she had spoken of in explaining her belated decision to testify. It was rumored that it was the product of her spiritualist beliefs and he wanted to probe her vision of the mysterious Linden Avenue stranger further.

Sterling spoke with equal satisfaction of his side's victories that long Thursday. Predicting the defense would rest its case by Saturday, he asserted, "We have proved beyond doubt that Mrs. George was not at all concerned in the killing of Saxton, and there is no need of uselessly prolonging the trial." Recalling his own Tuesday prediction, Sterling absolutely crowed over the impact of Dr. Eyman's testimony: "There was not much of Mrs. Eckroate, anyway, and now there is not anything."

Meanwhile, John Welty called reporters' attention to the woeful demeanor of Lizzie Miller on the stand. Trembling and pale throughout her examination, she had visibly tottered and almost collapsed as she staggered unsteadily out of the courtroom. It had all seemed a little too much like Christina Eckroate's shambling manner to the skeptical correspondents. But Welty explained that the conscientious Lizzie had actually risen from a sickbed to testify. Indeed, she had fainted dead away as soon as she walked from the courtroom to the court clerk's office and would have fallen to the floor if someone had not caught her.

Chapter 18 "Pleasant and Happy"

The defense team resumed their demolition of Christina Eckroate's credibility on Friday morning. Welty put Joseph Eckroate on the stand and asked him about his wife's drug habit:

"Does your wife use morphine or laudanum?"

"I cannot swear to that," said Eckroate cautiously. "She uses something. It is a white powder."

"How long has she used it?"

"Objection!" hollered Pomerene. "The defense has not yet shown knowledge that the witness knew his wife actually used morphine." Judge Taylor sustained the objection and Welty tried restating the question several times until Judge Taylor found his wording acceptable.

"When did you first see her have the powder and where?"

"In Navarre [Ohio], about twelve years ago. It was powder papers — doses — in our room."

"How long did you notice this in Navarre"?

"Two years. My children lived with us then."

"What effect did this powder have upon your wife?"

"It made her drowsy and irritable at first."

"Have you seen the same kind of powder since you moved to Canton?

"Yes sir, for the last ten years. It was in a bottle, kept about the house."

"What effect did you observe after coming to Canton?"

"She was irritable sometimes and drowsy."

Welty had arrived at the goal of his questions:

"What was the effect on her memory?"

"Her memory was not as good as it used to be."

"Has there been a change in her condition for the last six months or a year?"

"As near as I can tell she has been getting worse of late years."

Joseph Eckroate went on to state that Christina sometimes imagined that she saw things and blamed him for things he hadn't done.

Returning to his most bellicose form, Grant aggressively cross-examined Eckroate. Implying that he was prejudiced against his wife and the prosecution, Grant accused Joseph of changing his story:

"How long have you been married?"

"Somewhere between 20 and 23 years."

"During a good deal of that time you have had a good deal of domestic trouble?"

Welty objected before Eckroate could answer the question. Judge Taylor sustained him and Grant tried again:

"Have you any feeling against your wife?"

"No sir."

"You suggested this morphine matter to the defense?"

"No sir."

"You went to them and told them about it?"

"No sir."

"You talked to them?"

"I talked to Mr. Welty and Mr. Sterling at my store and I talked to Mr. Pomerene, too."

"Didn't Pomerene ask you what effect morphine had on your wife, and you told him it didn't have any effect?"

"No sir."

Grant insisted to Eckroate that he had, in fact, made that statement to Pomerene during a conversation over the telephone at his store:

"It's pretty hard for me to say just what I said."

"You said to Mr. Pomerene by telephone that it had no effect."

"I may have said that."

"When did you make up your mind to say that it did have an effect?"

"I made up my mind years ago."

"You have been talking to Welty and Sterling again!"

"I talked with Mr. Welty in his office this morning."

"You didn't tell Pomerene it made her drowsy and irritable!"

"Yes sir, I did. I told him night before last."

"You didn't tell him the first time he saw you!"

"No sir."

During Welty's redirect examination, Eckroate plausibly explained his lack of total candor with Pomerene over the telephone, saying that his telephone was in a public area and he was ashamed to talk frankly about his wife's drug addiction in the presence of his customers.

Canton druggist E. J. Schlabach took the stand. He stated that he owned a drug store on North Market Street. He said he had seen Christina Eckroate in his store six or seven years before as a regular customer. He recalled that she purchased morphine in 1/8 ounce bottles almost every week, sometimes every two weeks. During the last three or four years she had bought it less frequently; he believed she was buying it elsewhere. She always told him that she was buying it for someone else. During Pomerene's cross-examination, Schlabach explained that each of Christina's morphine bottles contained 54 grains of morphine, or about 270 adult doses. Pomerene confined his questions to challenging Schlabach's memory:

"You kept no record of the sale of morphine?"

"No sir."

"You are estimating from memory the quantity and frequency of her purchases?"

"Yes sir."

Grant's treatment of Harry Taylor, the next witness, was continuing evidence that the prosecution would fight a scorched earth battle over every remaining shred of trial testimony. Taylor, a Big Four Railroad passenger train brakeman, was a minor witness, to say the least. A cousin of Annie George's by marriage, his brief testimony was that he had seen both Annie George and

303

George Saxton on the train that took them to their Hotel Federal rapprochement on March 24, 1896. Taylor simply recalled that Annie had boarded the train at Canton, Saxton had got on at Alliance and that both of them had disembarked at Allegheny. Grant was relentless in cross-examination:

"You know they didn't leave the train together? She got off alone at one end and he at another?"

"Yes sir."

"Did you see them together after they left the train?"

"No sir."

"Did they occupy the same seat?"

"No sir."

"Did you see them talking together?"

"No sir."

"You were never introduced to this man?"

"No sir."

"You never coupled them together until after this murder?"

"I don't couple them together now."

"You talked with Mrs. George yourself during the trip?"

"Yes sir. I sat on the arm of her seat."

"Why did you notice this man closely?"

"Because he was watching me so closely."

Druggist Fred B. Shanafelt was examined by John Welty. He stated that Christina Eckroate had been buying 1/8 ounce and 1/16 ounce bottles of morphine at his Tuscarawas Street store for several years. The bottles cost fifty cents and her most recent purchase had been made this week. Shanafelt was followed by Dr. Alexander H. Garver. The Navarre, Ohio druggist testified that Christina Eckroate had bought morphine regularly at his store for two years before her family moved to Canton. Christina had purchased it every four or six weeks; she told Alexander that she used it in compounding a remedy for piles.

The defense next called H. M. Smallfield to the stand. Sterling asked the former policemen to recall the unhappy night in late 1894 when Saxton had ejected Annie from her suite in the Saxton block. When Sterling asked him what he had witnessed during that confrontation, Pomerene objected. Judge Taylor called Sterling and Welty aside, asking them privately what they expected to show by Smallfield's testimony. Judge Taylor then sustained Pomerene's objection, explaining that the incident was too remote in time from the murder and ordered Smallfield's brief testimony stricken from the record.

Miss Effie Darr, the daughter of previous witness Frank H. Darr, testified. She simply stated that she had passed Mrs. George while walking on South Market Street at about 5:20 p.m. on October 7. Darr was followed by Mrs. Ellen Fink. She said she had seen Annie talking to Lena Lindeman in front of the latter's house that day. During cross-examination Fink admitted to Pomerene that she had fixed the time at 5:30 p.m. after Lena talked to her about it the next morning. Fink added that there were lots of Spanish needles and burrs in the Lindeman yard.

Stark County commissioner James Summers then took the stand. Welty wanted to ask him if Sergeant Hasler's brother Mont had asked the county commissioners to offer a reward for the murder revolver. Pomerene objected and Summers' testimony was stricken from the record.

George and Sarah Finafrock of Waynesburg testified next. The couple had lived on a farm owned by George Saxton near Centerville, Ohio during the first years of Saxton's affair with Annie. They both testified that George and Annie often drove to the farm to have dinner between 1889 and 1892. Knowing that his next question would be ruled inadmissible, but wishing the jury to hear it anyway, Sterling recklessly asked Sarah, "Did Saxton come there with other women?" Pomerene and Grant simultaneously screamed, "*Object!*" and Judge Taylor, glaring at Sterling, ordered the question stricken from the record.

The last witness before the Friday lunch break was Alice Manabaugh. A resident of East Eighth Street near the Saxton block, Alice had known Saxton since his childhood and been acquainted with Eva Althouse for thirty years. She now testified that she had frequently seen the two of them entering the Saxton block together. She had often seen them go there on Saturday evenings and had seen Eva leaving the block on three Sunday mornings. She had seen Eva enter the building on October 1, the Saturday before Saxton's murder. Manabaugh's testimony added little information and no excitement until Sterling asked her whether James Grant had called upon her to inquire what she knew about the case. Judge Taylor had had quite enough. Showing more temper than at any previous moment in the trial, Taylor remarked that during the nearly two weeks of testimony the attorneys for both sides had laid great stress on the fact that witnesses had been interrogated by attorneys for the other side. "I have never before understood," remarked Judge Taylor reprovingly, "that it was an offense for a lawyer to talk to with witnesses before the latter took the stand. Inquiries along this line have wasted a great deal of valuable time." Court then recessed for lunch with Manabaugh still on the stand. During the break prosecutor Pomerene learned that Lizzie Miller was too ill to testify that afternoon but would try to be available for the Saturday sessions.

A minute after Manabaugh left the witness box at the start of the afternoon session, 26-year old Florence Klingler took the stand. By now everyone in the courtroom knew that she was Welty's long-promised super-alibi witness for Annie George. Up to now, neither Annie nor her defense witnesses had accounted for her whereabouts between 6 and 7 p.m. on October 7, the hour of Saxton's death. There was a critical gap[between the moment Annie left the streetcar at Hazlette Avenue and when Harry Noble saw her walking downtown on Fifth Street. It was the hope of Annie's defense that Klingler would fill that gap.

The well-dressed, if homely looking Klingler explained to the jury that she had known Mrs. George for some years and had lived at Mary Finley's boarding house while Annie roomed there. She recounted her visit with Annie to Saxton's office during the summer of 1896, and how they had retrieved and taken away scraps of torn-up letters from his wastebasket. Sterling then walked Florence through her timeline of the evening of October 7. She said she had been walking along Tuscarawas Street about 5:55 p.m. when Saxton passed her on his bicycle, traveling westward. Florence had continued on to her home at 311 Marion Street, more than a mile southeast of Lincoln Avenue. Klingler recalled that she had arrived home about 6:00 p.m. and remained there until 7:45 p.m. Sterling then led her to the nub of her memories:

> Mrs. George arrived at my house at about 6:20 or 6:25 o'clock. She remained until about 6:50 o'clock when, she said, she was going to Mr. Sterling's office. About 6:30 Mr. Howenstine [Klingler's date for the evening] came to the house. He was there until Mrs. George departed.

MRS. KLINGLER.
The alibi witness.

Witness Florence Klingler
(Cleveland Daily World, April 24, 1899)

Klingler added that she was making supper when Annie arrived and she asked Annie to eat with her. Annie had refused, saying she had already eaten and was going to see James Sterling at his office that evening.

If it could stand up, it was obvious that Klingler's testimony was the most devastating blow yet to the State's case against Mrs. George. It was an iron-clad alibi for a critical portion of the missing hour and it was sworn to by an ingratiating and seemingly ingenuous young woman. Better still, Klingler's story was studded with the kind of prosaic detail which accrues to real memories and renders their retelling plausible: she had seen Saxton "in front of the New Bank Building"; she was walking off the pavement because of debris caused by construction there; she saw Saxton riding on the west side of Tuscarawas Street near Cleveland Avenue; and she had heard the town clock strike six o'clock just as she unlocked her front door when she reached home.

The defense had almost everything its own way during Sterling's direct examination. The only tactical reverse came when Sterling tried to encourage Klingler to state that Mrs. George had been expecting to marry Saxton at the time Florence lived with her at Mary Finley's house. Pomerene objected and Judge Taylor called Sterling aside. Many of the defense witnesses had already testified to Annie's repeated complaints that Saxton had reneged on his promise to marry her. Many of the witnesses had also testified, and there was some ample documentation, that Saxton had treated and even addressed Annie as his "wife" during their sweetheart era. But Judge Taylor had had enough of such imprecision and he queried Sterling severely as to whether he had any hard evidence of Saxton's marital promises:

"What evidence of a promise to marry have you, aside from the defendant's statements in conversations with others?"

"I don't know that we have anything else. But we have those statements."

"Objection sustained," ruled Judge Taylor and Klingler's direct examination continued to its finish.

The unprecedented ferocity of Grant's cross-examination showed that he knew how much was at stake in the testimony of this key witness. It was a very angry man who confronted Klingler: he was angry that his friend had been murdered; he was angry at Annie George; and he was angry at this young witness, who seemed to him nothing more than Annie's morally repulsive accomplice. The *Cleveland Plain Dealer* correspondent described Grant as acting "like a caged beast" as he paced back and forth in front of the witness box, constantly glowering and frequently shouting at Klingler. His interrogation was brutal from its opening words and left no doubt that it was she who was on trial that afternoon:

"How old are you?"

"Twenty-six."

"Are you married?"

"No sir."

"With whom did you live on Marion Street?"

"With myself, except when my brother was with me"

"What's your brother's name?"

"Elmer Baxter."

"Just explain to the jury," shouted Grant, "how it is that, if you are an unmarried woman, your name is Klingler and your brother's Baxter!"

"I am separated from my husband."

"Then you're a married woman."

"I was."

"Where were you born?"

"Near Oil City, Pennsylvania."

"When did you leave home?"

"When I was eight or nine years old."

"Where did you go to then?"

"I went out as a nurse girl and I lived with my grandmother."

"How long did you continue as a nurse girl?"

"Until I was sixteen."

"What then?"

"I was married."

"Where were you married?"

"In Alliance in 1889?"

"Are you married now?

"I was married but I am not now. I was divorced in 1892."

Grant paused, then pounced: "Did not your husband secure a divorce from you on the grounds of *unfaithfulness,* and you made no answer to the petition?"

Welty and Sterling simultaneously leaped up, screaming in unison, "*I object!*" Judge Taylor responded quickly, trying to calm the charged atmosphere. "The objection is sustained. We are not trying a divorce case and we are not trying the witnesses."

There was a short lull in the dialogue as Grant quizzed Klingler on her employment over the past few years. He then resumed the direct attack:

"You are the *same* Florence Klingler who lived at the Idlewild [a notorious house of ill-repute in Canton]?"

"No sir."

"*What?!?*" roared Grant.

"No sir!" repeated Klingler vehemently.

"You have been to Charley Simmon's [another house of ill repute]?"

"No sir."

"You were often at Balser's?"

"No sir."

In response to his next question Florence admitted that she had once boarded with a woman named Kate Eyerle in Canton but she had left there three weeks later when she discovered what kind of place it was. Grant was sarcastically skeptical:

"Did it take you *three weeks* to find that it was a *house of pros-titution?*"

"I was not there all the time. I was in and out. I was not there half the time."

"I suppose not," sneered Grant. "That's the way you ply your vocation!"

Welty shouted, "Objection!" After Judge Taylor cautioned him on his language, Grant continued:

"Do you take patients at your house to nurse?"

Chapter 18 "Pleasant and Happy"

"No sir."

"Isn't it a *fact* that some of the nursing you do is the kind that follows *criminal operations* [abortions]?"

"Objection!" hollered Sterling and the question was stricken from the record.

Grant returned to the subject of whether Klingler had lived at various houses of ill fame until Sterling objected and Judge Taylor told Grant to stop it. Grant tried to but he couldn't resist one more shot at Klingler's reputation several minutes later:

"Why did you leave Mrs. Finley?"

"I went to housekeeping in a room in the Empire block with Lydia Bell."

"Didn't you leave Mrs. Finley's because Mrs. Finley told you to go on account of your conduct?"

Sterling again objected, forcing Judge Taylor to admonish Grant that he could not impugn Klingler's reputation in such piecemeal fashion.

Klingler stood up well under Grant's brutal assault, never yielding to tears or becoming unduly rattled by his insulting questions and antagonistic manner. Grant was unable to get her to modify a single fact of her testimony. And, just before leaving the stand, she loosed a Parthian shot of her own against the late George Saxton. When Grant asked her how well she knew Saxton, she replied, "pretty well." She went on to tell of one night the previous summer, when Saxton had followed her home on his bicycle. The impression left on the jury by the image of the portly, wealthy bicyclist roué stalking a young, working-class woman down the street could not have been an attractive one.

Florence Klingler's boyfriend Ira Howenstine followed her on the stand. He corroborated her testimony about the evening of October 7, stating that he had arrived at her house no later than 6:35 p.m. He had seen Mrs. George there for a few minutes and they had conversed briefly. He noticed nothing unusual about her manner. During cross-examination Pomerene could not shake Howenstine on the time he had seen Mrs. George at Klingler's.

Now occurred an episode of unintended comedy. Marshall C. Barber, Saxton's brother-in-law, appeared in court in lieu of his wife and stated she was too ill to appear. He added, however, that he and Austin Lynch, the lawyer handling George Saxton's estate, had repeatedly searched Saxton's papers but were unable to find the documents requested by the defense. The letters used in the replevin suit were a moot issue, as the court had accepted copies of the *Canton News-Democrat* clippings in lieu of the originals. But the copy of Annie's April 2, 1896 agreement to drop her lawsuits against Saxton was still missing. After listening once again to the description of the document, Grant conferred with Welty and then went to his office. He returned, somewhat abashed, several minutes later. He now confessed to Judge Taylor that he had not realized until now the nature of the document so eagerly sought by the defense. It had been in his office all this time and it was now offered and accepted into evidence.

Sterling next examined Henry Kettering. He had run one of George Saxton's Ohio farms between 1888 and 1892. He testified that Saxton brought Mrs. George with him on three or four visits to the farm in 1890 and 1891. His testimony merely supported the well-established fact that Saxton and Mrs. George had spent much time together during those years. Benjamin Beuter of the Zoar Hotel followed Kettering and testified that Saxton had occupied rooms at his hotel with both Mrs. George and Mrs. Althouse on several occasions.

The defense now returned to the happy task of demolishing Christina Eckroate's credibility. Michael Burke of Navarre, Ohio had known her when she lived there and the affable, loquacious Irishman now took the stand to answer Sterling's questions. Burke had run a saloon/grocery/dry goods store in Navarre and he vividly recalled the consequences of Mrs. Eckroate's chronic drug addiction:

"Did you know of Mrs. Eckroate using morphine?"

"Yes sir. I know she did."

"How did you learn it?"

"I saw her take morphine in my house and hers."

"What was the effect of the drug on Mrs. Eckroate?"

"Sometimes she looked wild and sometimes she was drowsy. She was inclined to be cross. I know she took it till it made her crazy sometimes and made her violent sometimes."

"Did you know it was morphine?"

"The girls [Burke's daughters] said it was morphine and it was the stuff she got drunk on."

Burke went on to say that Mrs. Eckroate had once left her husband Joseph and fled to Burke's home in Navarre. Burke had tried to persuade her to return to Joseph and stop using morphine. She told him she would use the drug as long as she lived. Burke told the jury he believed there had been much domestic turmoil in the Eckroate family because of Christina's drug abuse. He said that her step-daughters often fled to his house when she became abusive and her husband had told him that she would steal anything to get money for her morphine.

Grant had his hands full in his cross-examination of the personable, chatty Burke. His answers, often humorous and delivered in a thick Irish brogue, frequently made the jury laugh and his familiarity with Grant, whom he had know since boyhood, kept the prosecutor off balance. He finally became so frustrated with Burke's responses that he turned to Judge Taylor and complained, "I am going to have an answer if I can get authority from this court!" Judge Taylor looked hard at him. "*What do you mean by that?*" he as sharply barked back. Grant immediately backed down. "I want nothing, but I want the witness to answer," he replied meekly. Grant failed to undermine Burke's testimony but he did compel the interesting admission that the witness had not talked to anyone about the case until he had been subpoenaed at 5 a.m. that very Friday morning.

Burke's daughter Laura testified next. She, too, recalled the ill effects that morphine had produced in her neighbor Mrs. Eckroate. On one occasion, while Mrs. Eckroate was visiting the Burke family in Canton, Christina had gone berserk, knocked one of her stepdaughters down and threatened to kill her with a butcher knife. Laura had managed to take the knife away from her but Mrs. Eckroate had become violent again the same day. But the next day she couldn't remember the incident at all, or even that Laura had been at the house. Laura testified that sometimes Mrs. Eckroate had pretended that she didn't take morphine at all; on other occasions she had told her that she had tried to quit but couldn't. The witness said that Mrs. Eckroate had left her husband twice and that Joseph Eckroate had told Laura it was because of her morphine abuse. On cross-examination, Laura admitted to Pomerene that she had not seen Mrs. Eckroate in seven years and could not testify about her behavior during that period. But she added that Mrs. Eckroate had always acted "queer," except sometimes early in the morning.

SAMPLE GEORGE.
The former husband of the Canton prisoner.

Sample George
(Cleveland Daily World, April 21, 1899)

The last major milestone in the defense's presentation came mid-Friday afternoon with the calling of Sample C. George to the witness stand. As his name was called, Welty stood up, effectively blocking Annie's view of her former spouse as he sat down in the witness box. As much as possible, Welty remained in the same position throughout Sample's testimony. Annie, for her part, made no attempt to look at Sample but kept her face half-averted, her chin on her hand, which was clutching a handkerchief. It was said to be the first occasion that the entire Sample C. George family had been together in one room since its dramatic disintegration in 1889.

If the large crowd present had hoped to hear squalid details of his failed marriage, they must have been mightily disappointed by Sample's testimony. Examined by Welty, he said he had been married to Annie in 1878 and separated from her in 1889. Sterling then got right to the point:

"From the time of your marriage to the accused until the time you met George D. Saxton, what were your relations with your wife?"

Pomerene objected to the question but Judge Taylor over-ruled and the question was repeated, to which Sample George replied:

"They were pleasant and happy."

"How many children were born to your marriage?"

"Three."

"One is dead?"

"Yes sir."

"Is this one of them?" asked Welty gently, pointing to Charles Howard George, who was sitting with his brother by their mother at the defense table.

"Yes sir, and he is a good boy," said Sample with obvious emotion. For a moment the audience in the court room basked in what appeared to be beams of parental love flowing from both Annie and Sample to their two sons. Visibly moved to tears, Mrs.

George buried her face in her handkerchief. Then Welty said, "That is all," and turned the witness over to Grant.

By now the courtroom audience was used to Grant playing the heavy, and the spectators watched in fascination as he attacked Sample George's idyllic portrait of his pre-Saxton marriage days. Eager to show that Annie had already been unhappy and restless in her marriage before meeting Saxton, Grant took Sample George back to the early 1880s.

MRS. GEORGE WEPT WHEN HER HUSBAND TOLD THE STORY OF A BROKEN HOME.

Mrs. George Weeping as Her Husband Testifies
(Cleveland Daily World, April 22, 1899)

"You say your relations were always pleasant with your wife?"

"Always pleasant except for the ordinary troubles that come between man and wife."

"Did you not have trouble in Hanoverton?"

"No, sir."

"Didn't you quarrel there?"

"No sir; only the little quarrels such as every man and wife have."

"Where were you at the time of the birth of that child you say is a good boy?"

"At Salem."

"You were not with your wife then?"

"No sir."

"You were not there for some time after the birth?"

"I got home the same night."

"You had not been there for ten days or two weeks before?"

"It was over two weeks."

"She complained to you then?"

"No sir. I had left her in good care."

"Didn't you have differences for some time after this?"

"No sir."

"You remember the time you wanted her to go away from you and that you directed her to go back home?"

"No sir."

"You had trouble when you lived in the Saxton block?"

"We had trouble when we moved into the Saxton block."

After Sample stepped down the lawyers in the case finished their presentation of all remaining papers documenting the many lawsuits of Annie George and George Saxton that were relevant to the case. Finally, at 4:05 p.m. Welty intoned, "The Defense rests," and court adjourned for the day.

It had been one of the most eventful days of a tumultuous trial. The testimony from multiple witnesses concerning Christina

Eckroate's drug habit had been devastating to the State's reliance on her eyewitness identification of Mrs. George as Saxton's killer. Worse yet, Florence Klingler's provision of an alibi for Mrs. George's missing hour had provided the long-missing linchpin of her defense. Yet, the most important development of the day's voluminous testimony had been what was *not* said. After weeks of conflicting rumors, it was now finally clear that Annie George was not going to testify in her own defense. In the final analysis, only she could really account for her actions and whereabouts on the evening of October 7, 1898. And, now, for whatever reason, she had chosen not to testify. No one knew whether it would help or hurt her — but the disappointment in Canton was almost palpable.

Even more eloquent in its impact was what Sample C. George had not said in his testimony. Given the perfect opportunity to revenge himself on a faithless wife, he had taken the high road, essentially blaming her fall and his heartbreak on the murder victim. His silence on Annie's shame was a bonus to the defense and continuing evidence to everyone that it was really George Saxton, not Annie George who was on trial in courtroom No. 2.

MRS. GEORGE RECEIVING HER MAIL.

Mrs. George Attending to Her Mail in Court
(Cleveland Daily World, April 7, 1899)

Chapter 19 "Sensational Features of an Unseemly Character"

The Annie George trial had now consumed almost three weeks. As Saturday morning court opened, the audience in courtroom No. 2 could sense the rush to complete the presentation of testimony. Pomerene began by asking for the recall of Lizzie Miller to the stand. A certificate from her physician, a Dr. Marchland, was then produced, stating that she was too ill to appear in court. Pomerene agreed to complete the examination of the defense's witnesses, reserving the right to recall Miller if possible. The defense called Stark County surveyor John S. Hoover to the stand for his third appearance. He was not very helpful to the State's case. He testified that on the previous night, at the behest of the prosecutors, he had measured some distances between key locations discussed during the trial. According to his measurement, it was exactly 5416 feet from 319 Lincoln Avenue to Florence Klingler's home at 311 Marion Street. He also offered estimates of the length of other possible routes taken by Saxton's murderer. During cross-examination, however, he admitted that he had not included in his estimate of the route between Eva Althouse's house and Klingler's home the distance from Lincoln Avenue to Lawn Avenue or the route through the vacant lot that was the most probable escape route of Saxton's shooter. His estimates of other distances, including the route from 319 Lincoln Avenue to the intersection of South and High Streets, were objected to by Welty. After listening to his argument that the State had not proved that the accused had taken any of the specific routes measured by Hoover, Judge Taylor excluded his estimates from the evidence.

Judge Taylor didn't know it, but his decision throwing out Hoover's first measurement was supported by empirical experiment. Following Klingler's Friday afternoon testimony, five newspaper correspondents and a Canton lawyer had walked the route from 319 Lincoln Avenue to 311 Marion Street. It had taken them 20½ minutes to complete the trek, and they had walked faster than they thought Mrs. George could have done. As Florence Klingler's testimony only allowed Annie 15 minutes — at best — to sprint from the Althouse steps to Florence's front door, it seemed an unlikely route for her to have taken. Nor did it allow her any extra time for a detour to ditch the gun at High and South Streets on her way to Klingler's.

The presentation of rebuttal witnesses commenced. Michael Barr, the Canton post office money order clerk, once again returned to the witness stand. Contradicting Lena Lindeman's testimony, he swore he had seen Annie twice at the downtown Canton post office on the afternoon of October 7, once at 2:45 and again at 3:15 p.m. This was of little relevance to the State's case, except to impeach Lindeman's general veracity: where Annie was during mid-afternoon was not a critical element to either the State's case or her defense.

Barr continued his unlucky career as a prosecution witness as Pomerene asked him to authenticate two letters as being in Mrs. George's hand. The prosecutor's purpose here was to show that Annie had been friendly with other men, a contradiction of her supposedly exclusive passion for Saxton. One of the letters, written during her Dakota divorce sojourn, was addressed to a Canton man, whom she saluted as "Dear Jack." The letter expressed her longing for Jack and closed with "One big kiss for you." Although Barr identified the letters as being in Annie's hand, Judge Taylor, consistent with his policy of excluding testimony about other women or men involved with Annie and Saxton — always excepting Eva Althouse — briskly excluded the letters.

Grant essayed one final effort to destroy the credibility of Florence Klingler with an attempt to put the journal entry of her allegedly unsavory divorce into evidence but was rebuffed by Judge Taylor. Taylor likewise declined to allow in Mrs. George's affidavit from her 1891 Dakota divorce hearing, which set forth her reasons for ending her marriage. Mrs. George had stated at that time, in part to shield Saxton, that she had left Sample because of his "cruelty," rather than because Saxton solicited her affections. The State hoped to show by the affidavit that her state of mind at the time was far from the emotional, irrational frenzy suggested by the defense. Judge Taylor sensibly ruled it out as too remote in time from Saxton's murder.

Judge Taylor also excluded several State rebuttal witnesses ready to talk about Mrs. George's alleged relations with other men. One was J. C. Stanton, a Canton businessman who had received a letter from Annie while she was in South Dakota. The letter, while hardly explicit, might be interpreted as a request for an assignation. Stanton's obvious relief at not being forced to testify was considerably diminished when a vindictive James Grant leaked the text to newspaper reporters, who published the gist of the letter the following day. Pomerene tried once more, recalling Nettie McAllister to testify about Annie's relations with other men. Judge Taylor would not allow her testimony into the record and the defeated prosecutor promptly dismissed several other witnesses he had called for the same purpose. Judge Taylor's consistent policy of excluding testimony about the alleged relations of Annie George and George Saxton with other partners won the applause of the next day's *Cleveland Plain Dealer* account:

> All through the trial Judge Taylor has ruled to a fine point on all testimony degrading to the character of either Saxton or Mrs. George. It has been due to this attitude of the court that many sensational features of an unseemly character have been eliminated from the trial, and for this reason the gossip mongers have not been compelled to work overtime at any stage of the case. . . . If the court had allowed both sides to go as far as they stated they could go, the case would have fairly reeked with filth and shame. But, for the good of the community, it may be said these features are not portrayed.

Sample C. George was recalled, this time by the State. He was asked to authenticate the document recording the settlement of his alienation-of-affection suit again George Saxton. One of the most bizarre incidents of the trial occurred when Pomerene tried to enter it in as evidence. Welty initially objected to its admission, perhaps concerned that Annie's jury might perceive it as the triggering event for her long promised revenge. In the middle of his plea to Judge Taylor, however, Welty suddenly realized that the document actually worked as evidence *against* the State's case, as it constituted an admission that Saxton *had* lured Annie away from her husband. Without explanation, he suavely reversed field and graciously assented to putting the document in evidence.

Policeman Fred S. McCloud was recalled to testify by the State. He was prepared to say that he had seen Dr. Pontius removing towels from Mrs. George's corset during her physical examination at the Canton police station. The inference was that, contrary to Lena Lindeman's testimony, Annie could have concealed a revolver amid her ample figure enhancements. But Judge Taylor refused to allow McCloud to so testify, ruling that his testimony was inadmissible because Pontius' search had taken place when Annie was under duress.

Appearing as a State rebuttal witness, Cleveland private detective Jake Mintz finally made his long-anticipated appearance on the stand. Confronted with the evidence of his correspondence with Saxton—the pasted-together letters Annie and Florence Klingler had purloined from Saxton's wastebasket during the summer of 1896—Mintz cautiously denied authorship of them, parsing his words carefully: "I deny that I ever wrote those letters—at least I deny until I can look over my files and be sure about the matter." But Mintz was unapologetically frank about the nature of his work for Saxton, telling the jury:

Saxton asked me to shadow him and said that he was afraid that he was going to be murdered. He wanted me to put a man on the case and find out other cases in which Mrs. George had been intimate with men. Saxton was afraid of Mrs. George and wanted to get her mixed up with a certain restaurant keeper so that he could get away from her. I sent a man down there and he remained there for several days and then returned home. I asked why he had made a failure of the case and he told me Saxton wanted me to compromise Mrs. George. He anticipated her being intimate with other men and a restaurant keeper in particular and wanted to catch them together. When this first man returned I sent down another and by catching Mrs. George with some other man I expected to put her out of Saxton's way forever. That is the way I take that [letter], although at this time I deny that I wrote it.

Pomerene's attempt to enter Mintz's torn-up letters as evidence was overruled by Judge Taylor.

A Sketch of Jake Mintz
(Cleveland Plain Dealer, February 21, 1909)

Pomerene next made a strong effort to counteract Dr. Eyman's highly damaging testimony concerning Christina Eckroate's drug addiction. Dr. Austin C. Brant, who had already testified for the State, was recalled, this time as an expert witness. Stating his formal credentials and experience, Brant told the jury that he had devoted much study and practice to the use and effects of morphine and other opiates. More specifically, he said he had known Mrs. Eckroate for eight years, had observed her work as a nurse in families of his practice, and had been her personal physician at various times. He now told the jury that he and Dr. Austin B. Walker had examined her the previous Wednesday evening at Walker's office and at Mrs. Eckroate's home just the previous night. He stated to the jury that he had found Mrs. Eckroate normal in every respect: her eyes, pulse, temperature and nervous system seemed perfectly healthy, as was her skin tone. She could read rapidly and accurately. Better yet, Dr. Brant found that her memory was excellent; she even recalled nursing some of his patients whom he had completely forgotten. So far as he knew, said Brant, Mrs. Eckroate did not suffer from hallucinations. Summarizing his observations of Mrs. Eckroate, Brant swore under oath:

> If I relied on my examination, I would say that she
> never used any morphine at all. I did not see any
> symptoms of the use of morphine.

Speaking from his general experience, Brant stated that a person could take up to a grain of opiate without deteriorating effects, although after some years of use a large dosage would break down the patient and make her unreliable. But a small quantity taken over a period of years, as in Mrs. Eckroate's case, might not necessarily affect her truthfulness or reliability.

Welty had prepared himself well for Brandt's cross-examination. He began by reading extracts to him from medical authorities on the subject of morphine eaters. Every authority quoted affirmed that chronic morphine abusers had no idea of right and wrong and that no reliance could be placed on statements made by them. When confronted with these authorities, Brant replied that such had not been his experience. Welty quoted more authorities; Brant remained adamant. Finally, however, Welty wrung a significant concession from him:

"Is it not true, Doctor, that there may be no physical symptoms and yet the patient be a habitual user of morphine?"

"There may be such cases."

Pomerene recovered some lost ground during his redirect examination, when he got Brant to restate more emphatically his conviction that Mrs. Eckroate did not suffer from hallucinations.

Dr. Austin B. Walker was summoned to amplify Brant's testimony. He told the jury he had practiced medicine in Canton for 26 years and that he, too, had made a special study of drug addiction. Walker described the symptoms usually found in habitual morphine eaters: pallor, an impaired nervous system and muscle tremors. He said he had found none of these symptoms during his two examinations of Christina Eckroate. He said he could not tell that she had been using the drug for years. Walker qualified the statement slightly, saying that he thought she was addicted to morphine but that it had not a serious effect on her nervous system.

Sterling followed Welty's scholarly approach during his cross-examination of Walker, quoting numerous medical authorities on the unreliability and moral disintegration of habitual opiate abusers. Walker airily dismissed them, accusing Sterling of selective quotation from his sources. Finding Walker unyielding on medical grounds, Sterling tried a common-sense approach, appealing to the jurors' memories of Joseph Eckroate's vivid testimony chronicling his wife's drug-induced behavior:

Now, Doctor, I want to ask you this: Wouldn't a person living with a victim of the morphine habit for 10 or 15 years and observing such a victim day and night—might such a person be more competent to testify as to the effect of the drug than a doctor would be at the end of a half-hour examination?

"No," replied Walker emphatically. "Persons in her house," he continued, "might attribute her irritability and queer actions to morphine, when in fact they might be due to other causes. The physician would be the better judge."

The parade of rebuttal witnesses continued. J. J. Hawk was asked by Grant whether Ira Howenstine had been living at the home of Florence Klingler at the time of Annie's alleged visit on October 7. The defense objected and Judge Taylor ruled the question out of the record. W. H. Little was queried about Saxton's manner towards Mrs. George on an occasion when she entered the Saxton block to replevin some of her goods. Little stated that Saxton was not "unduly troublesome" and was excused.

During the noon recess Pomerene announced that the State would be unable to recall Lizzie Miller for rebuttal testimony, owing to her ill health. Once more, the State called Nettie McAllister to testify about Mrs. George's relations with men other than Saxton. Judge Taylor ruled such testimony out, as he did the words of the next witness, a Mrs. J. A. Giffin of West Virginia who had lived in the Saxton block during Annie's residency there.

The last three rebuttal witnesses were Samuel Kirk, Lena Mauger and Ida Hug. Kirk owned the Star Restaurant and Mauger and Hug were employed there as waitresses. Pomerene had already tried unsuccessfully to get their testimony into the record but had been twice rebuffed by Judge Taylor, who ruled that he should have examined them in direct testimony, not rebuttal. The chief prosecutor finally convinced Judge Taylor otherwise on Saturday afternoon, and his three witnesses were put on the stand to contradict Lena Lindeman's testimony that Annie George had remained at her home until 5:30 p.m. on October 7. They all testified that Annie had been at the restaurant between about 4:45

and 5:15 p.m., although Hug and Mauger persistently misidentified the date as October 17 instead of October 7.

And suddenly — it was over. At 2:38 p.m., Pomerene announced, "The State rests." "Is this all of your evidence?" asked Judge Taylor of the four attorneys. "We have nothing further," Welty replied. The defense had not called a single rebuttal witness. Judge Taylor asked the attorneys if they wished to begin their final arguments or put them off until 10 a.m. on Monday; they chose to defer them until then. Annie's jurors were admonished as to their duties, especially to keep silent and not discuss the case with anyone.

It had been another disappointing day for the State. As Arthur Sperry opined in Sunday's *Cleveland World*, they had continued to "get it in the neck" throughout that long Saturday. Virtually all of the prosecution's documents and witnesses pertaining to Annie's alleged relations with other men had been ruled out of evidence. But Pomerene put on his brave face for reporters, offering a confident summary of his three weeks' work:

> Mrs. George is manifestly guilty and the proof so shows. We are confident of her conviction. We have shown she was in the immediate vicinity of the crime, within 10 to 15 minutes before it was committed, at a point out of her usual haunts. We have shown the killing by two witnesses, one of whom swears positively to the very close resemblance of the party shooting to the accused. We have shown repeated threats by the defendant to kill the deceased, covering a period of three years, and even within seven hours of the crime. We have shown where she hid the revolver. She refused when arrested to make any statement, and she never has made any statement since that time. The defense has materially strengthened our case by their very weak effort at an alibi. The defense failed to account for

her during the half hour within which the crime was committed.

Pomerene ended his press conference by repeating his promise to move out of Stark County if Mrs. George were acquitted.

John Welty's summary comment to newspapermen was equally confident:

> Mrs. George is innocent of the killing of George D. Saxton and we have proved it. The state has proved nothing important. The state has not only not produced any evidence but has failed to establish any circumstances of guilt. The facts concerning her whereabouts the day of the killing conclusively prove her to be innocent. The only item of evidence connecting Mrs. George with the crime is what is sworn to by Mrs. Eckroate, and her testimony has been so completely discredited that the jury will not be warranted in considering it seriously. The alibi makes the proof of Mrs. George's innocence complete and absolute. She could not have been at the scene of the crime at the time it was committed, if the evidence of the witness was true. There was no need for Mrs. George to go on the stand in her own defense. Not only has the state failed to prove Mrs. George guilty, but we have proved her innocent.

Informed of Pomerene's renewed promise to quit Stark County if Annie was not convicted, Welty quipped, "He had better start packing."

Always her own best publicist, Annie contributed an upbeat gloss on the progress of her trial, singling out Judge Taylor and the press for special praise:

> I am satisfied. I have had a fair trial, and that is all I
> ever asked. Judge Taylor seems to me an ideal
> judge. His rulings have done a great deal to hasten
> the proceedings and his manner shows his absolute
> fairness. He may be a stern judge, but he is always
> fair. I want to thank the newspapers, too. They have
> all been very kind to me with one or two exceptions.
> I feel now that I am safe.

Annie's demeanor after she returned to her cell Saturday afternoon was consistent with her public stance, light-hearted and seemingly oblivious to the peril of her jury's impending decision. She entertained relatives in her cell that evening and the next day, laughing and joking as if she didn't have a care in the world. Her mood may have been infectious: the word of the Canton street was that she would get, at worst, a hung jury. More giddily optimistic souls were predicting that if she were acquitted she was planning to sue the Saxton estate for her one-third dower right, claiming it her desert as his common-law wife. Less sanguine souls dashed water on that startling idea, pointing out that Annie had probably forfeited any such claim when she withdrew her breach-of-promise suit in 1896. And the next morning's *Cleveland Plain Dealer* contained a chilling prediction, attributed to May Streeter, Annie's bosom confidante, that belied her calm public face.

According to May, the 40-year old defendant had determined to kill herself if convicted on any of the charges against her:

> She realizes her life has been blighted. She also realizes a term of penal servitude would leave her a decrepit old woman, with nothing to live for. Indeed, she has no home and, if acquitted, will be compelled to earn her own living. She has two handsome sons, but they have not lived with their mother for some years past.

When told of Streeter's alleged comments, Sheriff Zaiser laughed them off, saying Annie would never kill herself and that she was going to be acquitted anyway. Notwithstanding his optimism, the *Plain Dealer* writer morbidly enlarged on Streeter's direful prophecy, noting that Annie inhabited, by sheer coincidence, the "suicide" cell of the Stark county jail. It seems that in 1888 drunken Conrad Doll had killed his wife and son with a hatchet at the dinner table. His premeditated attack was so savage that both of the son's hands were cut off in vain attempts to protect himself. While awaiting trial, Doll hanged himself in his cell with his bed sheets. The jail turnkey had logged his death with the curtly callous entry: "Gone to hell by the hemp route."

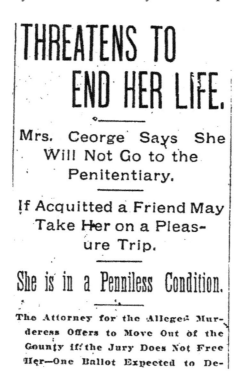

THREATENS TO END HER LIFE.

Mrs. George Says She Will Not Go to the Penitentiary.

If Acquitted a Friend May Take Her on a Pleasure Trip.

She is in a Penniless Condition.

The Attorney for the Alleged Murderess Offers to Move Out of the County if the Jury Does Not Free Her—One Ballot Expected to De-

Threatens to End Her Life
(Cleveland Plain Dealer, April 24, 1899)

Owing to Sheriff Zaiser's new rules, only relatives were allowed to visit Annie during the last weekend of her trial. Stung by criticism that his visitation policy had been too lenient to his celebrity prisoner — criticism highlighted in that Sunday morning's *Plain Dealer* — Zaiser reacted by sharply restricting the public's access to Mrs. George, defending his new policy thusly:

> The cranks, sharpers, fortune tellers and other fakers all over the country who have been writing letters to Mrs. George have taken to coming here now and if I allowed all of them to see her we would have the jail like a railroad depot. So I have decided to keep everybody out.

Chief among Zaiser's irritations was a 50-year old former stock raiser from Tuscarawas County. A regular attendee at Annie's trial, the prosperous retiree had written to Mrs. George and informed her that he was in love with her and wished to marry her. He was not discouraged by her failure to reply, or by Zaiser's refusal to let him visit Annie. He told Zaiser he supposed Annie thought he was a "crank" but was sure he would be able to persuade her otherwise if he had a chance to talk to her and lay his heart at her feet.

Meanwhile, more rumors percolated throughout Canton as the hours before the final arguments slipped away. It was said that Mrs. George was writing her autobiography. It was noised about that during Christina Eckroate's first appearance before the grand jury in January she had stated that she could not see well enough to say whether it was a man or woman by the Althouse steps. A little later, the story continued, she contacted Pomerene, saying she had just been commanded by the Lord in a vision to tell the truth about what she saw. She then confessed to the prosecutor she had clearly recognized Mrs. George as the shooter. The fact that Christina *had* appeared twice before the grand jury gave a certain structural plausibility to the claim she had changed her story. But the real explanation was that one of the grand jury members had become ill and missed a critical portion of Christina's first appearance, necessitating her recall for additional testimony. A more obviously false rumor, easily disproved by reference to the trial transcript, was that the State's attorneys had failed to ask witnesses who saw Mrs. George get off the streetcar at Hazlette Avenue which direction she then took. The latest gossip was that one of the witnesses had seen her walking west toward Lincoln Avenue. The witness had not stated this in court, it was said, because he wasn't asked.

Chapter 20   "Thus She Did It! Thus She Did It!"

Whatever her private thoughts, it was obvious to Annie's courtroom audience that she looked paler than ever as court resumed on Monday morning, April 24 at 10:00 a.m. When asked about the rumor she might commit suicide, however, she simply smiled and said, "Don't you believe a word of it!" The crowd, which had waited hours to invade courtroom No. 2, was the largest ever at Annie's trial. It spilled over into the section reserved for newspapermen and extra chairs were brought in to accommodate the overflow.

Shortly after Judge Taylor gaveled court into session, James J. Grant rose to make his final argument. Thereby hung a curious tale—if Canton gossips were to be believed. Rumor was that the two prosecutors had originally agreed that Grant would close for the State. It made some sense: Grant was at least equally celebrated as Pomerene for his oratorical force and it was felt that his love for Saxton and his contempt for Mrs. George would tell powerfully with her jury. Fearing that Grant would close, the defense had thereupon contrived a shrewd ploy to insure that Pomerene, not Grant, had the last word with the jury. To that end cunning John Welty had prompted his wife to spread the rumor that Pomerene was going to concede the glory and prestige of making the final argument to his assistant prosecutor. As intended, this rumor reached the ears of his wife, the formidable Mary Helen Bockius Pomerene. Ambitious for her husband, the incensed Mary Helen had given him a vigorous curtain lecture on the subject. The upshot came as the two attorneys dined together on the day before the closing arguments began. Out of the blue, Pomerene announced, "Mr. Grant, my wife is determined that I shall close this case." As the disappointed Grant allegedly later told friends, "There I was. What could I do?" So it was Grant, instead, who opened the closing arguments that Monday morning.

ATTY. GRANT'S POSES.

Attorney James Grant's Poses
(Cleveland Daily World, April 25, 1899)

The many lawyers who packed Judge Taylor's courtroom in anticipation of a memorable argument were not disappointed. Grant had waited a long time to push Annie George into the electric chair and he now made the plea of a lifetime. Often shouting, sometimes nearly sobbing, he stalked the courtroom like a man almost demonically possessed. Over six feet tall, and weighing an eighth of a ton, the imposing attorney alternately hung over the jury box or loomed like an avenging angel over the prisoner at the defense table. Sometimes he was so beside himself with emotion that perspiration run in rivulets down his face and saliva sprayed from his mouth. Experienced courtroom advocates present were said to rub their ears as Grant proceeded with his scorching condemnation of one he would only refer to contemptuously as "that woman."

Grant began by congratulating Annie's jurymen on their patience over the three weeks of the trial. He calmly took up some of the drier legal issues in the case, carefully defining for the jury the various degrees of murder and the concepts of malice and premeditation. He then turned to the Barberi case, which Annie's defense had offered as a legal precedent justifying testimony showing the state of mind of the accused. Maria Barberi had killed her lover in New York City after he had abandoned her. She had been convicted of murder but after much public controversy the verdict was reversed. During her second trial, testimony concerning her distraught state of mind was allowed and she was subsequently convicted of the lesser crime of manslaughter. It was an interesting precedent, Grant allowed, but it was particularly bizarre, he continued, that it had been cited by Annie's defense team. In the Barberi case, as he explained to the jury, Maria's defense team had consistently admitted to the *fact* of the killing — their only argument being whether her state of mind should lessen the degree of her guilt. But the case of Annie George, Grant insisted, was far different. Although it was true that Annie had pleaded not guilty, Grant told the jury, the fact that her lawyers placed so much emphasis on her state of mind constituted an implicit admission of her guilt.

Taking up the concept of premeditation, Grant argued that the period of time necessary to prove it need not be lengthy:

> Any time prior to the act is sufficient to constitute premeditation and deliberation, if sufficient to give the slayer an opportunity to consider and think about the act which he is about to perpetrate. A purpose and a design may be formed and constitute premeditation and deliberation without any particular period of intervening time.

Grant now came to the murder itself. He briefly reviewed the history of Saxton's troubled relations with Annie George, and recalled his own anguish and apprehension for his friend:

> For years I had seen the clouds gather over the path of the victim. Dark, dark and darker still, they grew. Two days before his death [when Sample C. George's suit was settled], light seemed to break. "It's settled at last," I said. "Old fellow, give me your hand; your trouble is over; I congratulate you." But I was mistaken; it was not settled. Then the dark purpose of that woman, who never faltered in her schemes from the first time she met him, was manifested.

Warming to his grim narrative, Grant reviewed the grisly facts of Saxton's murder, dwelling on the wounds in a manner which echoed Marc Antony's funeral oration over the corpse of Julius Caesar. Pausing for a moment, he raised his voice dramatically, and shouted, "I say now, as I shall say in the close, that in the light of the evidence on behalf of the state, I say the prisoner at the bar, Annie E. George, killed George D. Saxton!"

Welty was on his feet: "I object! Wait a minute! I want a stenographer to take that statement down, unless it is withdrawn!" Judge Taylor cautioned Grant, "Counsel has the right to argue in the case in light of the *evidence*." "I make the statement on behalf of the State, according to the *evidence*," shot back Grant. Welty challenged him again, "Do you withdraw it?" "I am not here as an individual," retorted Grant piously, "I speak for the State and of the evidence!"

Grant next discussed the aftermath of the killing, stressing the big crowds that had gathered at both the Althouse residence and Mrs. Oberlin's house. As he explained it to the jury, Annie's arrest was a perfectly logical outcome of widespread and justified suspicions against her:

The officers waited until she arrived, and she was arrested; then they dispersed and went to their homes — the murderess was found!

"Objection!" roared out Welty. "There must be some limit in this argument. He is talking about what public opinion was, and that is decidedly improper!" Judge Taylor didn't wait for argument. Turning to Grant, he said, "I shall take occasion to say to you and the jury that this lady is not to be convicted on suspicion." "But I expect to rely on the evidence," complained Grant. "That doesn't make any difference," returned Judge Taylor. "Public opinion hasn't anything to do with this woman's conviction."

Building his case for premeditation, Grant reprised Annie's repeated threats to shoot George Saxton. He reviewed W. F. Cook's story about seeing her with a revolver in the Saxton block, her threats in the presence of Mary Grable, Mary Finley, Nettie McAllister, Charles Lloyd and Perry Van Horne. Grant characterized Annie's Thursday night search with Dickerhoff as a stalking expedition, evidence that she was looking for Saxton to kill him. He brought up the threat to kill Saxton she made to John J. Jackson just seven hours before the murder. Grant sarcastically recalled in great detail her legal conference with W. O. Werntz, and how she cynically consulted with him about how to kill Saxton and get away with it. Grant soared into a blistering indictment of her character, ridiculing the idea of her supposed, enduring "love" for George Saxton and her pose as a loving mother:

> Werntz, like an honorable gentleman, told her if she had no respect for herself she ought to have for her two boys. I don't know how motherhood can forget the childhood it has created. She who has been consecrated to a mission, a cause peculiarly her own, I don't know how she can forget that. But even her love for her boys did not keep this woman from ful-

filling her purpose. The burden of the testimony you have heard shows that that woman would stop at nothing. . . . There this woman planned in cold blood the murder of the man they say she loved so well. She debated whether she should use one revolver or two. She considered whether she should throw a revolver at his feet. She would take his life and then throw a revolver at his feet to place him in the light of a would-be murderer. What a spectacle! And she would do this to the man she loved so well! Heaven keep you gentlemen and me, from such love as hers!

One of the chief obstacles for the State had always been to provide a clear-cut and unmixed motive for Annie's killing of Saxton. If it was partially her frustrated love for Saxton, as much of the defense testimony seemed to imply, it might be considered as a kind of mitigating temporary insanity by Annie's jury. So Grant directly attacked the claim that Anna had ever loved Saxton. "Her only purpose was *money*!" he screamed at the jury. Her goal, he continued, had been to get money out of Sample C. George's lawsuit and she believed it would lapse if she killed Saxton before it was settled. When she discovered it *was* settled, Grant continued, she decided to kill Saxton.

Continuing his character assault, Grant accused Annie of cowardice:

She said she would go in front of Saxton and make a "good job of it," so that all the world might know. She said she "would not go behind his back." Grant paused dramatically. "Where's that coat?!" he shouted. "We'll see whether the person who killed Saxton went behind his back!" The clothing worn by Saxton when he was killed was brought into the courtroom. Brandishing the coat just inches away from the faces of the jurymen, Grant shouted, "Look at the coat! See the powder burns!" Seizing Hasler's revolver, he grasped it in his right hand and acted out how Mrs. George had accosted Saxton at the Althouse steps. Holding the coat, he pantomimed how she had faced Saxton at the final moment. A second later, he walked over to Mrs. George and snapped the hammer of the revolver several times in her face, shouting, "Thus she did it! Thus she did it!" Annie didn't twitch a muscle as all eyes in the courtroom stared at the spectacle. Seemingly oblivious to Grant's towering belligerence, she appeared to be nonchalantly reading some newspaper headlines over Welty's shoulder. Her sister, Mrs. Sinclair, seated behind her, audibly wept as Grant confronted Annie.

Grant now turned to a more fact-based focus on some of the witnesses in the case. He singled out Mary Grable and Christina Eckroate for special praise, accusing the defense of unchivalrously blackening their characters:

> They showed nothing in their examination, and in their cross-examination, which Mr. Welty made very vigorous, but the infirmities of age, yet the defense has heaped calumny upon them and tried to prove that they were not to be believed; and that they were not reliable.

With a sobbing catch in his voice, Grant pitched his peroration perfectly to the jurymen, most of them middle-aged or older: "Is it not a pity that a woman must grow *old*?"

Moving on to the expert medical testimony, Grant carefully praised Dr. Eyman's qualifications but scoffed at his testimony, arguing that it should carry no weight because he had never

A Woman Scorned

personally examined Mrs. Eckroate. And he continued his vendetta against Florence Klingler, sparking the angriest assault in his 4½ hour diatribe: "True to her character," sneered the assistant prosecutor, "Mrs. George went to the home of the Klingler woman, the divorced woman, the woman who testified she lived for three weeks with an indecent woman!"

"Hold on there!" shouted Welty. "You can't call anybody indecent!"

"I didn't call anybody indecent," shouted back Grant, "and what I say I say from the evidence. I do not mean to say anything the evidence does not show!" Grant and Welty continued shouting at each other, nearly coming to blows before Judge Taylor calmed them down. "We must have order," he warned them, "or steps will be taken to secure it." By that time the disorder had spread to the courtroom audience and Judge Taylor had to make repeated threats to clear the room before the commotion subsided.

Grant did not forget the two mysterious strangers seen by Lizzie Miller and Jacob Adams. He dismissed Adams' sighting as "nothing" and went on to draw a highly skeptical conclusion about Miller's alternative suspect:

There was no blood on the strange figure, the he, she or it, which Mrs. Lizzie Miller saw on Linden Avenue. This evidence was drawn into the case to appear as something more than it was. This is a large city, gentlemen; there are many strange people walking along the streets.

Moreover, Grant continued, it was unlikely that the slayer of Saxton would choose such a public, noisy escape route as the Linden Avenue plank sidewalk.

Appropriately, Grant, the once dear best friend of George Saxton, saved his defense of the murdered man until almost the close of his impassioned plea. For three weeks he had listened painfully as many witnesses had repeated a decade's worth of

Annie's doleful tales about his wicked behavior to her. Grant's testimonial to Saxton was a moving tribute, if perhaps better than he deserved:

> George Saxton was a man. While there has been innuendo heaped upon George Saxton so black it can not be read, I want proof that has been introduced in these three weeks of trial or from anyone that George Saxton ever conducted himself as anything but a gentleman. You have nothing but the second-hand statements of this woman to the contrary. He never struck her.

Grant ended his passionate argument at about 3:30 p.m, after almost five hours of nearly volcanic oratory. Thanking the jury, he said he left the case in their hands with complete confidence that justice would be served. As he sat down, red-faced and exhausted, a phalanx of Annie's friends and relatives rushed to her side to give her support. It was reported that most of the half-hundred female spectators shook her hand and congratulated her on standing up so well to Grant's brutal attack. (They may, too, have been expressing empathic concern for Grant's cruelest charge against Annie George: that she was no longer young.) Noting the lateness of the hour and perhaps wishing to avoid an anti-climax, Judge Taylor announced adjournment for the day.

Whatever plaudits Grant garnered for his incendiary rhetoric that long Monday, it was, as usual, Annie who won the highest praise from the reporters in court, for her unflinching calm during Grant's marathon tirade. Jacob Waldeck once again complimented her in print for her "wonderful degree of self-possession" and the *Cleveland Plain Dealer* correspondent marveled at her imperturbability during Grant's vitriolic assault of "loathing, scorn and hate." Arthur Sperry, her most consistent press cheerleader, was unrestrained in his admiration of her unruffled demeanor as she basked in the sympathies of the female spectators who mobbed her after the day's adjournment:

> No happy hostess of a mansion could have received more gracefully or seemed more care-free and at her ease than did this wonderful woman who had been unstintingly attacked all day. . . . At the close of the day she shook hands pleasantly, almost merrily, with the crowd of half a hundred women who gathered at the front of the spectators' space . . . . The expressions of sympathy by the women . . . amount to an ovation.

JAMES STERLING,
One of the three attorneys engaged by
Mrs. George.

Defense Attorney James Sterling
(Cleveland Press, October 12, 1898)

Chapter 20 "Thus She Did It! Thus She Did It!"

When court reopened at 8:30 on Tuesday morning, Sterling promptly opened his final argument for the defense. Like Grant, he began slowly and calmly, citing almost an hour's worth of legal and medical authorities on the subjects of circumstantial evidence and morphine addiction. His key point on circumstantial evidence, which he hammered home hard to the jury, was that a chain of circumstantial evidence must be perfect to warrant conviction. "We shall show," promised Sterling, "that in this case several links are missing and others are very weak." Serving notice that he would attack Christina Eckroate's eyewitness testimony, he quoted eminent medical authorities to bolster his assertion that chronic morphine addicts were incorrigible liars.

Putting aside his law and medical texts, Sterling went on the offensive. He had barely begun speaking before it became clear that his final plea was consistent with the defense strategy pursued during the trial: the prosecution of the late George DeWalt Saxton. Citing Grant's characterization of Saxton as a "prominent" Canton citizen, he contradicted it head-on in phrases of stinging mockery:

> Grant has said that George was a prominent citizen of Canton. I grant it. He was a prominent citizen, but not prominent in anything that was noble, pure, true or good. He was the son of James A. Saxton and a brother-in-law of President McKinley. He was rich. While I do not charge that against him, I doubt the right of a man so situated, with all the beautiful women there are in this country, to live the life of a bachelor. He never legitimately called a woman his wife, though he often registered so with women under his own or assumed names. He never acknowledged a legitimate offspring. He was a deliberate, designing libertine and seducer. Happiness fled from the home of the defendant when George Saxton entered. Discord, sorrow and pain entered her

family. . . . There could be no such thing as a home in our land if all men were like Saxton. He died with his feet on the steps leading to a house of a woman of shady reputation. He defied public sentiment and Christian civilization. Although well bred, he never entered a house of worship, save in pursuit of his prey. He was a disgrace to his sister and all worthy persons related to him. He must have died unwept and unmourned, unless they mourned the manner of his death.

Such sulfurous rhetoric was enough, as Arthur Sperry later remarked, to make the late George Saxton "turn under his eight-ton granite marble tombstone." But Sterling went on to state what had been implicit in much of the testimony offered in Annie's defense. Referring derisively to the histrionic excess of "Grant's thundering tones" and "Grant's drama," he continued:

I have not the volume of voice of my friend Grant. But I will endeavor to give you a more truthful version of the drama he endeavored to put on the boards before you. It is my deliberate judgment that the death of George D. Saxton was to Canton a public benefaction. I say that the air is purer by his passing away, and our wives, sisters and daughters are safer because of his spirit taking its flight.

Observing the legal proprieties, Sterling followed his virtual endorsement of Saxton's murder with an obligatory disclaimer, piously stating:

I do not want to be understood as justifying the taking of a human life, unless it is in the interest of the public welfare and the protection of sacred interest.

Still, he felt compelled to add, just in case the jury missed the point: "An American jury has never convicted a man who took the life of a seducer."

Sterling's point, of course, was both irrelevant and untrue. The accused killer was not a cuckolded husband but rather the seduced woman herself. And Sterling was likely aware of the 1870 Galentine-Jones affair, in which Cleveland dentist Jay Galentine fatally shot physician William Jones, his wife's lover, a killing for which Galentine's jury briskly sent him to prison. [For a chronicle of the spicy Galentine-Jones tragedy, see the author's "Cold Lead for Breakfast" in *They Died Crawling and Other Tales of Cleveland Woe* (Cleveland: Gray & Co. Publishers, 1995)].

Having posited that George Saxton was the devil incarnate, or someone very much like him, Sterling began constructing his contrasting archangel, retelling the by now somewhat shopworn tale of sweet Annie's seduction. How the innocent country girl had enjoyed a happy life with her husband and two darling children until she came to Canton. How she had unknowingly moved into "Saxton's den of infamy, the Saxton block," and naively but understandably misinterpreted her landlord's interest in her. How she had then fallen helplessly in love with the blackguard Saxton, broken the heart of honest Sample George, shamed her children and disgraced herself in the eyes of the world. It was powerfully moralistic, melodramatic stuff, and the erstwhile Canal Fulton preacher dished it out hot:

> Like a serpent, he placed his vile arms around the wife of Sample George's youth. He gratified his lust, then drove her from his presence. He persecuted her. He had no thanks, no pity for the loss of her home, her happiness, her life. There are worse crimes than murder. If he had only killed Mrs. George, instead of seducing her, how much better it would have been for her, how much less the shame,

pain and disgrace for her husband; how much better in every way for her children.

Whatever its calculated bathos, Sterling told his tale superlatively: by the time he finished his narrative of Annie's temptation and fall, she herself was weeping uncontrollably, as were several dozen women and, more significantly, juryman Franklin C. Miller. Attired that morning with her usual impeccable care, Annie was wearing her dark hat with two black wings. "As she sobbed yesterday," Arthur Sperry recounted in the next edition of the *Cleveland Evening World*, "the wings fluttered as though they were beating themselves, appealing for freedom."

Confident that he had his audience in a receptive mood, Sterling attacked the prosecution directly. Scoring Grant's final argument, he blasted the prosecutor for virtually telling the jury that there was hardly need for a trial, as Annie George had already been convicted on the night of the murder by public suspicion, the Canton police and county prosecutor Pomerene. Accusing Pomerene of trying to "stampede the jury," Sterling stressed the ironies of the prosecutor's position as a lawyer representing the civil government, both before and after Saxton's murder:

> He wanted her convicted on suspicion, a remarkable talk indeed for one who is representing the dignity of the law. The State is not justified with in starting out with a presumption of guilt. All the presumptions of the law are in favor of the defendant's innocence.

What a contrast the State's rush to judgment was, Sterling continued, to the willfully blind eye it turned to Saxton's many misdeeds by the Canton powers-that-be and one James J. Grant:

> The public and the police knew who had been the victim of the wrong doings of George Saxton, who

346

had been the sufferer by his persecutions for years, persecutions in which he was assisted by the very man who is here today representing the State in this case.

Pausing for a moment, Sterling let fly his most scathing barb yet at the assistant prosecutor, sneering, "The mantle of George D. Saxton seems to have fallen naturally on James J. Grant." The usually touchy Grant, however, didn't seem to mind Sterling's personal barbs. While Sterling repeatedly impugned his honor, actions and arguments, Grant sat next to Pomerene, quietly reading over the testimony in the case. Occasionally, when Sterling said something particularly invidious about him, he would look at him with a bland smile.

Sterling next addressed Grant's bald statement that the defense's stress on Saxton's wrongs against her was a virtual admission of guilt by Mrs. George. It was nothing of the kind, insisted the former preacher, but was offered merely to show Annie's anguish and her state of mind at the time she made her specific threats to kill Saxton. Narrating the threats in sequence, Sterling stressed that Annie had been emotional and overwrought on each of the occasions she had made the threats, as testified to by the State's own witnesses. Each threat, moreover, Sterling stated, had always had a crucial "if" condition attached to it: Annie threatened to kill Saxton only *if* he did not keep his promise to marry her *after* Sample's suit was settled. And there was no evidence that Saxton had refused to do so after that settlement, or even that Annie had had the opportunity to talk to Saxton about it. Her unwillingness to violate Saxton's injunction against her, attested to by officer Dickerhoff and Judge McCarty, moreover, was strong evidence of her scrupulously law-abiding behavior.

One by one, Sterling addressed the elements of the State's case. In their haste to railroad Annie to the electric chair, he asserted, Pomerene and Grant had not even bothered to establish a consistent, coherent motive for her alleged crime. It had spent most of its time documenting her threats — threats which could only be used as evidence of premeditation and malice, not as proof she committed the murder.

Nor had the State proved that Annie was even at the murder scene, continued Sterling. Their witnesses took her as far as the corner of Tuscarawas Street and Hazlette Avenue — and not a step farther. He asserted the evidence that she had even walked towards Lincoln Avenue was so meager as to not meet the evidentiary standard required in a civil action, much less a criminal trial with a woman's life at stake. Moreover, if Mrs. George had walked from the streetcar towards Lincoln Avenue she would have been seen by Jacob Adams. "So far as the proof is concerned, gentlemen, I say — and I say it in perfect confidence — you have no proof that Mrs. George was on Lincoln Avenue on that night. Nothing has been presented that would warrant you in holding that opinion."

The assistant defense counsel could not resist dragging in the absent Eva Althouse. Although she had not testified a word at the trial, Sterling darkly hinted that she knew much about Saxton's murder that the State would not like to hear told. And why, sneered Sterling, had the State taken such pains to provide an alibi for the missing Eva, a telling contrast to its persecution of Anna George?

Sterling vented particular scorn on Sergeant Hasler's revolver-in-a-sock tale, calling it "about the weakest, silliest story that could have been manufactured." He noted that it was so insubstantial that Pomerene had not even mentioned it in his opening statement, despite the fact that he had known of its existence three months before the trial opened.

Taking up the eyewitness testimony, Sterling singled out various witnesses as credible or not. He dismissed Laura Huwig's sighting of a "form" at the murder scene as worthless. "Why, you would not forfeit the life of a *dog* on such evidence," he told the jury. He recalled that even the young eyes of Russell Hogan could not tell whether the shooter was male or female. On the other

348

hand, he allowed that Lizzie Miller's "mysterious stranger" might have been the real killer. As for the pathetic Christina Eckroate, well, she was simply an object of pity. Speaking of her appearance on the stand, Sterling even insinuated that Doctors Austin Brant and Alonzo Walker were guilty of grossly unethical behavior:

> It is to be remembered that a woman's complexion is not always what it seems. I will not pretend to say that she was given just enough of the accursed stuff to brace her up and make her appear natural. I will not pretend to say that her tongue was not clean, her eyes not bright. Doctors know just how much of the stuff to give to produce the desired result; they knew how to patch her up so she could walk a chalk line and pass the examination… This is a matter of life and death, gentlemen. It is not an old horse trade. Will you pay any considerable attention to such testimony as this? I undertake to say, gentlemen, that you wouldn't convict anybody or anything on such testimony.

Sterling ended his evaluation of the witnesses by denouncing Grant for his no-holds-barred cross-examination of Florence Klingler, characterizing her, perhaps too generously, as an "unfortunate girl" thrown on her own resources at a young age but, notwithstanding unjustified suspicions and slurs about her actual vocation, a clear, honest and credible witness. And her testimony, insisted Sterling, when taken with that of Charles Huth and John Freeman about the delayed streetcar, proved conclusively that Annie would not have had sufficient time to either walk from Hazlette Avenue to 319 Lincoln Avenue or from 319 Lincoln Avenue to Klingler's home at 311 Marion Street within the timeframes posited by the prosecution. Sterling also insisted on the utter truth of Lena Lindeman's assertion that Anna had stayed at her house until 5:30 that Friday afternoon, simply ignoring the rebuttal testimony of the Star Restaurant employees.

Shortly after 3 p.m. Sterling began wrapping it up. It had been a long day and he and quite a number of spectators were feeling unwell in the hot, stuffy, overcrowded courtroom. Pleading with the jury to help in preserving the safety and sanctity of the family, he told them that Annie's acquittal would aid that sacred cause. Sterling once again reminded them that Annie deserved the presumption of her innocence. And for all of the State's claims and witnesses, he concluded, "The only thing the state has established positively is that George Saxton is dead." Growing hoarser all afternoon, he finished at 3:05, his voice almost a whisper:

> The life that George D. Saxton led had but one end — and that end was in blood. Who knows how many outraged hearts there were who were wishing for the death of Saxton? Who knows that some revenge-seeking person slew him, knowing that when he died that blame would be placed upon the prisoner. You are not the gentlemen to find a victim, but to decide whether, beyond a reasonable doubt, Annie E. George was the slayer of George D. Saxton. The law says it is safe to err on the side of acquittal, but that it is dangerous to err on the side of conviction. My hope is that you will come to such a conclusion as you will never have cause to regret.

After such a scenery-chewing finale, it was little wonder that James Grant turned to Arthur Sperry and commented acidly, "They're talking justifiable homicide now."

Chapter 21   "We Do Not Ask for Mercy!"

It had been a taxing day for everyone in the courtroom. James Sterling was drained as he fell back in his chair and his fatigue and emotional exhaustion were mirrored in the faces of many sitting in the packed, almost airless courtroom. It was already after 3 p.m. and Welty could probably have easily persuaded Judge Taylor to adjourn for the day. But he decided to go ahead with his plea immediately, probably calculating such a strategy would give him two shots at the jury, the last when they were fresh and alert the following morning.

John C. Welty was a lawyer for his time and place. Although lacking the oratorical flash of Grant, Sterling and Pomerene, he had learned from years of experience as a prosecutor and defense attorney what worked with the relatively unsophisticated, common-sense jurors of Stark County. Although not immune to the temptation of making emotional appeals — if effective — or larding his arguments with sentimentality, he preferred dealing with practical reasoning and hard, cold facts. No one present would have been surprised to learn that the argument he made now for Annie George would come to be considered as the greatest plea ever made at the bar of Stark County.

Like Grant and Sterling, Welty began with a discussion of some of the key legal issues involved in the case. He explained the intricacies of circumstantial evidence to the jury, stressing, like Sterling, that there had to be a perfect chain with no broken links. He talked of reasonable doubt, especially with reference to Mrs. George's threats to kill Saxton. He then discussed the possible verdicts in the case: first-degree murder, second-degree murder, manslaughter, assault and battery and simple assault. Asserting Annie's complete innocence, he scorned the idea that she deserved special consideration or mercy because she was a woman:

This woman stands charged with the gravest offence recognized by the laws of our state, murder in the first degree. The penalty for this under the law is death or imprisonment for life. If you, gentlemen, shall find her guilty and recommend her to mercy the penalty will be imprisonment for life. But for her sake and for my sake I beg of you that if you do find her guilty of murder in the first degree that you do not recommend her to mercy. Send her to the chair. We do not ask for mercy; we do not want it!

Welty knew how to have his cake and eat it, too. While demanding impartial justice for the accused, he simultaneously appealed to the well-known local prejudice in her favor, saying, "The people do not demand that you convict this woman! They do not want it!"

Welty now returned with relish to the defamation of George Saxton, the strategy that had served Annie's defense so well for three weeks. The late Saxton, he said, was like a noxious Brazilian tropical vine, known to the locals there as "The Murderer":

This vine creeps over the ground until it reaches a tree or plant, and insidiously entwining itself about it, chokes it to death. All along its course is death and ruin to plant life; its seemingly innocent tendrils carry destruction through the forests.

So, too, Welty told the jury, was the course of George Saxton through Canton. And, like Sterling, he suggested that Saxton's murder had been a public blessing:

Call in the mourners! Call in the victims! Call them from the grave or wherever they may found, and ask them whether it is better that a man whose whole aim is to wreck homes should live. I believe in the purity of the home, and the nobility of womanhood. I am not one of those who believe that the course of a libertine and an adulterer should be winked at.

Welty now recalled to the jury the fate of Philip Barton Key. Key, the son of national anthem writer Francis Scott Key, had been the adulterous lover of Teresa Sickles, wife of U. S. Congressman (and later inept Civil War Union general) Daniel E. Sickles. Sickles had shot Key to death in broad daylight in Lafayette Square, Washington, D. C. in 1859. Welty didn't have to tell Annie's jury that Sickles, defended by a crack defense team (including future Civil War Secretary of War Edwin Stanton), had been acquitted by his jury. (Welty did *not* remind the jury that Sickles himself had been a notorious violator of conjugal vows.) Warming to his theme of family sanctity, Welty movingly quoted some lines from John Howard Payne's "Home, Sweet, Home," that popular staple of sticky Victorian sentimentality:

How sweet 'tis to sit 'neath a fond father's smile,
And the cares of a mother to soothe and beguile!
Let others delight 'mid new pleasures to roam,
But give me, oh, give me, the pleasures of home!
Home, Home, sweet, sweet Home!
There's no place like Home! There's no place like Home!

Welty paused. "George Saxton never read those words," he sententiously sniffed. He paused again. "If you vote this defendant guilty," he warned the jury, "I want the mothers and daughters to know why. You should acquit this defendant. You should serve notice on the homewreckers that no premium is placed on that line of conduct!"

Moving smoothly from the general to the particular, Welty repeated the now familiar trope of a sweet country girl's downfall, helpless against the wiles of the practiced city libertine. His bathetic, if effective narrative lacked only the sound of a tinkling parlor piano in the background. First he painted an idyllic scene of the George family home in Hanoverton, a halcyon domestic Eden "the sort of home in which you have the right to expect when you leave in the morning that your wife will be safe from the advances of libertines and adulterers." Then came the move to Canton and that fatal hour when the sinister and licentious eye of George D. Saxton fell upon his vulnerable prey:

> Shopping in the store there marked the beginning of her fall. There she was seen and admired by Saxton. He was told she was the wife of Mr. George and a dressmaker. There, his inquiries should have ended. He wanted to get acquainted with her. She was unsophisticated, a novice; he an expert. The husband was away at work. The intruder was invading the home, telling her of her fitness for a higher station and beguiling her with the comforts and luxuries wealth could buy. For two long years and more she tried all she could to ward off that feeling that was growing and growing. It finally overcame her. This woman fell before the blandishments of the man experienced in the breaking of homes, but she has been punished for it, punished severely. Saxton had gained her love.

And it was *real* love, Welty insisted, not the vulgar pecuniary motive that prosecutor Grant had claimed. If it was money Annie wanted, then why would she have killed Saxton? She had no hope of getting anything from his death. No, she had loved him truly, said Welty, and to the "hour of his death." And he had loved her, too—at least for a time. Welty here quoted from his letters to her in Dakota, dwelling on his use of the word "wife" and his terms of endearment. "They say Saxton never loved her," said John Welty sarcastically. "If he didn't, his letters are very deceptive."

Welty now took up the multiple threats Anna had made to kill Saxton. He repeated Sterling's assertion that the jurors must first be persuaded by the evidence that Mrs. George murdered Saxton before they considered the weight of such threats with regard to malice and premeditation. Unless the State could prove Annie murdered Saxton, Welty continued, the threats were completely irrelevant. And how serious could those threats have been? Those made before 1896 were both remote in time and had been obviated by Annie's reconciliation with Saxton in March of that year. And most of the threats made after that meeting, Welty told the all-male jury, could be dismissed as merely the gossip of careless women. Typical of those threats was the one made at Mary Nauman's quilting bee in 1897, when Annie had been so cruelly baited and provoked by the teasing of her so-called friends. Her pulling a revolver on Saxton, too, was only a theatrical gesture; how serious could it have been if Saxton so easily gained possession of the gun? Recalling for the jury Grant's dramatic showboating with the revolver the previous afternoon, he jeered, "Why, Grant; you ought to have been there with your gun to show them how to flourish a revolver!" (Sadly for Welty, Grant missed this sarcasm, having stepped out of the courtroom for a moment). As for Annie's threat to "raise hell" at the home of Eva Althouse, who, demanded Welty, could blame her for that?

> I don't know any place nearer hell than that house. There could be no more fitting place for a libertine to die or an adulterer to pay the penalty of his vice than at the threshold of the woman with whom he consorted.

Having brought up Eva's name, Welty took the opportunity to point out that she was still missing. She had run away, he said, "rather than be exposed or forced to give evidence that would help clear Mrs. George." Why, he demanded, hadn't the police searched the house of this shady character, the "fair Eva," with the same energy they had displayed in their dragnet for Annie after Saxton's murder? Finally, he dismissed Eva with contempt, bracketing her with the late Saxton as a public moral nuisance:

> But we don't care where she is. I, for one, am glad she's gone. Canton's better off without her and I hope she will stay away.

Welty stopped speaking at exactly 4:30 p.m. and the spent crowd rushed out of the courtroom. Annie, who had wept again during Welty's description of her once happy family, seemed more depressed than at any time during her trial. One of the first spectators to chat with the reporters was Annie's stockman suitor. Confident of her acquittal, he said he was ready to offer her his hand in marriage. That night Canton shook as a powerful electrical storm pummeled the city.

Another overfull house greeted Annie as she was brought into court on Wednesday morning. It was another hot, stifling day. The crowd was so large and anxious that they practically knocked bailiff George Bowman down as they rushed through the door. Welty resumed his argument by returning to Annie's threats, beseeching the jurymen to see them in the context in which they were made. All of them were wrung from her overfull heart while she was, by the testimony of many witnesses, beside herself with love of Saxton and jealousy of Eva Althouse. Almost every threat, Welty insisted, was conditional on Saxton not marrying her after the settlement of Sample George's suit. "Who has not," Welty asked the twelve jurymen "at some time in his life threatened vengeance if thus and so did not occur?" All of Annie's threats were idle, all made in the heat of the moment and all equally irrelevant to the question of whether she killed George Saxton. The fact that she was hesitant to break the law, carefully observing the terms of the injunction against her during her search with officer

Dickerhoff and her promise to Judge McCarty, only a half-hour before Saxton's murder not to break them, constituted telling evidence that Annie George was a pacific, law-abiding woman. And her tender words about Saxton to Lena Lindeman, uttered scant hours before his death were profound proof of her passionate love for him. And the earliest threat, William Cook's memory of Annie standing before Saxton's door with a revolver, Welty dismissed as the product of Cook's overactive imagination.

Welty now began to try to demolish the chain of circumstantial evidence against Annie. The chief elements were her whereabouts at the time of the crime, the circumstances of her arrest, the alleged murder weapon, her shoes, and the burrs and Spanish needles. He began by stating there was no evidence Annie had been on Lincoln Avenue, much less at the murder scene. There was no real identification of her; even the State's so-called eyewitnesses generally spoke of having seen a "form" or "shape." Indeed, it seemed to Welty that the descriptions of the mysterious stranger offered by Lizzie Miller and Jacob Adams were far better matches for the killer than Annie George. "I don't know whether he was a father, or husband, or brother, or sweetheart," suggested Welty. "But it was not a woman that killed Saxton." And, given the testimony about the lateness of her streetcar and her arrival at Florence Klingler's house, Annie would not have had enough time to get from the streetcar stop to the murder scene at 319 Lincoln Avenue or from there to Klingler's home.

Welty stated that the testimony of the police officers and Dr. Pontius likewise supported Annie's claim of innocence. Pontius had specifically denied that she smelled gunpowder on Annie's hand during her police station examination. The policemen testified that her shoes were not muddy; yet the alleged escape route of Saxton's murderer was through a rain-soaked vacant lot. And the burrs and Spanish needles could be easily explained as having come from Lindeman's backyard or the weedy lots along Tuscarawas Street where Annie walked on her return to Mrs. Oberlin's house and her later trudge to the police station.

DEFENDER WELTY—"IF YOU FIND EVIDENCE THAT MRS. GEORGE OWNED THIS REVOLVER CONVICT HER."

If You Find Evidence that Mrs. George Owned this Revolver
(Cleveland Daily World, April 26, 1899)

Welty reserved his most derisive words for Sergeant Hasler's "murder weapon," denouncing its uncertain provenance and directly excoriating the prosecution for its failure to connect it to the accused:

> Why did you not learn where this gun came from; the factory that made it; where it had been purchased, and in short, learn something about it? You had it long enough in your possession! Who ever sold it to Mrs. George? No person testified that she ever had it. It is not identified as ever being in her possession. Any officer, who with a full knowledge that the whole town was being searched for the gun

that shot George Saxton, and finds it, takes it to his home and hides it in an old stocking for months in the garret of his house; I will ask you to think about it, gentlemen: What is there about this revolver that connects Mrs. George with this crime?

Turning to Pomerene, Welty shouted, "Hasler planted that gun himself, in the hope of securing a reward! If you believed his story and had confided in him, why did you send him to Mrs. George with a lie in his mouth? He went there to entrap her! She was alone in her cell with her misery! The job you set up on this woman should damn any prosecution! And I mean what I say!"

Welty picked up the revolver from the table and brandished it over the heads of the jury. "Mr. Grant has said this revolver is the real arbiter of the case. So say I! Let this revolver decide the issue. If you find that Mrs. George owned this weapon, find her guilty!" He also gleefully noted that Werntz had testified that Mrs. George said she had a double-action revolver in her trunk. "This revolver, gentlemen," Welty crowed to the jurymen as he held it aloft, "is not a double action gun. This is a self-acting gun."

Putting down the revolver, Welty moved on to a consideration of the two key eyewitnesses: Christina Eckroate and Florence Klingler. His treatment of Mrs. Eckroate was a shrewd combination of compassion, common-sense logic and ridicule. Her identification of Annie, Welty insisted, was only a hallucination of a morphine-addled brain. It was a dark night, the lighting was poor and her view was blocked by the cherry tree. Why had she waited three months to tell anyone what she had seen? Would they, the jurors, have concealed that kind of knowledge for so long? Citing the learned testimony of Dr. Eyman, Welty recalled the testimony of Michael and Laura Burke:

They say she wouldn't harm anybody. They say she wouldn't harm a member of her own family. But she did try to harm one of them, as is shown by the testimony, and when her attention was called to it the next morning she remembered nothing of it. Mrs. Eckroate did not want to tell a lie. She did not willingly tell a lie, but as the experts say, when morphine is taken, as it had been by her for years, the brain becomes diseased and irresponsible.

Welty ended his consideration of Christina Eckroate with a troubling rhetorical question for the jurymen, "Gentlemen, when you retire to the jury room put yourselves as nearly as possible in Mrs. George's place. How many of you would like to be convicted on the testimony of a morphine fiend?'"

Following Sterling's lead, Welty hotly defended Florence Klingler, sharply reproving Grant for his vicious assaults on her character:

> They have undertaken to abuse Florence Klingler. They have insulted her. They have called up her unfortunate domestic trouble. She was cast upon her own resources at a tender age. She, as many others, has had an unfortunate marriage, but a fairer, clearer and more direct witness has not testified in this case. Her cross-examination was an insult to her, and would be an insult to any respectable person.

Welty spoke until just after 2:00 p.m. Reiterating Mrs. George's complete innocence for the last time, he told the jury they would be committing legal murder if they found her guilty of Saxton's murder. The State, he insisted, had not produced one scintilla of evidence that she had. He ended with a final plea for justice:

> I am not here to ask you to do what I would not step into the box and do myself. I am not here to ask you to perjure yourselves by rendering a verdict at vari-

ance with the facts as you view them and the law as the court shall give it to you. But I am here to demand justice for this defenseless woman and to say to you that poor as she is, she is an American citizen and entitled to the rights guaranteed to every such citizen.

Welty sat down and Pomerene immediately commenced the final argument of the trial.

ATLEE POMERENE,
PROSECUTING ATTORNEY OF STARK COUNTY.

Prosecutor Atlee Pomerene
("Coe," Canton's Great Tragedy)

The Stark County prosecutor drew the largest crowd yet for his final peroration, a testament to his renowned oratorical prowess. When the doors opened to admit spectators for the afternoon session, there was a stampede of anxious women, who almost trampled each other in their haste to obtain a seat for the show. One of them was Mary Helen Bockius Pomerene, who hung on every word uttered by her husband during the next 150 minutes. A violent thunderstorm rattled the courthouse as he began to address Annie's jury.

Like his predecessors, Pomerene began his appeal with a sober discussion of some of the legal issues in the case. He first addressed a list of seventeen propositions that the defense had asked Judge Taylor to include in his final charge to the jury. (Pomerene did not mention that the State had submitted fourteen such demands of its own.) Most of the defense's demands were standard legal cautions regarding the presumption of innocence, the insistence that a chain of circumstantial evidence be unbroken, that the silence of the accused not be held against her, and the irrelevance of threats — except with regard to premeditation and malice — in determining whether someone actually had committed murder. It was propositions thirteen and fourteen that attracted Pomerene's ire and initially distracted him from a more general summary of the case. In those two propositions Welty and Sterling had asked Judge Taylor to caution the jury:

> 13) [P]ersons addicted to the habitual use of morphine or like drugs of which class are opium and laudanum, as a stimulant, are usually unreliable and untrustworthy, and the habitual use of such drugs for any considerable length of time, generally produces a diseased and distorted condition of the perceptions and imagination; and such persons are generally devoid of a proper regard for truth.

14) It is for the jury to determine whether the witnesses for the State, Christina Eckroate and Mary Grable, have used morphine or like drugs, in such quantity and for such a length of time as to affect their moral perceptions and imaginations and reliability for truth telling; and whether any, and if any, what weight is to be given to their testimony, or the testimony of either of them.

Atlee Pomerene was still counting on Mrs. Eckroate's testimony and he angrily chastised Welty and Sterling for their effrontery in attempting to shape Judge Taylor's instructions to the jury. The Court could not so instruct the jury, insisted Pomerene; whether Mrs. Eckroate's drug taking affected her veracity was a question that only Mrs. George's jury could decide on their own. Pomerene then took up the charges against Mrs. George, the possible verdicts and the by now familiar topics of premeditation, malice and reasonable doubt.

The chief prosecutor next mocked the emphasis that Welty and Sterling had placed on Saxton's alleged mistreatment and the purported sufferings of his "victim," Mrs. George. "It seems that the main idea of the defense is to prove a justification for the crime," said Pomerene. He told the jury that he understood how the defense might want to argue that there was some provocation for Saxton's murder and that it was in some moral sense justified by his conduct. But both defense lawyers had strayed far over the line of legal sense and common decency, virtually praising the murder as a "public benefaction." "I was appalled," Pomerene thundered in shocked tones:

[W]hen I sat here and heard Brother Sterling declare George Saxton was rightfully killed! Think of it! A lawyer at the bar, defending *murder!*

A Woman Scorned

Accusing Welty of shedding "crocodile tears" during his melodramatic recitation of Saxton's misdeeds, Pomerene said the defense portrait of the murdered man was an untrue, inaccurate caricature. "They overdid their work," he said, "they presented only a picture, not a likeness. The painting black of the dead man's character was simply to divert attention from the facts. They talk to me of the villainy of George Saxton!" Pomerene cried. "This Saxton was not the Saxton that I knew!" He continued angrily:

> They say he caused graves to be filled. You will con-
> sider how much testimony there has been on that
> point. It has not and it could not be shown that
> George Saxton ever insulted any virtuous woman.
> Such reflections exist only in the minds of the revil-
> ers of his character. How many hearts ached for him
> when he died? Is there any man who is all evil and
> no good? Even if he was as black as painted his life
> was as dear to him as yours is to you. He had as
> much right before the law. None of these crimes
> were charged to him until this woman appeared on
> the scene. Is there any testimony that he injured her
> or any other woman?

Leaving such questions ringing in the jurymen's ears, Pomerene turned to deconstructing Welty and Sterling's sentimental myth of an innocent country girl debauched by a hardened Canton libertine. In the strongest attack on Annie's character yet uttered at the trial, Pomerene scoffed:

> What virtuous married woman would permit a man
> to make advances to her without immediately tell-
> ing her husband? Oh, she was a *lovely* woman, this
> *loving* and *virtuous* wife, this indulgent *mother!* Ra-
> ther, I would say, a *vile, designing woman,* who was
> not content with her lot! No woman can be led from

her husband and children, unless she is willing; unless she wants to be. No man is bold enough to force himself on a pure woman, who raises her hand and says, "Thus far shalt thou go, and no further." *A lovely, pure woman,* this, truly!

Turning to the jury, Pomerene asked rhetorically challenged: "Would anyone have dared to have insulted *your* wives?" Referring to the reported language of some of Mrs. George's threats, language so foul some of the witnesses refused to repeat it, Pomerene jeered again, "*This* is the lovely woman, the *pure, virtuous* woman, whom the *vile* Saxton ruined!" Several times during his vituperative assault, Pomerene confronted Mrs. George directly, pounding his fists on the table next to her, as he shouted in her face, "Mrs. George, if you should meet yourself on the street as you really are, you would pass by a stranger!" He begged the jury to see Annie as the stonehearted killer she really was, "not as an elegantly dressed woman who appeared in court with constant changes of costume, as though she were attending an operatic performance." As was her wont, Annie stood up well to his histrionics, staring at her hands with an impassive countenance as Pomerene screamed his moral condemnation in her face.

The chief prosecutor tried hard to compensate for the fact that much supposedly damning testimony about Annie's character — particularly her alleged relations with other men — had been excluded from the trial record by Judge Taylor. Pomerene now offered his apologies for this omission to the jury:

> I said when I opened this case we would show that this woman by her conduct had forfeited any confidence Saxton or any other man could have had in her. Mr. Welty in his argument said we didn't prove it. No — we didn't prove it. But we were ready to prove it. Our witnesses as to this conduct were called but Mr. Welty said, "I object," and the mouths

of our witnesses were silenced. That is why we didn't prove it.

The record was clear, however, Pomerene stated, that Mrs. George had perjured herself about the facts of her marriage and conduct in the evidence she submitted to obtain her South Dakota divorce. And the claim that she had loved Saxton was ludicrous: her motives from 1887 to the moment of Saxton's death had simply been: "her vanity, her ambitions and desires."

Turning to the murder victim, Pomerene sought to counter the hours of vituperation heaped upon his memory by defense counsel. Recalling the days of the early 1890s when George and Annie had "honeymooned" in various South Dakota and Iowa hotel suites, he argued that the defense's demonic portrait of Saxton was simply the malicious, mendacious creation of Anna George:

> Was he the sinner and she the saint? Was he all black, and she all white? Was he all corruption, and she all incorruption? It is but one side of the story. George D. Saxton is lying cold and silent in his grave, and cannot speak for himself. Will you judge him by that woman's tongue? There was not a single witness that testified that Saxton had ever harmed Mrs. George, and all the testimony that was given as to his conduct came from her own lips. . . . Seven hours before the bullets sped their way into the vitals of Saxton, you were telling the negro Jackson that you would kill him, and that he would get his deserts in Hell! *You who loved him so well!*

Pomerene did not spare the absent Sample C. George in his florid denunciations. Remarking on Sample's summary of his early marriage years as "pleasant and happy," Pomerene inquired mockingly, "*Where* was that devoted husband while [Saxton's] advances were going on?" Blaming Annie for her son Newton's ordeal on the witness stand, he lamented:

> We have had a spectacle here that I hope you and I
> will never be called upon to witness again. I refer to
> the calling of a woman's own flesh and blood to the
> witness stand to testify to her shame.

Completing his gallery of the principal characters in the Saxton tragedy, Pomerene defended the absent and much-maligned Eva Althouse. He was amused, said the prosecutor, that the defense attorneys would dare to object to the State's witnesses furnishing her an alibi for the murder moment, yet at the same time complain that she had not shown up for the trial. "Perhaps," said Pomerene, turning to Welty," she kept away to avoid your abuse and calumny." Turning to Mrs. George, he declaimed, "Speak of Mrs. Althouse as you will; at least *her* hands are not stained with *blood!*"

Focusing on the keystone of Anna's alibi, Pomerene poured out his contempt for Florence Klingler, a fit companion, he sneered, for the accused. "You tell us we haven't proven the character of this Klingler woman!" he shouted, glaring at Welty and shaking his fist. "When we tried to, you wouldn't let us!" The wily Welty refused to rise to the bait, merely riposting calmly, "Anything you had a right to prove the court permitted."

Court was adjourned at 4:30 p.m. with Pomerene's final argument unfinished. It had been an incredible performance for both the prosecutor and Annie George. Arthur Sperry's summary paid fulsome tribute to both antagonists but gave the laurel, as usual, to Mrs. George:

> Through it all Pomerene went on. His thin figure vi-
> brating with emotion, his lean fists clenched and
> raised high in the air only to be beaten with re-
> sounding whacks on the rail of the jury box, the wit-

ness box, the tables, on whatever happened to be nearest him when he wanted emphasis, Pomerene's voice rose shrill and weird, above the crash of the thunder as he demanded the life of the white-faced woman who sat before him with her head bent forward so that he could not look into her eyes. As he talked Pomerene sprang toward Mrs. George and shook his clenched fists in her face so close that it seemed as though he must hit her but she never moved a muscle. Again he shook his bony finger at her until it almost touched those black wings on her hat but she did not look up. Pomerene, after one of his fiercest climaxes, stepped back to prepare for another rush toward her, a rush that would have frightened a ghost even, and then, in a fraction of a second, was given one of the finest exhibitions of nerve ever seen in a court room. The white-faced woman with her great mysterious eyes that glitter or blaze as her emotions change, this woman they are already strapping into the death chair, according to Pomerene's view, this wonderful Mrs. George, she yawned. Right before Pomerene's staring eyes, right before his face livid with hate and earnestness, she put her handkerchief up to her mouth and indulged in a well-bred but unmistakable yawn. It was a masterpiece either of acting or unconcern. It broke Pomerene all up and he did not get under full headway with his torrent of vitriol before court adjourned for the day.

Jacob Waldeck was likewise impressed by the unstinting level of Pomerene's animosity, writing that his scorn "would bore holes in boiler iron and the contempt would wither an evergreen."

When court resumed the next morning at 8:30, Mrs. George was screened from the view of most of the spectators by a gigantic bouquet of roses. The card on it read, "From Sincere Friends." The rumor circulating through the courtroom audience was that a Canton medium had summoned the ghost of George Saxton to a recent séance. Saxton's ghost, however, had refused to disclose the identity of his murderer, saying only that he forgave whoever it was.

The chief prosecutor now turned from his portraiture of the personalities in the case to a consideration of the circumstantial evidence. It alone, he insisted to the jury, was enough to convict Mrs. George of Saxton's murder. The most critical element was the timeline. Pomerene argued that Mrs. George had gotten off street-car No. 21 no later than 6:00 p.m., leaving her enough time to get to Lincoln Avenue for the murder at 6:10. Indeed, Pomerene claimed that the defense had trapped itself by insisting that she had disembarked from the streetcar no earlier than 6:05 p.m. If that were true, Pomerene said, Annie would not have had enough time to walk from Hazlette Avenue to 311 Marion Street by 6:25.

Thanks to Judge Taylor's exclusionary rulings, Pomerene didn't have much physical evidence to discuss with the jury. He defended Hasler's behavior after finding the alleged murder weapon and characterized it as a legitimate piece of evidence. Pushing that claim to an extreme, he dubiously insisted that Annie's jailhouse request that Hasler talk to Welty about the weapon constituted an admission that the revolver belonged to her. In this connection, he also gratuitously demanded to know why ex-Mayor Rice had not been called by the defense to refute Hasler's gun story in person. Welty immediately objected, invoking Judge Taylor's repeated exclusion of testimony about Mayor Rice from the trial record. Predictably, Judge Taylor sustained the objection and Pomerene moved on to try to neutralize some of the damage done to the State's case by one of his prime witnesses, Dr. Maria Pontius. Pontius, he now told the jury, had stated that she didn't smell gunpowder on Mrs. George's hand. That didn't prove, the sly prosecutor argued, that it wasn't present—it just meant that Pontius, a female not likely to be familiar with firearms, didn't recognize the smell. As for the burrs on Annie's skirt and her unmuddied shoes, there could be only one explanation:

> She could have got them in Pike Township--but she wasn't there. She could have got them, and she *did* get them, in the vacant lot near the Althouse place. Again, they claim that her shoes were not muddy. It is no wonder. There was no mud. It was not raining at the time the shooting occurred, and there was no mud along the route over which she passed. The policemen, the streetcar men, the women who testified, say that they did not get their shoes muddy.

Then there was the matter of her peculiar conduct after she was arrested. Aware that her silence could not be used against her, Pomerene nonetheless harped on her passive, mute demeanor, arguing it could only be explained by a consciousness of guilt:

> She must have heard of the killing of Saxton; she must have heard it discussed. Yet, when apprehended, she was stoically silent. When placed in custody, she could have, had she been innocent, cried out, "What did I do; why do you arrest me?" Instead of that she merely said, "I will go with you," and she would "talk when the proper time comes." She did not ask why she was made a prisoner.

The real scenario, Pomerene stated, was a simple story. It had nothing to do with Lizzie Miller's "mysterious stranger" or Jacob Adams's phantom pedestrian. What had happened was that Mrs. George, by sheer chance, had spotted Saxton as he was bicycling westward on Tuscarawas Street on the evening of October 7. Surmising his destination, she had boarded a streetcar and arrived at Hazlette Avenue before he did. Walking to 319 Lincoln Avenue, she had ambushed and slain him when he arrived at Eva

Althouse's front steps. Returning to the murder timeline, Pomerene stated that there remained a critical half hour that Annie would not account for and her lawyers could not explain. Even if Annie *had* walked to Florence Klingler's home, it was obvious that Florence must have been mistaken or lying about the time she arrived there. Moreover, the State had a good eyewitness, Christina Eckroate, who had recognized Annie at the scene as the shooter. At this juncture, Pomerene alluded to his previous claim to reporters that a defense witness had tried to intimidate Christina and prevent her from testifying. He didn't name Joseph Eckroate but Welty became livid as he listened to Pomerene impugn the ethics of defense counsel:

"Wait a minute! I object to that. We have had about enough of this! There should be some regard for the testimony in this argument. That is absolutely false and unfair! Do not state to the jury that there was any attempt to intimidate a witness!"

"I did not so state," replied Pomerene.

"Yes — you — did!" shot back Welty, clapping his hands aggressively.

"I beg your pardon. I did not so state!"

"Yes, you did!"

The wrangling continued for several minutes, until Judge Taylor had had enough and told both attorneys to calm down. Pomerene then restated his accusation in milder terms, sarcastically baiting Welty, "Now you may object if you want to." "That is all right; I have no exception," replied Welty. "Yes, your skin is too thick for that," retorted Pomerene.

Returning to Christina Eckroate, Pomerene disparaged Dr. Eyman's testimony about the effects of her morphine addiction. Eyman's experience with addicts, Pomerene argued, was confined to asylum lunatics, not respectable housewives. Unlike physicians Walker and Brant, he had not personally examined Mrs. Eckroate. No witness had testified that Mrs. Eckroate had hallucinations, nor was there any convincing evidence that she attempted to conceal her drug use, a trait Eyman had characterized as typical of morphine addicts. True, her pallor and irritability in court had been noticeable, conceded Pomerene. But, he continued humorously, many present had remarked the same qualities in "Brother Sterling." Yet no one, to his knowledge, said the prosecutor, had yet accused Sterling of being a drug fiend. Here Sterling took objection to Pomerene's jabbing and more sarcastic byplay followed until Judge Taylor sternly ordered them to confine their arguments to the testimony and the case on trial.

The chief prosecutor again pooh-poohed Lizzie Miller's mysterious stranger sighting. Regretting that he had been unable to complete her cross-examination, he ridiculed her story of an eerie pedestrian on Linden Avenue:

> Let us see. She thought she saw a woman, then a man, and then it faded away. She said she had a "strange impression." I don't know whether she had just come out of a trance or not, but I suspect this ghost story will not be believed by you.

The same was true, he continued of Jacob Adams' testimony about a strange man:

> There are forty thousand people in Canton. It would be no uncommon thing for a person to meet a man along a sidewalk. Adams did not say that the man he had met had any connection with the Saxton tragedy, nor was there any testimony to show that he had.

Mindful that Annie's threats constituted a critical part of the State's case, Pomerene gave them ample attention. He told the jury that they constituted clear and weighty evidence of both her raging malice against Saxton and her brazen character. Reprising the catalog of her verbal and written threats, he asked her jury:

Were these threats, these flourishes of the revolver, this letter, these "messages of love," evidence of love and affection? She sent for a newspaper reporter and asked him to publish to the world her encounter with Saxton. Would any refined and virtuous woman, who became engaged in a fight, rightfully or wrongfully, seek to have the details of that fight paraded before the public? She wanted to annoy him, and humiliate his family and friends! She wanted Saxton *roasted,* she said. . . . She told these witnesses, time and again, that as soon as the case against Saxton was settled that she would kill him. Why did she say this? What was in her mind? Why was she saying these things, if she did not intend to do so?

Before ending, the chief prosecutor couldn't resist one final attempt to put Annie's post-murder behavior before the jury. "When she left Florence Klingler's," he stated, "she said she was going to see lawyer Sterling. What did she want —

"Hold on!" yelled Welty. "That conversation was ruled out on the ground that it occurred after the crime charged!" Judge Taylor promptly sustained Welty's objection and Pomerene soldiered on.

The prosecutor finished his argument at exactly 11:11 that Thursday morning. Summarizing the evidence and testimony one more time, Pomerene picked up the gauntlet hurled by Welty when he begged Annie's jury to send her to the electric chair if they could not entirely exonerate her, saying, "If you find this woman guilty, send her to the chair. If you don't find this woman guilty beyond a reasonable doubt, acquit her." He ended his plea with another appeal for justice to the dead George Saxton:

The fact still remains that he had not an enemy on earth who desired his life, except the prisoner. Granting that Mrs. George had wrongs, that Saxton mistreated her, the courts were open to her. But she had made up her mind to kill him — and kill him she did. Is she now to go acquitted and incite others to commit crime?

Aware of the acrimony excited during the trial and aware, perhaps, of his own culpability in hot-tempered courtroom outbursts, Pomerene disclaimed any personal animus against Annie George:

> I want to say in the beginning that this defendant never did me any harm. She never had the opportunity. I bear her no ill will; I bear her no malice. I am here as the prosecuting attorney to discharge the duty I have been sworn to perform.

Thanking the jury for its patience, Pomerene told them to remember the sanctity of the law and asked that their verdict be a vindication of that law.

To the surprise of many in the courtroom, Judge Taylor did not call for a lunch recess but immediately delivered his instructions to the jury, some 5500 carefully reasoned words. He noted that Annie George was charged with first degree murder and that she was to be presumed to be innocent until proven guilty. If there was a reasonable doubt of her guilt in the mind of a single juror, he warned, she could not rightfully be found guilty. Judge Taylor cautioned the jurymen that the fact that Annie had been charged with the crime and almost universally suspected of committing it could not affect the presumption of her innocence. It is fair to say that Judge Taylor could not have been more scrupulously emphatic in his cautions to the jurymen that they respect the legal presumption of Annie's innocence: he employed the phrase "reasonable doubt" 32 times and used the conditional "if" no fewer than 56.

Judge Taylor carefully addressed the issues of circumstantial evidence, explaining that it alone was sufficient for conviction but had to constitute a perfect chain. He then elucidated the possible verdicts in the case, with special reference to the elements of premeditation and malice. After a lengthy analysis, he turned to the question of Annie's threats against Saxton. As the defense had requested, he stressed that the testimony they had heard about them was admissible, but only with respect to determining malice and motive. Mindful, too, of the vitriolic character-assassination engaged in by Grant and Pomerene during their final arguments, Judge Taylor warned:

> The question of the general character, or general reputation of the defendant for chastity, virtue or morality is not an issue in this case, and testimony as to this question was not admissible. The fact that such testimony was not offered is not to be considered as a circumstance against the defendant.

Judge Taylor was scrupulously careful, too, in dealing with one of the most violently disputed issues in the case, the weight to be given to the testimony of the two drug addicts, Mary Grable and Christina Eckroate. After discussing the testimony of the medical experts, Judge Taylor, as per the State's request, left it entirely to the discretion of the jury to decide what weight to give to the testimony of the two women. He also stressed that Annie's decision not to testify at her trial could not be held against her as evidence of guilt. Nor could her failure to prove an alibi — if there were such a failure — be considered proof that she was present at the murder scene. Judge Taylor completed his instructions in 35 minutes and dismissed the jury to its deliberations at 11:50 a.m. Annie followed the jury out of the courtroom, returning to her cell. There she began her fateful vigil in the company of her son Newton, various Hanoverton relatives and friends. Chatting mostly of personal matters, it was said that she seemed the gayest, happiest, most unconcerned person in the room.

VERDICT

THE CHAIR

OR LIBERTY?

NOT YET

Mrs. George's Case at Last With the 12 Men Good and True.

One Ballot Taken at Once, but Its Result Is as Yet Unknown—Stormy Scenes as Prose-cutor Pomerene Finishes His Fierce Argument.

Verdict: The Chair or Liberty: Not Yet
(Cleveland Daily World, April 27, 1899)

When Annie's jury retired on Thursday morning, it was as-sumed by most persons that their verdict would be a quick one. Public opinion in Canton was nearly unanimous that Annie should be, and would be speedily acquitted by her jury. Many interested persons, too, were well aware that the legal position of the jury and the physical circumstances of the jury room were favorable to quick verdicts. The law governing Ohio juries in capital cases dictated that there be no physical separation of the jurors between the time they were charged by the court and when they returned a verdict. There were no cots in the stuffy, square little room on the third floor jury room of the courthouse, and if the jurymen were locked up for the night, they would have to sleep sitting up in hard, straight-backed chairs or on the floor. So most of the several hundred spectators in courtroom No. 2 stayed in their seats, not wishing to miss the dramatic moment when the verdict came in. But the slow hours passed by without any news. Judge Taylor left the courtroom at 5:30 p.m., leaving word that he would be available at his hotel until at least midnight. His exit precipitated a general rush to dinner, with many of the original spectators replaced by new faces as the afternoon waned into evening.

With no information leaking out of the jury room, there was little for the assembled reporters, lawyers and spectators to do but swap rumors. The word on the street as darkness descended was that the jury was deadlocked with eight for acquittal, three for first degree murder and one for manslaughter. Sterling and Welty remained calm, telling one and all that they thought it would be either an acquittal or a hung jury. Welty admitted, however, that they had already prepared an appeal, in case the verdict went against them. But, he assured his listeners, "We have not anticipated such action will be necessary." Little could be seen of the interior of the jury room from nearby buildings, except that various jurors were pacing up and down as they thrashed out their verdict. It was noticed, too, that they gradually doffed their coats, vests and collars as the hours went by in their uncomfortable quarters. When word came at 3 a.m. that the jury had been locked up and that there would be no verdict before morning, the remaining spectators left and the bailiffs locked the courtroom doors.

The departure of the crowd was a welcome respite for the four bailiffs in courtroom No. 2. The daily deportment of the trial audience had always left something to be desired, but that behavior had deteriorated further as the anxious spectators waited for the verdict. Many who had stayed to the end of the night vigil had consumed chewing tobacco, cigars, peanuts and fruit to pass away the time. The resulting organic debris had gradually been churned by the pressure of many feet into rancid mulch on the courtroom floor. It took bailiff Holman three hours to clean up the mess but he had the courtroom in presentable condition by the time he opened the doors to the public at 8 a.m. Meanwhile, back at the Stark County jail, Annie and her supporters fretted away the long hours. Occasionally, she would ask if there was any news of the jury, only to be told there was no verdict as yet. Her only public comment was, "Well, I don't believe they will hang me at any rate, but it is hard to tell what twelve men will do." She spoke dispassionately of the verbal roasting Grant and Pomerene had given her in their final statements, saying she thought such vituperation was counter-productive to persuading her jury. She had nothing but kind words for her attorneys and most of the witnesses, excepting Mary Nauman and John J. Jackson, who she said had lied on the stand. She also stated that if she were convicted she would not ask for a new trial. She conversed with her friends until 11 p.m., and sat up until 2 a.m. to await the verdict. She then slept soundly until 7 a.m., arose and ate a hearty breakfast. She told her first visitors she still expected nothing worse than a hung jury, particularly because of the prolonged deliberations.

The first word from the jury came at 7:15 a.m., when they ordered breakfast. Two more hours drifted by. At 9:15 a.m., the jury bell rang and the crowd milling in the courthouse corridor rushed into courtroom No. 2. Outside, hundreds more, waiting in the Canton streets, dashed from all directions to the court house entrances. Judge Taylor ran through his private entrance to the court, ready to receive the verdict. All soon learned it was a false alarm; bailiff Holman explained that he had merely been testing the jury bell. More than one of the disappointed spectators suspected that the harried bailiff was having some fun at their expense. Ducking away from small objects thrown at his head by the miffed crowd, he promised it wouldn't happen again.

A Woman Scorned

The four attorneys and Judge Taylor were all in their seats by 10:00 a.m. The courtroom was completely filled with over 200 spectators and probably four times that number spilling out into the courthouse hallways and into the surrounding streets. When the jury bell rang again at 10:25, Judge Taylor sent Holman to the jury room. He returned, saying that the jury had formed its verdict. Word was sent to the county jail, where Annie heard the news. Rising from her jail cot, she said calmly, "I am acquitted," and marched with one of Sheriff Zaiser's deputies to the courtroom. As she stepped to the defense table, John Welty leaned over and whispered to her not to worry, even if the verdict was against her. She was extremely pale but calm.

A few minutes later the twelve jurymen filed slowly into the room and into the jury box. They looked, said one thoughtful observer, like men who had spent the night tossing upon the surface of the ocean. After they were seated, Judge Taylor sternly cautioned the crowd that there was to be no public demonstration after the verdict, no matter what it was. He warned that the bailiffs in the courtroom would enforce his order. He turned to Clerk of Courts Thomas C. Casselman and said, "Inquire the jury." Casselman then called the jury roll, each man answering "Present." When he finished, Casselman asked, "Gentlemen of the jury, have you agreed on a verdict?" Jury foreman Julius Zang answered, "We have." He passed over the sealed paper to Casselman. He opened it and read aloud in a clear voice:

> We, the jury impaneled and sworn to well and truly
> try, and true deliverance make, between the State of
> Ohio and the prisoner at the Bar, Annie E. George,
> do find the defendant Not Guilty.

There was a split second of silence. Then the courtroom exploded in pandemonium as the crowd leaped to its feet, cheering the acquitted Annie George. The demonstration spread through the crowd waiting outside, into the streets, as hundreds shouted and screamed their joy at Mrs. George's deliverance. Judge Taylor and his bailiffs looked on helplessly as the tumult went on for a good ten minutes before subsiding. Finally, when Judge Taylor could be heard, he said, "The accused is discharged and may go hence." He then thanked the jury, discharged them, and asked that the next case be called.

Mrs. George is Free!
(Cleveland Daily World, April 28, 1899)

Annie's face lit up like a lamp as the words "Not Guilty" were pronounced. She was instantly smothered by about ten women, most of them friends and family. When she could free herself from their embraces, she walked to the jury box and personally thanked each member of the jury. She then stayed in the courtroom for a good hour, holding an impromptu reception for the many well-wishers who surrounded her. After shaking hands with hundreds, she went for a brief walk up North Market Street, her first unrestricted ramble since the night of her arrest, six months before. Owing to the fact that she had had little exposure to sunlight during her incarceration, Anna was forced to wear tinted spectacles during her first outdoor forays. She then returned to her jail cell to thank Sheriff Zaiser and collect her personal belongings. She had spent 222 days in jail and the total cost of her confinement came to $158.70.

Followed by a worshipful crowd, Annie walked from the county jail to Sterling's office for a legal conference. There, she was mobbed by 300 persons, most of them women and all of whom wanted to shake her hand. Among the crowd was juror George Steinmetz, who told her that her acquittal had left him with a clear conscience. Then it was off to the Hotel Conrad to greet more well-wishers. Already, an "extra" edition of the *Canton Repository* proclaiming her acquittal was being cried by newsboys in the streets.

The celebratory turmoil in the streets of Canton continued for several hours. Most observers judged that it was simply a spontaneous eruption of public approval for the most popular jury verdict ever rendered in Stark County and the greatest public tumult since McKinley's election in 1896. As a *Cleveland Plain Dealer* scribe noted, however, it was difficult to say "what would have been the effect upon that crowd in the court room had a verdict of guilty as charged been returned." His comment reflected an angry but generally unarticulated populist subtext to the Annie George trial: sheer rage at the plight of a working-class woman who had suffered at the hands of one of Canton's "swells." As one unidentified court official put it to *Cleveland Press* reporter Jacob Waldeck:

> This demonstration is an indication of what might have been expected if the verdict had been first degree murder. The crowd were so wrought up that they would have swooped down on the jury box like a cyclone. It would have been a scene that would not have been forgotten in the history of the county.

Some details of the jury's deliberations began leaking out that Friday afternoon. Annie's jury had been out for 23 hours and 45 minutes. They had taken a total of 23 ballots to decide her fate. The first ballot, an informal "test" vote, was taken at 12:30 p.m., immediately after the jury went out and lunched in the jury room. That test ballot showed four votes for conviction of first degree murder and eight for not guilty. The four jurymen voting against Annie were Brenner, Erb, Zang and Howald. The second and third ballots, taken at 2:00 and 2:45 p.m. were the same. The fourth at 3:15 p.m. showed two for first degree murder, seven for not guilty, one for second degree murder and two for a manslaughter conviction.

The fifth ballot at 4 p.m. was eight for not guilty, four for manslaughter. Ballots five through fifteen continued the same. The sixteenth ballot, taken at 4:55 a.m., Friday morning, showed nine for not guilty and three for manslaughter. The seventeenth ballot at 6:15 a.m. showed eight for not guilty, three for manslaughter and, oddly, one for assault and battery. The eighteenth ballot at 8:45 a.m. showed eight for not guilty, four for manslaughter.

Annie's big break came on the 19th ballot at 9:15 a.m., almost 22 hours after the jury went out. It showed ten for acquittal and two for manslaughter. The next ballot slid back to nine for acquittal and three for manslaughter. But ballots twenty-one and twenty-two showed eleven for acquittal and only one holdout, Foreman Julius Zang, for manslaughter. Minutes later, Zang finally conceded and the jury voted for the twenty-third and last time, 12-0 for acquittal, at 10:22 a.m.

The reactions of the principals in the case were predictable. Speaking to reporters at the Hotel Conrad, Mrs. George was graciousness itself:

> Pleased with the verdict and with my treatment in court? Indeed I am. I have always confidently expected the verdict to be just what it is, but nevertheless it is a great comfort to actually realize it and to be at liberty. I am very grateful to the court and to the officials for the kindness and consideration shown me. And to you boys of the press I am especially thankful. You have been very kind to me, treated me fairly and shown me much sympathy which I can never forget. I can find no words to express my feelings towards my attorneys. I feel that I cannot ever repay them for what they have done. There was nothing that could have been done that they did not do. No words can over praise them.

GO, AND SIN NO MORE

The Merciful Verdict of the Jury in the Case of Mrs. Annie E. George.

CROWD IN THE COURT ROOM CHEERED THE VERDICT.

An Immense Demonstration That Indicated That the Jury Had Returned the Popular Finding.

RADIANTLY HAPPY, MRS. GEORGE THANKS THE JURYMEN.

She Tells Them That She Is Grateful That They Gave Her Life and Liberty—Dramatic Close of One of The Most Famous Lawsuits in the History of the Country—The Freed Woman Going Home to Her Mother—The Ballots.

Go and Sin No More
(Stark County Democrat, May 4, 1899)

Asked what her plans were, Annie was understandably vague. She had made no plans while sitting in jail for a half a year, she told the reporters, because she didn't know what the outcome of her trial would be. She thought she would visit her mother in Hanoverton first, accompanied by her two sons. After that, she had a standing invitation to be the guest of her friend May Streeter at a seaside summer resort.

Annie also discussed what her feelings had been during the long vigil awaiting the verdict. She told a *Cleveland Plain Dealer* reporter she had almost lost hope of acquittal as the jury stayed out into the wee hours of Friday morning. But she had never thought the verdict could be worse than manslaughter, although Welty and Sterling had cautioned her not to be too confident of acquittal. Thanking her attorneys, Judge Taylor, her twelve jurors, the press and the public anew, she concluded her interview with the most open display of her heart she had shown throughout her long public ordeal:

> God only knows or ever can know, what I have suf-
> fered during the last eleven years of my life. I have
> been through temptation, darkness, persecution and
> even the shadow of death. I have suffered more than
> a thousand deaths, and many, many times would I
> have gladly laid down in the grave. But now the
> darkness is over and I shall forgive my enemies and
> persecutors and am fully resolved to live an upright
> life.

Among the first to greet Annie as she held court in the parlor of the Hotel Conrad that afternoon and evening was juryman Franklin C. Miller. After she thanked him again, he told her that he had been her supporter from the very beginning of her trial. He stated that he would have stayed in the jury room all summer rather than vote to convict her. Annie promised Miller that he and his family would always find a welcome in her home.

The public comments of the four attorneys were predictable and consistent with the characters they had displayed throughout the trial. James J. Grant took the verdict the hardest and had the least to say. He was seen to scowl when he heard the words "Not Guilty," and his immediate response to a reporter's request for a statement was a curt "Nothing." When the reporters persisted, he added, "We have tried Mrs. George and she is acquitted. That is all to be said." His final comment on the subject as he left the courtroom was characteristically sardonic: "What do I think of it? I only care to say what Mark Twain said of his dog: 'It speaks for itself.'" Cynical Canton souls suspected, however, that Grant's disappointment was tempered by his abiding anger over Pomerene's refusal to let him close for the State.

Atlee Pomerene had fully expected a conviction for first-degree murder. When he heard Casselman read the verdict, he fell back in his chair and seemed utterly crushed. Exhausted by his labors, he soon left the courtroom, saying to reporters only, "I have nothing to say, I have done my duty." He then turned to the two Dr. Brants, both of whom had testified for the State and one of whom was his brother-in-law." "Which of you doctors was it," he inquired with indelicate sarcasm, "that performed the criminal operation on the goddess of justice that resulted in this miscarriage?" He then went home and took to his bed, refusing to see reporters or anyone else.

The Stark County prosecutor was more expansive after 24 hours rest. On Saturday, April 29, he gave his considered views on the trial to newspaper men:

> I feel that the State made out a clear case of first degree murder. I did my duty. The responsibility rests with the jury. The verdict can have only one effect, and that is to lower the standard of public morality, of regard for law and order.

There was at least one other person who agreed with Pomerene's fearful prophecy. Writing to the *New York Times* two days after Annie's acquittal, the anonymous "M. L. H" deplored public sympathy for her and predicted the verdict would serve as a virtual green light to like-minded homicidal females:

> How much is her acquittal due to the merits of her case and how much to the fact of her sex? Mr. Saxton had no opportunity to state his side of the case. His slayer took care that he should not. There is no more helpless thing than a dead man. A live woman has far more power. The acquittal of "Mrs. George" is a hint to certain kinds of women how to proceed when they allow the spirit of murder to take possession of them.

Befitting their status as the legal victors, Sterling and Welty were happier, more forthcoming and analytical in their post-trial public comments. Obviously ecstatic at the outcome of his first murder trial, James Sterling's immediate response was, "It was the only legitimate verdict that could have resulted from all the evidence given to the jury." The following day, he offered a sympathetic view of his client and perceptive criticism of his judicial adversaries:

> The outcome of the trial is just what it should have been. The so-called direct evidence of the state was entirely annihilated and the chain of circumstantial evidence was lacking many links. Prosecutor Pomerene, who is a good lawyer and a conscientious man, was led to believe in the guilt of Mrs. George and was unconsciously led to adopt the vindictive spirit of Mr. Grant, who was Saxton's attorney, intimate friend and associate. Mrs. George, to my personal knowledge, has been a much abused woman.

She was dominated over and then persecuted by
Saxton, and the time never was, up to the hour of his
death, that she would not have believed in him if he
had uttered but one kind word to her.

Sterling denied, however, that the defense had relied on
pity for Annie, insisting that the jury had decided the case strictly
on the evidence, despite the State's exploitation of the general
public opinion that she had killed Saxton. Citing Saxton's "fascina-
tions, lust and brutality," Sterling expressed the hope that his fate
would be a "stern warning to evildoers." Sensitive to Pomerene's
charge that the verdict would lower public regard for law and
order, Sterling was deeply skeptical that Annie's acquittal would
encourage would-be and brazen female killers.

More particularly, Sterling addressed what he identified as
the two most challenging facets of the case for the defense. The
first was Sergeant Hasler's revolver. Although the prosecution was
never able to link the gun to Annie George, he said that the jury
had agonized mightily over the implications of the defense suggestion that the revolver story had been contrived by Hasler with
the complicity of prosecutor Pomerene. Sterling believed that the
jury, simply unable to believe that a public official could be a party
to such an unethical act, eventually concluded that Hasler had
made up the revolver story all by himself.

Intriguingly, neither Sterling nor Welty publicly discussed
what may have been their private suspicions about the actual
provenance of that revolver. They weren't the only trial observers
who thought it distinctly odd that the prosecution had made no
attempt to trace the alleged murder weapon, despite the fact that it
had a legible serial number. The unstated inference was that
Pomerene and Grant knew or at least suspected that the Hasler
gun actually belonged to *Saxton*, not Annie George. If that were
the case, then they perhaps believed that the most likely shooting
scenario was that Annie, as per her nightly routine, had confronted Saxton at the Althouse steps. Exasperated to his limit, he had

drawn his revolver on her—but she had gained possession of it during the ensuing struggle and shot him, initially at least, in self-defense. Such a scenario would explain why the prosecution had no genuine interest in tracing Hasler's weapon to its owner and the defense, likewise persuaded that it was not Annie's gun, was content to have the prosecution fumble with its alleged provenance. This theory, of course, did not address the improbability that Mrs. George could have seized the revolver from the burly, more powerful Saxton. A variant of this hypothesis was that Saxton was shot by some "mysterious stranger," most likely a vengeful husband, who wrested Saxton's revolver away from him with the same fatal consequence.

The second critical challenge for the defense, Sterling continued, was the demolition of Christina Eckroate's testimony. It was the only important eyewitness testimony the State possessed, and Welty's most effective tactic in parrying it was when he asked the jurymen if *they* would like to be convicted on the evidence of a "morphine fiend." Tellingly, the jurymen threw out Mrs. Eckroate's testimony very early in their deliberations. But, notwithstanding the force of Sterling's post-trial analysis, it is possible that Mrs. George's prosecutors *never* had a realistic chance of clinching their case against such a sympathetic defendant. Way back at the beginning of the trial, on April 5, before any of the evidence was presented, canny *Cleveland Press* correspondent Jacob Waldeck had prophesied the verdict that came three weeks later:

> Your average prophet is disposed to take a general view of the case, rather than to bother with the legal technicalities. He says that the state will be unable to prove conclusively that Mrs. George did the shooting and that, even if she did do it, a jury, taking into consideration that her home had been broken up and her life blighted by Saxton would not declare that the deed was murder.

"Justice has triumphed once more," was Welty's initial comment in the instant after the verdict. He, too, however, expanded on his victory during the weekend that followed Annie's acquittal. Like Sterling, he thought that the discrediting of Christina Eckroate's testimony and Hasler's revolver story had been decisive turning points in the trial. But after post-verdict discussions with some jury members, Welty concluded that Annie's fate had actually been determined by the testimony of three seemingly minor witnesses:

> It was the testimony of express man Huth and his wife and Treeman, the target man at the Valley Railway crossing, that helped us most. They showed that the car on which Mrs. George was could not have reached Hazlette Avenue until about 6:07. The shooting occurred at 6:10 and the margin of time was so small that the state could not crowd murder into it.

Asked about the effect of the verdict, Welty expressed the ambitious hope that it might deter licentious behavior and even abate the sexual double-standard governing the behavior of men and women. His secular sermon exhibited quite the feminist slant:

> You ask me what effect it will have. I can only say that I hope it will have the effect of making the adulterer more cautious in his career of vice. It should mean, and I hope it will mean, the elevation of woman to her proper place in the home. Some men should be more cautious, hereafter, and other men can go and come from their homes believing that their wives and daughters are safe from the intrusions of the destroyers of homes. It not only emphasizes the virtue of woman and the manhood of man, but the legal rights that surround and protect the

home. It should have another effect, and that is this — that all people will stop and consider whether or not the acts and conduct of men and women should not be judged and determined by the same rules. If a woman commits one indiscretion, the bars of society are closed upon her, but men can indiscriminately commit like indiscretions and society winks at it. The verdict means that parents should be more guarded as to the character and habits of young men who are entertained in their homes as proper and suitable associates for their daughters. It means, I hope, a step toward the purification of morals. It will have the effect of lessening the number of home wreckers. Yes, I believe in doing everything possible to make all homes happy and virtuous, and I sincerely hope that the results of this trial may lead to that end.

Welty ended his uplifting homily by discounting Pomerene's concern for the future of law and order and prudently lauding the man whose name, usually loudly unspoken, had loomed so large throughout the almost month-long trial:

This verdict does not mean that, as the prosecution argued, there will be more killings. There will be no outbreak of lawlessness on account of this verdict. Mrs. George was not proven guilty. There is, too, the added fact that the libertine takes his life in his hand when he follows his miserable work as much now as he did at any time in the history of civilization. There were many homes that wept at the name of Saxton. But there are other considerations in connection with the trial that afford more pleasant food for thought. One of the things at which I am most deeply gratified is, that the name of the president was not mixed up in the case, as I feared at first that it might be. President McKinley was the chairman of the county Republican committee at the same time that I was chairman of the Democratic, and though political enemies we have been personal friends for a great many years. He is an ideally clean man, and it is a source of great satisfaction to me that he was not dragged into the trial of this case at all.

Welty's final remark on the case was to dampen public speculation that Annie would sue the Saxton estate for her dower rights. The very mention again of the idea provoked verbal apoplexy in Marshall Barber, who subsequently vowed to a reporter:

We would fight a case of that kind to the finish and there would be no let-up on that woman. I say that if President McKinley and I did not exhaust every legal means in a case of that sort we would be cowards. There would be no mercy for this woman in that event. However, I do not anticipate such a suit.

Barber further denounced the trial verdict as an "outrage." Accusing Judge Taylor of bias against the State, he deplored the atmosphere of the trial, alleging the defense had hired women to drum up sympathy for Anna on the streets of Canton and packed the courtroom with a phalanx of partisan "shouters." He insisted that the McKinley family had never desired a verdict more severe than manslaughter. He also uttered some last kind words for his dead brother-in-law:

If George D. Saxton had ever promised to marry that woman he would have kept his word. He had his faults like other men, but he was an honest, loyal and devoted friend and his death was an awful tragedy.

Pomerene, Grant and the George D. Saxton's relatives weren't the only persons chagrined by the trial verdict. The final cost to the Stark County taxpayers for the trial was between $6,000 and $7,000, much of it eaten up by witness fees. By the provisions of Ohio law covering acquittal in criminal cases, Sheriff Zaiser and Clerk of Courts Casselman did not receive any extra compensation for their labors in the case. But it could have been worse: if Anna had chosen to testify, the State would have countered with more rebuttal witnesses and the resulting fees might well have boosted the trial costs past $10,000.

Annie continued to bask in public acclaim for some days and she and her lawyers continued to receive a blizzard of congratulatory telegrams from all over the nation. But such happy auspices for Anna George were deceptive. As Saturday morning, April 29 dawned, Annie's present seemed triumphant and her future promising, if not outright golden. From the moment she exited the courtroom she was solicited by offers to tell her story on the lecture and theatrical circuits. Typical of such propositions was one from H. Walter Van Dyke, the manager of the Board of Trade Auditorium in Columbus, Ohio. His telegram on Friday read: "Will pay $500 for your appearance in drama next week." When Annie failed to respond immediately, Van Dyke showed up in Canton the next morning, begging her to tread his boards. He stated he wanted her to speak for ten minutes before each performance of his scheduled drama. The drama, naturally, would present some of the more vivid incidents of her life. Annie was tempted by the offer but eventually yielded to Welty and Sterling's advice that she forego the stage.

Mrs. George was more receptive to the blandishments of lecture circuit promoters, particularly if their offers tickled her vanity. She might be forgiven if her celebrity now slightly turned her head. For half a decade she had merely been George Saxton's scorned doxy, a purgatory succeeded by six months of excruciating shame, agony and peril. Now she was free, and her lawyers and other interested parties were trumpeting her acquittal as something bigger than her personal survival: a victory for wronged women and a potent blow against the sexual double standard. As token of her new-found role as a feminist exemplar and icon, Annie accepted the offer of one Madame Blanchard to deliver a lecture on "Woman's Rights" in Pittsburgh on May 9 at the Fifth Avenue Theater. Madame Blanchard, no fool, carefully stipulated in her contract that Annie's performance include a stimulating narrative of her Saxton ordeal.

Simultaneously, Annie began positioning herself for her new political role during an interview with a *Cincinnati Enquirer* correspondent. Her comments contained what sounded to some readers like a virtual admission that she killed George Saxton:

> I want to say that my misfortunes and bitter results should be a warning to designing men. Oh, if I could only go into every home and tell each wife, sister or daughter, and warn them against trusting any man with their virtue! I would say to them that no man, however fair he may seem, can be trusted with their dearest possession. I would warn them to be careful of their associates; to guard themselves against this temptation that dragged me down. . . . The verdict, I believe, will be accepted as a declaration that the home is a sacred place that cannot be violated with impunity. I feel that here in the city of Canton and elsewhere in the country the general people stand by that sentiment. Why, I have had countless letters from all parts of the country upon that very subject. Many of them came from ministers of the gospel, and a large number from women and girls. They were comforting in tone and offered me not only support but sympathy.

More prosaically, Annie told reporters that women should be allowed to vote and serve on juries. Still, she assured them that she thought it was the duty of every woman to marry and have a home, and promised that her lectures would address these issues. She was understandably non-committal on the oft-asked question of whether she would marry again. James Sterling, also known for his feminist sympathies, publicly announced that he approved of Annie's decision to lecture and would assist Annie in the preparation of her talks. Sterling also hinted that the tutoring of professional elocutionists would be enlisted to polish Annie's platform skills. He was at least as aware as Annie of the potential remuneration from such performances, having been paid nothing for his labors on her behalf, save his modest public defender's fee.

STAGE? NO.

MRS. GEORGE SAYS SHE WILL TAKE THE PLATFORM INSTEAD.

Believes in Women's Rights and Will Lecture on That Subject.

HER SUIT AGAINST SAXTON ESTATE WOULD BE VIGOROUSLY CONTESTED.

Stage? No.
(Cleveland Daily World, April 29, 1899)

The weekend following Annie's acquittal was a gratifying continuation of her royal progress through Canton. Saturday morning she again received well-wishers at Sterling's office and then returned to the Hotel Conrad to resume her adulatory levee there. Hoping for a triumphant visit to the First Methodist Church (the McKinley family's home church!) on Sunday, she was ultimately deterred by warnings that she would be mobbed by an unseemly throng during her devotions. She did, however, enjoy a number of public promenades, at least one of which took her past the Barber home at 333 South Market Street.

Annie left Canton on Monday for a promised visit to her mother in Hanoverton. Leaving her sons there, she returned to Canton on May 4 to pick up the threads of her life. Coincidentally, she shared part of her return train ride with Eva Althouse, who was seated in the same Pennsylvania Railroad passenger car when Annie boarded it at Alliance. It was reported that the two women studiously ignored each other's presence, and Eva waited until Annie exited the car at Canton before disembarking.

Annie's career as a lecturer on Woman's Rights was brief, unimpressive and disappointing. Whatever her ideological pretensions or personal hopes, she had been aware from the start that her public appeal was based on her notoriety, rather than her personality or beliefs. "I suppose they want to see me a great deal more than they want to hear me," she had confessed to friends at the outset. Typical of her few lecture appearances was a performance at the Grand Opera House in Akron on May 11. There was a paid audience of only 127 present when she came out on the stage at 8:30 p.m. Attired in a dark skirt and dark blue shirtwaist, she was greeted with an uncomfortable silence after her introduction. Reading stiffly from a manuscript, she narrated the story of her life, with particular emphasis on the Saxton years and her trial. It was the familiar melodrama adumbrated by Sterling and Welty: the innocent country girl, the humble carpenter husband, halcyon married days, the vile serpent Saxton's seduction, her tribulations, arrest, trial and final vindication.

Annie's reception by the audience at the Grand Opera Hall was tepid, but relatively kind, compared to that of the *Akron Beacon Journal* reporter sent to review her performance. Describing her manner as "shameless," the unidentified scribe served notice on Annie that her press honeymoon was over and that she had resumed her erstwhile status as "fallen woman" and object lesson:

> She does not hide the fact that she is an outcast from society, but posing as a martyr, she presumes to warn other women from falling into the snare of which she had become a victim.

Crueler still was the reporter's inference that Annie's speech was an implicit admission that she had, in fact, murdered George Saxton:

> Mrs. George handles Saxton without gloves .... Her whole story seems to have the earmarks of an excuse for the killing of Saxton, and she bounds lightly over his death without denying that she is the author of the crime of which she has been acquitted.

Annie probably read that review, it being her inveterate habit to both evoke and consume newspaper coverage of herself. If so, she may have realized its import that her acquittal had been something of a Pyrric victory. Whatever her jury's verdict, like Lizzie Borden of the same decade or O. J. Simpson a century later, she had been found guilty in the court of public opinion. Perhaps the unkindest cut of all, however, was the anonymous Akron journalist's comment on Annie's fading personal charms:

> She is a very tall and handsome woman, who in her younger days must have been called pretty, but who now bears evidence of the terrible trials through which it has fallen to her lot to pass.

Annie's manager angrily denied reports of poor attendance at her lectures but her platform career was over less than a month after her acquittal. As a *Cleveland Plain Dealer* editorialist commented, she had "evidently mistaken her calling" and it was time to find a new life. Meanwhile, a report that missing eyewitness Russell Hogan had turned up created a brief, if inconsequential commotion. According to a *New York Times* account in that paper's July 24, 1899 edition, Hogan had just been arrested and charged with disorderly conduct in a Chicago juvenile court. Arrested under the pseudonym of "Richard McKnight," Hogan had readily confessed to being the long missing witness to the Saxton murder. Given the prohibition against double jeopardy, Hogan's reported statement about the night of October 7 remains worth nothing as evidence but is offered here as a tantalizing curiosity:

> I was standing right across Lincoln Avenue from Mrs. Althouse's place and saw Mr. Saxton on the porch and saw Mrs. George shoot him. I was afraid they might do something to me if I told what I had seen, so I left home and have traveled all around the country since then.

Nothing more was heard of Mr. Russell Hogan, if the Chicago miscreant was, in fact, the fugitive Canton youth. But another reluctant, if hitherto unknown witness, a Miss Clark, now came forward to offer her belated two cents. Clark, a Canton book canvasser, claimed to have seen Mrs. George at lawyer James Sterling's home shortly after Saxton's murder and about an hour before her arrest. Her recollection was that Anna had knocked on the door while Sterling's family was at supper and subsequently conferred with Sterling. Clark recalled that Anna was "cool and calm," and she explained her belated testimony with the odd excuse that she had remained silent because she wanted to avoid notoriety.

Epilogue

Following the collapse of her abortive lecturing career, Annie George tried resuming her former life, minus its destructive obsession with George D. Saxton. She returned to Canton and took up her vocation as a seamstress once again. The evidence of subsequent Canton city directories attests that she pursued her needlework career at least as late as 1902. But with the exception of one dramatic episode, she succeeded in disappearing into private life. Her sons, reared mostly by relatives in Hanoverton, grew to maturity and made successful lives for themselves. Newton, the elder, became a career United States Navy officer, serving honorably in World War I and later enjoying a successful business career.

On May 15, 1903 Annie George married Dr. Arthur C. Ridout at a ceremony in Wheeling, West Virginia. Ridout, just a year younger than Annie, had previously been a physician in Salem, Ohio with a successful practice, a wife and three daughters. Ridout was said to have known Annie from the days of her early marriage, when she and Sample lived for a while in Salem. He was also said to have deserted his wife Minnie and his children, but whether Annie was the cause of that is unknown. In any case, their marriage license identified her as a "widow" and him as a "widower."

Little would likely be known about Annie's second marriage were it not for the spectacular way in which it ended in 1906. There are conflicting stories of Arthur Ridout's demise. He and Annie were then living in a house in Ravenna, Ohio, at the corner of Main and Meridian Streets. They had only been there since June, having previous lived in Salem, Warren, Ashtabula, Akron and Brocton, New York, where Dr. Ridout's parents and some of his siblings dwelt. Apparently a chronic problem drinker, Ridout had been anxious for some time about his financial difficulties. According to witnesses other than his wife, he had also been talking about suicide, even inquiring as to which policies did not exclude self-destruction. Sadly, although he had filed for insurance polices worth $50,000, however, he had not paid the premiums and Annie realized nothing material from his death.

FOUL PLAY IS SUSPECTED.

Relatives of Ravenna Physician Do Not Believe He Killed Himself.

SPECIAL TO THE PLAIN DEALER.

BUFFALO, N. Y., July 23.—According to word received here from Brockton, N. Y., there is likely to be a sensational investigation of the alleged mysterious suicide of Dr. A. C. Ridout, who died in Ravenna, O.

The remains reached Brockton from Ravenna last night and were taken in charge by the father and brother of the dead man. The father is a retired preacher of the Methodist Episcopal church. It is reported that before the body is buried there will be a post-mortem examination held.

Dr. Ridout's relatives, it is alleged, are not of the opinion that he killed himself. Believing that he was not the kind of man who would commit suicide, they suspected foul play in

Foul Play is Suspected
(Cleveland Plain Dealer, July 24, 1906)

According to the *Cleveland Plain Dealer* account, Annie came home on the afternoon of Saturday, July 23 and found her husband had hanged himself. "It was regarded as a singular thing," continued the item, "that the body was not discovered earlier, for it hung from a chandelier in a front room of the residence with the window open on Main Street, the principal street of the village." A less dramatic account in the nearby Ravenna newspaper had it that Ridout had hung himself with a trunk strap from a gas fixture in a second-floor bedroom after several days of binge drinking.

Annie, bringing him some mid-afternoon coffee, had discovered the body and run screaming into the street. The same account stated that although his feet were resting on his bed when found, he had nonetheless slowly strangled to death. Ridout's New York relatives were reported to be suspicious about the circumstances of his death, but the Portage County coroner, sheriff and the Ravenna marshal agreed it was a clear case of self-destruction. Ridout's body was hastily shipped for burial to his New York kin and Annie disappeared into obscurity again. None of her Ravenna neighbors had known that Annie was "the woman" mixed up in the notorious Saxton murder. But newspaper readers of inquiring mind were probably not surprised to learn that it was reported that there had been unspecified "troubles" in the marriage of Arthur and Annie Ridout.

The years flew by. President McKinley, the He-Who-Must-Not-Be-Named specter at Annie's trial, was shot and fatally wounded by a Cleveland anarchist while shaking hands at the Pan-American Exposition in Buffalo, New York on September 6, 1901. Ida McKinley, grieving to the end for her family dead, died in 1907. Two decades after her brother's murder, her family was once again scandalized by a messy divorce and murder. In 1919 George D. Saxton's nephew, namesake and heir George Saxton Barber sued his wife Bernice after she was named as a correspondent in the divorce action of Mrs. Lillian K. Geissenhainer. Barber's suit for divorce ended disastrously, however, when his own extramarital misbehavior resulted in his suit being thrown out of court. George and Bernice Barber were never reconciled and he died in 1921. Several days after his death, a young man named Peter Bender was found gravely wounded on the estate of Bernice Barber in New Jersey. There was a bullet beneath his heart and the circumstances were considered highly scandalous.

Three more years passed. On June 25, 1922, Annie C. Ehrhart George Ridout died at the age of 63 at the Methodist Episcopal Hospital in Brooklyn, New York. Admitted there four days earlier, she died of colon cancer. She had been living on Hoyt

Street for an unknown period of time and was buried without publicity in Greenwood Cemetery. The date, circumstances of her death and her burial place were only brought to light during the 1990s by Saxton tragedy buff Karl R. Harsh, whose discovery of the last facts about Annie George was a prodigy of research.

There were a few more modest echoes of the Saxton murder. Eva D. Best Nighman Althouse lingered in Canton for a few years before departing to parts unknown. And sometime in the 1930s or '40's Edwin G. Miller was building a new back porch on his home on the west side of Lincoln Avenue. While clearing the ground for construction he raked out a small .38 caliber handgun. Bob Miller, Edwin's grandson, would later recall in a 1992 interview that the weapon still had a bullet in one of its six chambers. A small handgun appropriate for a woman, it could well have been the murder weapon — especially if those witnesses who heard five shots on Lincoln Avenue, instead of four, were correct. And the location where it was a found was adjacent to the famous vacant lot at side of the Quinn house, the presumed escape route of Saxton's killer.

Sample C. George was the last of the Saxton tragedy principals to die. A cabinet maker for most of the remainder of his days, he expired at 7:10 a.m. on August 1, 1944. He had survived the defining scandal of his life by almost half a century. The father of five daughters by his second wife, Sample was also survived by Newton Robert and Charles Howard George. His second wife, Lucy, died on December 11, 1950. The house at 319 Lincoln Avenue still stands, albeit much altered from its appearance on the night of October 7, 1898. The murder of George DeWalt Saxton has never been solved.

GEORGE SAXTON'S TOMB.

*Sketch of George Saxton's Tombstone in
West Lawn Cemetery, Canton
(Cleveland Daily World, April 12, 1899)*

Notes on Composition and Sources

A Woman Scorned is the result of a decade-long obsession with the murder of George Saxton and the trial of Annie George. Although I must have run across it during an adolescent reading — circa 1961 — of Margaret Leech's mesmerizing *In the Days of McKinley*, Saxton's slaying had long since been forgotten when I stumbled across it again in 1998, while auditioning, as it were, murder stories for *The Corpse in the Cellar,* my third book of northeast Ohio woe. My initial intention, indeed, was to include the Saxton slaying in *Corpse* — but I was thankfully dissuaded from that foolish impulse by my beloved wife Laura, who emphatically questioned my sanity for even flirting with such a notion. I remember our spirited colloquy now as if it were yesterday: after hearing my two-minute summary of the story, she vehemently insisted that this incredible story and its larger-than-life characters deserved greater exposition than the kind of narrative "shorts" I had been constructing for my crime and disaster anthologies. Justly chastened, I soon began the prolonged research which has at last culminated in this full-length treatment of my all-time favorite crime suspense story. I will not immodestly boast of its merits, save the Shakespearian avowal that it is "mine own" — and to gratefully confess that it would never have come about save for Laura's love, belief and support. Not content with saving my life, she has saved this story time and again.

Owing in part to the fact that the George Saxton murder scandal touched the family of a United States president, sources for this story are frustratingly sparse. Premier McKinley scholar Margaret Leech could not find any trial record of the Annie George prosecution during the researches for her 1959 McKinley biography and I have had no better luck. As should be obvious from my narrative, virtually all of the research for this book is based on the wonderfully voluminous and florid journalism of the newspaper correspondents who covered the Saxton murder and Annie George's trial. A large debt, too, is due to the often brilliant newspaper sketch artists who covered the trial and whose drawings so deftly captured the memorable characters and high drama of this improbable story.

During the period of her incarceration and trial it was repeatedly rumored that Anna George was writing her autobiography, but no such manuscript has ever surfaced. The only book ever written specifically about the Saxton murder is the quickie account by "Coe," [Canton journalist Thurlow K. Albaugh], *Canton's Great Tragedy*, published soon after the trial in 1899 and it likewise was largely grounded in newspaper coverage of the events it chronicled. I am indebted to the staff of the William McKinley Presidential Library and Museum in Canton for their aid in locating some of the other meager resources for this story, with special thanks to Bill Bockman, who shared his knowledge of the Saxton tragedy and kindly escorted me to my first view of the murder scene. Thanks, too, to Deborah D. Edwards for introducing Laura and me to the enchanted realm of Kindle publishing.

As this account is intended for the general reader rather than the scholar, it does not include the 533 footnotes which still buttress my original manuscript. All quoted material contained in *A Woman Scorned* comes from the original sources, although the precise order of the sentences written or spoken may have differed slightly in the event.

One final thought. Like many a reader, I have had occasion to wrestle with the hoary question of whether truth is stranger than fiction. That puzzlement was much on my mind as I stitched together the unlikely events of the Saxton story. Some time after finishing the narrative I finally got around to reading Mark Twain's first novel, *The Gilded Age*, which he coauthored with Charles Dudley Warner in 1873. A major character of that satirical tale is Laura Hawkins, a beautiful Washington lobbyist. As a naïve young girl, she had falls in love with caddish Confederate Army Colonel George Selby, who requites her affection by stealing her virtue *via* a fake marriage ceremony and then abandons her. Years later, Laura renews their affair, and when Selby refuses to divorce his wife, Laura shoots him dead at a New York hotel in front of witnesses. Not to worry: During her subsequent first-degree murder trial, Laura's copious tears and dazzling pulchritude beauty utterly seduce her jury, her shrewd lawyer harps on her girlish sufferings and the depraved character of her victim — and she is triumphantly acquitted. Like Anna George, Laura tries to capitalize on her notoriety with a lecture tour, which likewise proves a disaster. Unlike our beguiling Anna, however, Laura dies of a broken heart, edifying contrite at the last.

Sources consulted in the composition of *A Woman Scorned* include:

BOOKS

"Coe" [Thurlow K. Albaugh]. *Canton's Great Tragedy: The Murder of George D. Saxton.* (Wooster, OH: Clipper Printing Co., 1899); the undated reprint version available from the William McKinley Presidential Library and Museum, Canton, Ohio includes Karl Harsh's most informative essay, "What Happened to Annie George?" (pp. 309-315)

Leech, Margaret. *In the Days of McKinley.* (New York: Harper & Brothers, 1959.

McElroy, Richard L. *William McKinley: A Pictorial History.* (Canton, OH: Stark County Historical Society, 1996).

Ohio. Adjutant General's Department. *The Official Roster of Ohio Soldiers, Sailors and Marines in the World War 1917-18, Volume XX* [Columbus: The F. J. Heer Printing Company, 1926-29].

Additional information was gleaned from the following sources:

Brown, Gary. "Murder That Reads Like a Movie Plot," *Canton Repository*, October 31, 1988, p. B1.

Cain, Mary. "Whatever Happen to Annie E. George?" *Stark County Free Press*, May 31, 1992, p. A6.

_____ . "McKinley's Past: Governor, Congressman, President—and Brother-in-Law of Murder Victim, *Stark County Free Press*, May 31, 1992, p. A7.

_____ . "Hearts, Homicide: Playing the Playboy Turns Fatal for Ida Saxton McKinley's Brother, *Stark County Free Press*, May 31, 1992, p. A7.

_____ . "Everybody Loves a Mystery, Especially an Old Mystery," *Stark County Free Press*, 1992.

Goldsmith, Greg. "A Canton Killing That Shook the White House," *Massillon Evening Independent*, October 6, 1973, p. 2.

Goshay, Charita. M. "Saxton Murder Still a Mystery 100 Years Later," *Canton Repository*, July 9, 2000, pp. B1, B4.

McGrew, Dottie. "Death, Sex, Intrigue: It Is All Here," *Akron Beacon Journal*, September 22, 1996, pp. AA1, AA6

Shaffer, Dale E. "Playboy's Murder Stuns Ohioans," *Salem [Ohio] News* "Yesteryears," December 27, 1994, pp. 1, 7.

NEWSPAPERS

Canton Evening Repository
Canton Sunday Repository
Canton News-Democrat
Cleveland Daily World
Cleveland Sunday World
Cleveland Press
Cleveland Plain Dealer
New York Times

DOCUMENTARY RECORDS

U. S. Federal Census Records: 1860, 1870, 1880, 1900, 1910, 1920.

West Virginia Marriage Records

ILLUSTRATIONS

Almost all of the illustrations are taken from newspapers and other print sources more than one hundred and ten years old. Owing to their antiquity, there is some distortion in some of the images, particularly with regard to newspaper headlines. Any such imperfections are more than compensated for by the period flavor these images add to the Saxton murder story.

ABOUT THE AUTHOR

Photo by Laura A. Serafin

John Stark Bellamy II is a former librarian and a son, grandson and great-grandson of newspaper journalists. He grew up hearing stories about the fabled murders and disasters of his northeastern Ohio region and eventually chronicled them in six collections of Buckeye State dismalia: *They Died Crawling, The Maniac in the Bushes, The Corpse in the Cellar, The Killer in the Attic, Death Ride at Euclid Beach, The Last Days of Cleveland* and two anthologies (*Women Behaving Badly* and *Cleveland's Greatest Disasters.*) He has also perpetrated *Vintage Vermont Villainies*, a collection of the Green Mountain State's most celebrated murders and mysterious disappearances. He currently abides in central Vermont with his wife, Laura, and their diverting dog, Clio.

CPSIA information can be obtained at www.ICGtesting.com
Printed in the USA
BVOW11s1905071215

429634BV00015B/414/P

9 781456 541941